o Baekela... ...rs-Lee

amuel ... Marie

rothea ... Einstein

Sigmund Freud • Betty Friedan

ndhi • Johannes Gutenberg

rtin Luther King, Jr. • Alfred

enthal • Toussaint Louverture

o Marconi • Karl Marx • Margaret

ick • Elon Musk • Isaac Newton

• Branch Rickey • Jacob A.

aki Shikibu • Benjamin Spock

or • Nikola Tesla • Ted Turner

Whitman • Frank Lloyd Wright

THE
DISRUPTORS

Confucius (551 BCE–479 BCE) * Sun Tzu (544 BCE–496 BCE) * Martin Luther (1483–1
(1819–1892) * Frank Lloyd Wright (1867–1959) * Jackson Pollock (1912–1956) *
* Gregor Mendel (1822–1884) * Louis Pasteur (1822–1895) * Sigmund Freud (1856–1
James Watt (1736–1819) * Samuel Colt (1814–1862) * Otto Lilienthal (1848–1896) *
* Henry Ford (1863–1947) * Guglielmo Marconi (1874–1937) * Clarence Birdseye (1886
(1955–2011) * Jeff Bezos (1964–) * Elon Musk (1971–) * Johannes Gutenberg (c. 1400–1
Louverture (1743–1803) * Dorothea Dix (1802–1887) * Karl Marx (1818–1883) * Jacob A
king, Jr. (1929-1968) * Branch Rickey (1881–1965) * Alfred Kinsey (1894–1956) * Bett
* Madonna (1958–)

THE
DISRU

saki Shikibu (c. 973–c. 1014) * Leonardo da Vinci (1452–1519) * Walt Whitman
c. 287 BCE–c. 212 BCE) * Galileo Galilei (1564–1642) * Isaac Newton (1642–1727)
Curie (1867–1934) * Albert Einstein (1879–1955) * Richard Feynman (1918–1988) *
slow Taylor (1856–1915) * Nikola Tesla (1856–1943) * Leo Baekeland (1863–1944)
n Turing (1912–1954) * Tim Berners-Lee (1955–) * Kevin Mitnick (1963–) * Steve Jobs
et Mead (1901–1978) * Benjamin Spock (1903–1998) * Salman Khan (1965–) * Toussaint
1914) * Mohandas Gandhi (1869–1948) * Margaret Sanger (1879–1966) * Martin Luther
1–2006) * Louis Armstrong (1901–1971) * Ted Turner (1938–) * DJ Kool Herc (1955–)

50 PEOPLE WHO CHANGED THE WORLD

ALAN AXELROD

STERLING
New York

PTORS

STERLING
New York

An Imprint of Sterling Publishing Co., Inc.
1166 Avenue of the Americas
New York, NY 10036

ISBN 978-1-4549-3031-0

Distributed in Canada by Sterling Publishing Co., Inc.
c/o Canadian Manda Group, 664 Annette Street
Toronto, Ontario M6S 2C8, Canada
Distributed in the United Kingdom by GMC Distribution Services
Castle Place, 166 High Street, Lewes, East Sussex BN7 1XU, England
Distributed in Australia by NewSouth Books
45 Beach Street, Coogee, NSW 2034, Australia

For information about custom editions, special sales, and premium and
corporate purchases, please contact Sterling Special Sales at 800-805-5489
or specialsales@sterlingpublishing.com.

Manufactured in China

2 4 6 8 10 9 7 5 3 1

sterlingpublishing.com

Design by Lorie Pagnozzi
Cover design by David Ter-Avanesyan
Illustrations by Alexis Seabrook

CONTENTS

Introduction *vii*

INTRODUCTION

CREATIVE DESTRUCTION, DESTRUCTIVE CREATION

Until recently, *disruption* was a bad word, plain and simple. The 1928 edition of the *Oxford English Dictionary* defines it as "The action of rending or bursting asunder; violent dissolution of continuity; forcible severance." Linguists know that the meanings of words often change over time. They may be subject to what language historians call amelioration, a change from pejorative to neutral or pleasant. For instance, in the days of Geoffrey Chaucer (c. 1343–1400), the *Oxford English Dictionary* tells us that the word *nice* meant "foolish, silly, simple" or "ignorant, senseless, absurd." By about 1500, however, the meaning began to undergo amelioration, morphing at this time to "requiring or involving great precision or accuracy." By the 1800s, *nice* meant "kind and considerate, friendly." More frequently than amelioration, words undergo pejoration, a linguistic downgrading from positive to pejorative. Take *silly*. Go back to Chaucer again, and it essentially meant "happy, blissful, blessed." Over the years, it got uglier, coming to mean "empty-headed, senseless, foolish."

In the case of both *nice* and *silly*, the amelioration and the pejoration took hundreds of years. The amelioration of *disruption*, however, happened almost instantly and pretty much because of the way one man, Harvard professor and business consultant Clayton M. Christensen, used the word in a 1997 book, *The Innovator's Dilemma: When New Technologies Cause Great Firms to Fail*. In this volume, Christensen coined the phrase *disruptive innovation*, which describes something new that creates new markets and new relationships between businesses while simultaneously displacing old markets as well as the leading firms and products associated with markets. Disruptive innovation is creative destruction—or, if you are on the wrong side of the disruption, destructive creation. In 1997, thanks to Christensen, the word *disruption* was itself disrupted, undergoing an instant amelioration to something good, positive, and productive.

The amelioration of the term *disruptive* is recent, but the concept behind creative destruction and destructive creation is as old as humankind. The discovery of fire, for instance, disrupted everything about human life—both for the better (warmth and light through the cold, dark night) and for the worse (get too close to the fire and you get burned). Anyone who has raised a child from infancy, or even just knows someone who has, understands that one of the most consequential and dramatic days in a family's life is the day the baby stops crawling, struggles to stand, and then begins to take his or her first steps. To watch the process of those first steps is to witness disruption in its post-Christensen sense. Each step is a disruption of the status quo we call "standing." Each step is a falling forward—the coordinated use of gravity to defy the painful consequences of gravity. Each of us who learns to walk learns an act of disruption.

Disrupting the status quo with every step is a *common* human attribute. Carrying such a disruption into other human activities can be an *uncommon* human attribute, the lofty province of heroes and geniuses. We admire and envy the disruptors among us because they represent the best, the most spectacular achievements of which human beings are capable. The disruption that is two-legged upright walking takes you from place to place. The kind of disruption created by history's great disruptors takes all of humanity from place to place. In the process, it destroys certain features of society and civilization while creating new ones. Creating new possibilities usually requires clearing away some of the old.

This book profiles fifty disruptors, from Confucius, who lived in the sixth century BCE, to Elon Musk, who was born in 1971. The disruptors in this book are drawn from the fields of philosophy and religion, art and literature, science, technology, enterprise, education, society, and popular culture. By definition, they are all innovators, because all disruption (in Christensen's ameliorative sense of the word) is, perforce, innovative. But not all innovators are disruptors, because not all innovations are disruptive. The IBM Selectric typewriter, introduced in 1961, with its interchangeable typing element (its "typeball") was highly innovative, but it did not disrupt the market for typewriters—even those that had the traditional individual rising and falling typebars. The advent of the personal computer was a disruptive innovation, which rapidly destroyed the market for typewriters. Both innovators and disruptors make and build. But disruptors also change how we think, act, do business, learn, and live. The most profound disruptions change civilization itself. And in this book you will meet fifty creators of just such disruptions. Some of the names will be familiar, others not so much.

My chief criterion for choosing disruptors for this particular Hall of Fame is that the candidate's disruption or disruptions (many disruptors produce more than one—they just can't help themselves) unarguably transformed philosophy, religion, art, literature, science, technology, enterprise, education, society, or popular culture sufficiently to leave a mark on civilization, on the way we live and think and experience the world around us. I have no illusion that my selection will settle any arguments. On the contrary, I expect it will start some. That's fine with me. But remember that fifty human beings plucked from some 2,700 years of global history cannot possibly be more than a mere sample. I invite you to gather some of your own disruptive heroes, thinkers, inventors, and innovators. Maybe build your own book, blog, vlog, feature film, interactive game, or thought experiment. Perhaps start a club, a foundation, a religion, a cult, or a country. Or begin more modestly. Next time you walk your dog, pot-bellied pig, or ferret, walk him or her around the block counterclockwise or around a different block clockwise. We all need disruption.

1

PHILOSOPHY AND RELIGION

CONFUCIUS
(c. 551 BCE — c. 479 BCE)

Active in China during the sixth century BCE, Confucius created the philosophy named for him. Confucianism may be regarded as a humanistic religion, which has served as the basis for society, government, and a simplified, virtuous way of life. Few individuals have been more influential in history, since Confucianism has influenced, even shaped, millennia of Chinese and other Asian civilizations from ancient times to the present. Mao Zedong was profoundly influenced by the teachings of Confucius. As a moral force, Confucius may be compared to any major Western religious figure, since the emphasis of his teaching was on living a life of virtue informed by extreme reverence for one's ancestors. Where the subjects of rule and government were concerned, Confucius wrote of the moral responsibility of rulers, whose duty, he believed, was to be frugal and benevolent, embodying an inner harmony that would of necessity be reflected in the harmony of the people they governed.

As pervasive and influential as it has been, nothing about Confucianism is truly settled. As a body of concepts, the philosophy remains subject to lively debate and discussion. It is, therefore, a living body of thought. The breadth, depth, scope, and longevity of Confucianism would identify Confucius as a great disruptor, but the philosopher's disruptive legacy is even more profound and elemental. He is generally considered the first teacher in the history of civilization—preceding Socrates by nearly a century—and so he brought to light the basics of the creation, propagation, and transfer of knowledge.

* * *

As with so many other figures of the distant past, little is known of the life of Confucius. He is believed to have lived from c. 551 BCE to c. 479 BCE in the state of Lu, modern Shandong or Shantung. The earliest written record of Confucius dates from four centuries after his death. According to these records, he grew up in the city of Qufu and was employed by the prince of Lu in a number of administrative roles, including as director of public works (503 BCE) and director of the justice department (501 BCE). He traveled extensively in China before returning to Qufu, where he established a school intended to disseminate the teachings of the ancients. In his conception of himself, Confucius created the role of teacher—not as the originator of new knowledge, but as the transmitter of existing knowledge. He also created the model of the ideal teacher, someone who opened the doors of his school to all classes of society, rich and poor alike.

Confucius's thought may be divided into three major areas: Ethics, Politics, and Education. His teachings in the area of ethics are set down in the *Analects* (also known as the *Lunyu*), a work that was assembled in its present form sometime during the second century BCE. Confucius believed that the Supreme Power—perhaps a Supreme Intelligence, Supreme Being, or simply nature itself—sets the boundaries of each person's life. Within those boundaries, however, an individual's life is not predestined. People are responsible for their own actions and, most especially, how they treat others. Our span of life is fated—predetermined—but how we fill that span is up to each of us.

The social philosophy of Confucius is centered on *ren*, or "compassion." The ethical person deliberately deprecates himself in practicing concern for others. As in many religions, those possessed of *ren* follow a form of the Golden Rule, which Confucius expressed in this formula: "What you do not wish for yourself, do not do to others." Confucius taught that society is made harmonious by extending into society as a whole the harmonious structures of a well-run family. Roles had to be defined within the family and extended outward through neighborhood, community, political bureaucracy, guild, and even through philosophy itself (as a chosen "school of thought"). Social cohesion ultimately rests on the altruism of the individual, a quality that requires hard-learned self-discipline to achieve and maintain. Ritual, therefore, takes on tremendous importance and value as a means of instilling and maintaining discipline. In this sense, ritual is necessary to the survival of society.

Self-discipline is also at the core of Confucian political philosophy. A ruler must acquire self-discipline so that he may, with virtue and benefit, govern his subjects by his own example. His behavior toward his people, the philosopher wrote, should be regulated by an attitude of love and concern. Confucius did not believe that the compulsion of law was an effective tool for governance. Under pain of law, people will devote themselves to escaping punishment and therefore will fail to develop an inward sense of shame, a conscience. If a ruler leads not by compulsion but by virtuous example, however, and instills discipline through ritual, the people governed will acquire a sense of rightful shame, which will propel them voluntarily and eagerly into the embrace of the ruler.

Based on his expressed concerns, Confucius appears to have lived at a time in which political institutions had largely broken down. The problem, as he saw it, was the failure of the members of society to recognize and then live out their proper social roles. "Good government," he said, "consists in the ruler being a ruler, the minister being a minister, the father being a father, and the son being a son." To assume titles of authority without sufficient competence was, he believed, the source of social decay. One must be true to one's role, even as one must be truthful in all things. Confucius called the absence of truth, the disconnection of facts from the words associated with them, *zhengming*, which describes a pathological severing of word from reality. Bring word and thing closer together, and you can begin to "rectify" the behavior of people. Do this diligently and thoroughly, and you will remold the prevailing social reality. A leader must be truthful in both desire and deed. "If your desire is for good, the people will be good," Confucius wrote in the *Analects*. "The moral character of the ruler is the wind; the moral character of those beneath him is the grass. When the wind blows, the grass bends."

The desire for good is the seed of *de* ("virtue"). Confucius conceived of *de* as a moral power by which a ruler wins a following, rather than compelling it. To be virtuous as a leader is to create a virtuous people, who will automatically emulate their ruler. Confucius did not rely on some supernatural force of virtue, but on an array of social rituals, such as toasting at meals, bowing in greeting, yielding the way to others, and exchanging gifts. Done correctly and faithfully, such ritualistic acts create the magic that is harmonious social order.

In society, Confucius saw the reflection of the individual. For this reason, he elevated education and study to a lofty place. He put little stock in inborn instinct or intuition, arguing instead for the value of understanding that is based on long and hard study. *Study*, however, was to be carried out not alone, but through the interaction of the student with a teacher. Indeed, the ideal student was the one who most faithfully emulated the words and acts of his teacher.

For Confucius, the teacher's function was to be the living, speaking, acting memory of the very best acts and thoughts in history as carried into the present from the ancients. Lessons were wisdom transmitted from antiquity. In ancient wisdom was to be found the truth, and his job, as a teacher, was merely to convey that truth. Confucius recognized the essential subjects fit for study as morality, proper speech, government, and the refined arts, in addition to what he called the "Six Arts" (ritual, music, archery, chariot-riding, calligraphy, and computation). Chief among them all was morality.

In his writings, Confucius detailed his pedagogical methods. He did not lecture, but instead asked questions, recited passages from classic works of Chinese literature and philosophy, and proposed analogies to the subject at hand. This done, he would fall silent and wait for his students to work out the correct answers. His belief was that frustration was indispensable to learning. Once sufficiently frustrated, a student would be ready to accept a prompt from the teacher—a starting place from which to learn. This was the modest goal Confucius set for the teacher: to provide a starting place from which the student might learn.

The purpose of education was not to acquire knowledge for its own sake, but to acquire the mental elements that, together, create a person who is fit to perpetuate a harmonious, refined society. Each educated human being is to be a microcosm of social excellence, moving with grace, speaking with eloquence and correctness, and always exhibiting integrity.

If many of the precepts of Confucius strike us as self-evident and even pedestrian, it is because we ourselves have been brought up in a society that accepts the value of teaching. A society in which knowledge is *not* conveyed from one generation to the next seems to us inconceivable, precisely because Confucius and others like him invented the disruptive concept of knowledge as a definable body of intellectual material that must be acquired through education. The acquisition of this material, moreover, constitutes the very tissue of civilization. Without the likes of Confucius, the lives of human beings on earth might have stretched on across who knows how many millennia without direction or purpose, and our species, *Homo sapiens*—"Wise man"—would not be worthy of its name.

BRINGING HIGH-LEVEL STRATEGY TO WAR, BUSINESS, AND OTHER ASPECTS OF HUMAN ENDEAVOR AND ENTERPRISE

SUN TZU

(544 BCE–496 BCE)

On an April 2001 episode of HBO's *The Sopranos*, mob boss Tony Soprano (James Gandolfini) told his psychiatrist, Dr. Melfi (Lorraine Bracco), that he had been "reading that—that book you told me about. You know, *The Art of War* by Sun Tzu. I mean here's this guy, a Chinese general, wrote this thing 2,400 years ago, and most of it still applies today! Balk the enemy's power. Force him to reveal himself. You know most of the guys that I know, they read Prince Matchabelli"—he meant Machiavelli—"and I had [my wife] Carmela go and get the Cliff Notes once and—he's okay. But this book is much better about strategy."

B eginning the day after the episode aired, sales of the book—more like 2,500 years old, by the way—exploded. Oxford University Press, publisher of the most authoritative English translation, instantly blew through its entire stock of 14,000 units. The publisher pulled the trigger on another 25,000 copies and took out a *New York Times* ad: "Tony Soprano fears no enemy. Sun Tzu taught him how. *The Art of War*. The book for bosses."

And then there are these ripples and waves—

- From the 1960s through the 1980s, *The Art of War* became a reading staple for Japanese business leaders during the height of the postwar "Japanese economic miracle." In 1980s America, which was staggering under a seemingly intractable recession, executives in search of a winning strategy bowed to Japan's example and started reading Sun Tzu as well as books and articles adapted from Sun Tzu. Once again, pop culture showed the late twentieth-century preeminence of this 2,500-year-old military thinker when Gordon Gecko (Michael Douglas), corporate raider par excellence, trades Sun Tzu quotes with his protégé Bud Fox (Charlie Sheen) in the Oliver Stone film *Wall Street* (1987).

- On the softer side, *The Art of War* also inspired a raft of self-help titles, such as *The Art of War for Dating: Master Sun Tzu's Tactics to Win Over Women*, *The Art of Love: Sun Tzu's The Art of War for Romantic Relationships*, and *The Art of Parenting: Sun Tzu's Art of War for Parenting Teens*.

- In 2002, Armed Services Editions, which shipped millions of books to GIs during World War II, was revived to send books to troops serving overseas. Among the first volumes sent? *The Art of War*. Following the terrorist attacks of September 11, 2001, Sun Tzu was also nominated as a strategic ally in books with titles such as *The Art of War on Terror: Sun Tzu's Art of War for Countering Terrorism*.

● ● ●

Today the most familiar name in military strategy (eclipsing that of the nearest runner-up, the nineteenth-century Prussian Carl von Clausewitz) and among the most widely read *business* strategists (sorry, Malcolm Gladwell), Sun Tzu, the man, is a dim specter in the darkest shadows of distant history. There is disagreement on where in China he was born—perhaps in Qi, perhaps in Wu. Although they disagree on his birthplace, *The Spring and Autumn Annals* (official record of the state of Lu) and *Records of the Grand Historian* (a history of ancient China completed about 94 BCE by a Han official named Sima Qian) do concur that he was born late in what is called the Spring and Autumn period, roughly between 771 and 476 BCE. Both sources also identify him as a general and military adviser or strategist serving King Helü of Wu beginning about 512 BCE. The two histories suggest that Sun Tzu was a victorious commander, whose success moved him to write *The Art of War*. Sima Qian specifically cites the Battle of Boju, a great Wu victory over Chu in 506 BCE. The trouble is, however, that the *Zuo zhuan*, a text that predates the *Records*, gives history's most detailed account of the Battle of Boju—yet makes no mention of Sun Tzu.

In any event, *The Art of War* gained its first notoriety and authority during ancient China's Warring States period, which followed the Spring and Autumn period. As the name suggests, this period was an era of virtually continual warfare. It spanned 403 BCE to 221 BCE and saw seven nations—Zhao, Qi, Qin, Chu, Han, Wei, and Yan—all battling for control over eastern China. *The Art of War* was, in effect, a strategic manual for generals of this period.

A few anecdotes concerning Sun Tzu have been frequently repeated, although their historicity cannot be corroborated. In the most famous, it is related that King Helü tested Sun Tzu by ordering him to transform his harem of 180 concubines into troops. Sun Tzu took up the challenge, dividing the 180 into two companies and appointing as their commanders the two concubines he knew to be the king's favorites. This done, Sun Tzu issued his first order: *Right, face*. When the ladies responded by giggling, Sun Tzu modestly turned to the king and said that it was the responsibility of the general—namely, himself—to ensure that soldiers understood the commands given to them. With this, he repeated his order. Again, the women giggled. Sun Tzu then issued his second order—for the immediate execution of both company commanders, the king's favorite concubines. When the king objected, Sun Tzu patiently explained that if the general's soldiers understood their commands but failed to obey, the officers were to blame. Moreover, once a king appointed a general, it was the general's absolute duty to accomplish his mission—even over the objections of the king. With that, the women were summarily put to death. Sun Tzu appointed their replacements, and *Right, face*, as well as every subsequent order, was obeyed with precision and alacrity from that point on. Sun Tzu had turned a harem into an army.

That the book exists and is genuinely ancient is beyond doubt. But by the twelfth century, some Chinese scholars questioned the very existence of Sun Tzu, regarding the legend of this strategic genius and author as either an error of confusion with other commanders or an outright fiction.

• • •

In the end, the historicity of Sun Tzu the man matters less than the disruption created by the concepts collected in the brief book that bears his name. Consider: Mao Zedong credited his 1949 triumph over Chiang Kai-shek and the

Nationalists in the Chinese Civil War to *The Art of War* (at least in part). This assigns to the book a key role in the birth of a Communist China, the single most disruptive world event in the postwar era until the collapse of the Soviet Union in 1991.

The Art of War without doubt influenced Mao's thinking about asymmetric, or guerrilla, warfare, which has been the dominant mode of armed conflict since the end of World War II. Ho Chi Minh ordered a Vietnamese translation of the book, which he distributed to all of his military officers. Ever since its wartime encounters with Japan, North Korea, and North Vietnam, the United States military has made *The Art of War* required reading for all officers.

The truth is, however, that the book is first and foremost a study in applied Taoist strategy—an emphasis on naturalness and "effortless action" to assert one's will in the world—and only secondarily a work of military strategy. The ease with which the book has been adopted from military applications to an array of civilian uses is evidence that *The Art of War* was conceived as a book of persuasion, of winning hearts and minds, of Taoism—applied to war, but also applicable to every other aspect of life and work. When Sun Tzu wrote "Every battle is won or lost before it is ever fought," he was clearly setting the battle space not in the field but in the minds and imaginations of those engaged. The action finally fought out was almost superfluous because, as Sun Tzu saw it, the outcome was virtually inevitable.

War as practiced by Western armies has generally been about killing people and breaking things. Sun Tzu suggested that warfare was really about moving hearts and minds, thereby asserting personal will, or the will of the sovereign, with the smallest cost in lives and treasure. Taoism has been called a philosophy of parsimony, of doing the most with the least, of achieving one's ends while doing the least harm in the process. The truly disruptive impact of *The Art of War* should be measured by the degree to which it brought ancient Chinese Taoism to a wider range of the human family, from Mao Zedong to Tony Soprano.

CHALLENGING RELIGIOUS
AUTHORITY, CREATING
A REFORMATION THAT
SHIFTED ISSUES OF
FAITH, MORALITY, AND
EVEN GOVERNMENT
FROM INSTITUTIONS TO
INDIVIDUALS

MARTIN LUTHER

(1483–1546)

On October 31, 1517, Martin Luther—a monk, theology professor, biblical translator, and ecclesiastical composer—sent Albert of Brandenburg, Archbishop of Mainz, Germany, a momentous letter: ninety-five "theses" challenging the authority and morality of the Catholic Church's practice of selling forgiveness of sin: "indulgences." That day is today commemorated by Protestants worldwide as Reformation Day. It has long been believed that, on this same day, Luther also nailed his *Theses* to the door of All Saints' Church and other churches in Wittenberg. It is by no means certain that he ever posted the document in this manner, but, if he did, it was not until sometime in November.

O n the face of it, Luther had nothing more than a bone to pick with his church, the Church of Rome. He was a theologian, after all, and thus predisposed to finely parsing articles of faith. In fact, the entire dispute may well have been aggravated by the monk's chronic and apparently intractable constipation. He himself referred to *"a secretus locus monachorum hypocastum"*—a toilet—where he contemplated, one fateful day, a theological problem as intractable as the difficulty with his bowels. Luther included an account in a sermon, which the British playwright John Osborne portrayed in his 1961 play *Luther*. As rendered by Osborne, the monk preached to his congregation:

> Who'll speak out in rough German? . . . It came to me while I was in my tower, what they call the monk's sweathouse, the jakes, the john or whatever you're pleased to call it. I was struggling with the text [from the Epistle of Paul] I've given you: "for therein is the righteous of God revealed, from faith to faith; as it is written, the just shall live by faith."

Osborne's Luther relates how, sitting on the toilet,

> he seemed to sense beneath me a large rat, a heavy, wet, plague rat, slashing at my privates with its death's teeth. . . . And I sat in my heap of pain until the words emerged and opened out. "The just shall live by faith." My pain vanished, my bowels flushed and I could get up.

● ● ●

Get up Martin Luther did. He realized the truth in Scripture, that the just shall live *by faith alone*, not by paying any church or any priest for forgiveness. All a sinner needed was "my sweet redeemer and mediator, Jesus Christ," not an institution corrupted by money.

After his revelation, Luther realized that *his* reading of the Bible simply could not be reconciled with the practice of the Roman church. For Luther, a sinful believer in God is made righteous by faith in God's mercy, not through his own good works or his money. Luther's epiphany was much more than a theological dispute or a fit of constipation—if the message of Christ is that believers can turn directly to God through prayer at any time, then there is no need for priest or church or any other middleman. Not only did this challenge the Catholic Church, the most powerful religious and political force on earth at the time, it challenged the very concept of organized religion and of the nations, societies, and civilizations based on it. Luther's message was that under God, all people of faith are equal; the individual's relationship to God is supreme; and the individual conscience of a person of faith is the ultimate and unimpeachable source of morality and right versus wrong.

The implications of Luther's argument were vast and enormously disruptive. Luther's beliefs affected not just how religion was conceived and practiced in the Western world, but the role of law and ethics in societies, and even how governments were created and knocked down. Historically, the Protestant Reformation launched by Luther's *Theses* unleashed more than a century of war in Europe. The continent was riven with religious conflict that began in 1524 and culminated in the cataclysmic Thirty Years' War (1618–1648). Violent disputes between Catholics and Protestants continued sporadically into the twentieth century, most familiarly in "The Troubles," a low-intensity civil war that wracked Northern Ireland from 1968 to 1998.

• • •

Born on November 10, 1483, in Eisleben, Saxony, Martin Luther was the child of a prosperous family. Martin was educated at the University of Erfurt, from which he received a master's degree in 1505. His father wanted him to become a lawyer, and Martin dutifully enrolled in the law school at Erfurt. But the already headstrong young man quickly left, complaining that the study of law was the study of "uncertainty." What the young man demanded was truth, *certain* truth, and so he dived into philosophy. When this field failed to satisfy him, he turned finally to religion. The story Luther himself tells is that while returning to Erfurt on July 2, 1505, he was very nearly struck by a bolt of lightning. The close call provoked him to cry out "Help! Saint Anna, I will become a monk!" And so he dedicated himself to the Augustinians. Ordained in 1508, he was chosen by the dean of the newly founded University of Wittenberg to teach theology, and in 1512 he was awarded the degree of doctor of theology.

A monk-turned-professor, Martin Luther was also a zealous preacher and proselytizer. His *Theses* were rapidly printed in pamphlet form and as placards. During 1517, several hundred copies of the document were printed and, thanks to the rapid rise of the movable-type printing press, introduced by Johannes Gutenberg less than seventy years earlier, the document was soon widely broadcast across Germany and Europe. The Wittenberg-based artists Lucas Cranach the Elder and his son Lucas Cranach the Younger painted several portraits of Martin Luther that were widely reproduced. Colleagues of the theologian circulated admiring stories about him as well. Thus, it was a combination of the ideas *and* the personality behind the ideas that gave the Reformation its early momentum.

Rome did not take the challenge lying down. In June 1518, Luther was summoned to stand trial in Augsburg on charges of heresy. Under intense interrogation from the papal envoy Cardinal Thomas Cajetan, Luther refused to renounce his assertions. In 1519, Charles V (1500–1558) became the new Holy Roman emperor and swore to protect the Catholic Church against the likes of Luther. Nevertheless, Luther persisted in believing that he could reform the Catholic Church from the inside. He wrote a series of three works, considered foundational texts of the Protestant movement. The central of the three, "On the Freedom of a Christian," held that a "Christian is a free lord of all, subject to none. A Christian is a dutiful servant of all, subject to all." In these two sentences, Luther liberated the Christian believer from all arbitrary earthly authority, religious or secular—though he explicitly renounced armed rebellion. In January 1521, Pope Leo X excommunicated Martin Luther. Four months later, Luther was compelled to defend himself before Charles V. He told the Holy Roman emperor that he would take back his words if—and only if—scriptural fact could be shown to disprove them. To act against his own conscience, he told the emperor, was a thing he could not do: "Here I stand. God help me. Amen."

Unimpressed, Charles V issued the Edict of Worms, banning Luther's writing and proclaiming him an outlaw of the empire.

But Luther was not alone. Frederick III, prince of Saxony, arranged for Luther's "abduction" as he journeyed back from Worms. Frederick had the theologian brought to his Wartburg Castle, where, under the prince's protection, he continued to write—albeit under a pseudonym. In the space of ten months at Wartburg, Luther wrote various statements on issues relating to the Reformation, and he also worked intensively to complete a German translation of the New Testament. In contrast to the many error-ridden translations that others had made from the Latin text, the scholarly Luther used the ancient Greek testament as his source. His was the first translation from the original Greek to the German—and it was a masterpiece of literary translation. Printed in 1522, his New Testament was both a spiritual and commercial success, even though Pope Leo X's excommunication of Luther the previous year had effectively banned his writings, including his biblical translations.

Despite his having been declared an outlaw, Luther returned to Wittenberg in 1522. Having been excommunicated from the Catholic Church, he considered himself freed from his monkish vow of celibacy. In 1525, Luther married a former nun, Katharina von Bora, with whom he raised a family of six children. In 1526, the Reformation enjoyed a political triumph when the Imperial Diet (the legislative body of the Holy Roman Empire), meeting at Speyer, issued a decision that allowed princes and states to determine for themselves whether to remain Catholic or become "Lutheran." This opened the way for the creation of the first officially sanctioned Lutheran churches and "Protestant" schools.

As the Reformation gained traction, Luther, recognizing that the religion he had fostered was populist rather than dictated by a clergy, embarked on an effort to educate Germans in the principles of Christian belief. In 1529, he wrote and published a "Small Catechism," aimed at informing the common layman, and a "Large Catechism" for the new Protestant priesthood.

● ● ●

Remarkably—and despite his excommunication, Luther persisted in clinging to the hope that Protestantism would reform the Catholic Church and remain unified with it. During the summer of 1530, a nervous Charles V convened an imperial diet in Augsburg, hoping to avoid the breaking apart of the Holy Roman Empire. Because the emperor had both outlawed and banned him, Luther dared not attend the diet. Instead, Luther deputized his friend and colleague Philip Melanchton to represent him. At Augsburg, Melanchton made a valiant but doomed effort to earn Catholic recognition of the Protestant denomination—which was not formally named Lutheranism until 1597. Nevertheless, the result was no victory for Charles V, either. With the Islamic Ottoman Empire aggressively threatening all of Christian Europe, and especially his own Habsburg (Austrian) regime, Charles did not dare risk the political unity of the Christian states. Accordingly, he granted Protestants religious freedom in exchange for the military participation of the Protestant states in the Ottoman-Habsburg wars.

While Luther made this critical political headway, he turned his attention to translating the Old Testament directly from Hebrew into German. Completed in 1534, the result was another literary masterpiece. What the King James Bible of 1611 would become to the English language, the Lutheran translation of the Old Testament of 1534 became to the German tongue: a source of innumerable sayings and idioms intimately woven into the fabric of the common language.

This is evidence of the pervasiveness of Luther's translations. More than any vehicle before them, his New and Old Testaments conveyed Christianity to people of virtually every class, bringing to practical fruition his dream of creating a Christian religion unmediated by a corrupt and corruptible institution and clergy.

2
ART AND LITERATURE

DISRUPTION:
CREATING THE
NOVEL, A RADICAL
LITERARY FORM FOR
"ORDINARY"
PEOPLE

MURASAKI SHIKIBU
(c. 973–c. 1014)

Westerners tend to believe that they know who wrote the first novel: the Spaniard Miguel de Cervantes (1547–1616), who published *Don Quixote* in 1605. In fact, Cervantes was beat by several centuries. Murasaki Shikibu, a lady-in-waiting in the court of Emperor Ichijō during Japan's Heian period, wrote *The Tale of Genji* some six hundred years before *Don Quixote*. There is ample reason to call this literary masterpiece not only the world's first novel but the world's first *modern* novel. It is, the great Argentine writer Jorge Luis Borges said, "written with an almost miraculous naturalness." This quality of naturalism helps define a novel as unique, compared to a play or an epic poem. It is literature brought down to earth. As Borges wrote, *The Tale of Genji* is "what one would quite precisely call a psychological novel," a book of emotion, motivation, and character. When the modern Japanese novelist Yasunari Kawabata became the first Japanese writer to receive the Nobel Prize for Literature in 1968, he remarked in his acceptance speech that *The Tale of Genji* is "the highest pinnacle of Japanese literature. Even down to our day there has not been a piece of fiction to compare with it."

ittle is known of the world's first novelist, not even her "real" (personal) name, since Murasaki Shikibu is a descriptive "court" name. It is believed she was born into the Fujiwara clan, and may have been Fujiwara no Takako, the daughter of a provincial governor, who had a reputation as a scholar. Her intelligence was such that her father allowed her to study alongside her brother, so that, unlike the vast majority of Japanese females, even of high birth, she became acquainted with the classics of Chinese literature, greatly admired in Japan.

In her early twenties she was married to a distant relative, with whom she conceived a daughter who was born in 999. Her husband died in 1001. Sometime after this, she was invited to live in the imperial court of the Emperor Ichijo in what is today Kyoto. Some authorities believe that another of her relatives, Fujiwara no Michinaga, who was the regent and power behind the imperial throne, invited her in 1006 to become the lady-in-waiting, companion, and tutor for the Empress Shōshi. It is further believed that she already had a reputation as a writer—she composed poetry—and was known for the brilliance of her conversation. From the time of her arrival in the imperial court and for the next two years, we have a vivid picture of her life as a lady-in-waiting. She kept a meticulous diary, in which she revealed herself as essentially dissatisfied with the frivolity of the court, which, she wrote, focused on everything but the governance of Japan.

Given the length and complexity of *The Tale of Genji*—modern English translations comprise 54 chapters across well over a thousand pages—it is widely assumed that Lady Murasaki began the work before she came to court. Doubtless, however, much of it is based on what she saw and heard while she was the empress's lady-in-waiting. Yet the tale it tells is unmistakably a work of fiction. Its hero, Genji, does not exist in history. In the novel, he is the son of a fictional emperor and his favorite concubine, Kiritsubo. Although a Korean wise man at court foretells a wonderful future for him, Genji's mother, the object of great envy in the court, falls ill and dies young. The emperor becomes obsessed with a new concubine and demotes Genji to the status of commoner. This is not only a key turn in the plot of the novel, but a breakthrough in literature, marking the novel as a literary form that, even when devoted to court life, is not about just the highborn—those nearest to the gods in status—but the concerns of the "ordinary" man and woman. *The Tale of Genji*'s invitation to its readers to identify closely with the narrative and characters creates a level of vicarious intimacy between author and audience that is almost absent in other literary forms at the time.

Genji grows into a handsome and accomplished young man who enjoys great success as a lover but is feared by some at court as a potential rival for imperial favor. Much of the novel concerns his amorous adventures and eventual return to power within the court. The longest section of the novel details the growth of Genji's influence and how he orchestrates the rise of his children and grandchildren in the imperial administration.

Unlike the works of the ancient Greek bard Homer, which were composed and delivered orally, *The Tale of Genji* was written down—yet it was meant to be shared, read aloud to groups, serially, over long periods. The original manuscript is lost, and the novel survives in a twelfth-century transcription. Doubtless, innumerable audiences relished the individual tales, but they were eager most of all for the window the novel provided into the life and mind and heart of the imperial court.

Like any good novel, *The Tale of Genji* is a vision of life in a particular time and place. It conveys the human values of that time and place, as well as the thoughts and motives of characters, not just their outward actions. In this, Lady Murasaki set a high literary standard not reached in the West for many centuries, and not equaled until the rise of the English novel in the late eighteenth and early nineteenth centuries. Although the line from *The Tale of Genji* to the modern novel is hardly unbroken, the impulse common to most great works of fiction—namely, to convey the sheer living complexity of life—is abundantly present in this first novel.

● ● ●

Of Lady Murasaki's later life, following the death of Emperor Ichijō in 1011, little is known. Some believe she left the Imperial Palace to live in retirement and seclusion in a convent, where she devoted her declining years to religious study and to Chinese literature. She may have sensed that the days of imperial rule were numbered and, with it, the decadent life of the upper class. The overthrow of imperial rule by the samurai and the creation of the shogunate's feudal military government would indeed come, but not until 1192, long after Lady Murasaki's death. Whether or not she wrote it as a kind of elegy to a life she believed was doomed to pass, her *Tale of Genji* not only created the novel, but serves as an early monument to Japanese as a written rather than as a predominantly oral language. In this sense, her work of fiction may be regarded as the birth of Japanese history written by a Japanese writer in Japanese, rather than the dominant court language, Chinese. Through her book, she left the world an intimate portrait of Heian Japan, the last and perhaps most glorious period of classical Japanese history and culture.

LEONARDO DA VINCI
(1452–1519)

The period we call the Renaissance—fourteenth through seventeenth centuries in Europe—gave its name to the polymaths who created it. The phrase *Renaissance man* evokes a type of genius that the fifteenth-century Italian humanist, author, poet, philosopher, architect, master of languages, priest, and part-time cryptographer Leon Battista Alberti (1404–1472) described this way: someone who "can do all things if he will." Alberti and others of the era did not conceive the ideal of the polymath as a mere showoff. Rather, the ideal was walking, thinking, showing that human beings possess a capacity for limitless development.

The word *renaissance* is French for "rebirth," and it refers specifically to the rediscovery of classical (mostly Greek and Roman) philosophy and science, which had been suppressed as pagan and all but lost during the Middle Ages. Among the ancient philosophers rediscovered during the Renaissance was Protagoras (c. 490 BCE–c. 420 BCE), who is best remembered for having proclaimed "Man is the measure of all things." During the Middle Ages, such a statement would have been heresy, since God and the changeless moral law of God were the measure of all things, the ultimate source of truth and value. In reviving the formulation of Protagoras, the thinkers of the Renaissance sharply distinguished themselves and their age from the religion-bound philosophers of the Middle Ages. The focus became human-centric: humanistic.

No symbol of the Protagoras formulation is more powerful than the one created by the ultimate Renaissance Man, Leonardo da Vinci. Drawn by the artist in 1490, "Vitruvian Man" depicts a male figure in two superimposed positions, his arms and legs apart inside both a square and a circle. It is both an artist's study of ideal human proportion and the superimposition of man upon nature, showing that the human being fits the universe so perfectly that it may serve as its very measure. More than a representation of a perfectly proportioned nude figure—perfect because it fits a mathematical model of nature—"Vitruvian Man" is a demonstration that nature is perfect because it fits humankind. Man, not an invisible God and not churchly interpretation of that God, is the measure of all things. This belief was the core of Leonardo's genius and the summation of his life's work.

• • •

It is helpful to think of Leonardo's work as having a summation, given how dazzling its scope and breadth are. Through the centuries, Leonardo was considered chiefly a painter. His *Mona Lisa* and *Last Supper* are the most iconic artworks of the Renaissance—perhaps in all of Western history. But he was also an architect, inventor, technologist, and precursor of the modern scientist.

His inventions and scientific work are contained mainly in his notebooks, some 13,000 pages of manuscript material, which were not only unpublished in his own time, but written in mirror-image cursive script. Whether Leonardo wrote in this manner from a motive of secrecy or because he happened to be left-handed and therefore found it easier to write backward, we cannot know. But the technique kept most of his inventions, observations, and theories from wide distribution for centuries. Only in relatively recent times has the full extent of his cross-disciplinary disruptive genius been appreciated. Drawings and notes on human flight, designs for a helicopter and a fixed-wing glider aircraft, many advanced engines of war—who knows what effect these expressions of his innately futuristic imagination would have had if more of his contemporaries had seen them?

• • •

Leonardo da Vinci was born on April 15, 1452, in Vinci, a town in the Tuscan republic of Florence. He was born out of wedlock to Ser Piero Fruosino di Antonio da Vinci, a prosperous notary, and Caterina, a peasant woman. His father married four times, unions that produced a dozen half-siblings, who were born over a long span of time—the last when Leonardo was a middle-aged adult of forty.

Little is known of his childhood, except that he was educated in mathematics, geometry, and Latin. He himself related an illuminating incident from his youth in which he was exploring in the Tuscan countryside, where he found a cave. Although terrified that it might be the lair of some monster, Leonardo wrote, his irrepressible curiosity compelled him to venture inside. Whether or not this memory was real, it seems a fitting emblem for Leonardo's life. He dared to explore, whatever trepidation he may have felt.

From 1466 to 1476, Leonardo was an apprentice to the great artist Verrocchio (Andrea di Cione, c. 1435–1488). The artist's workshop was staffed by some of the greatest painters of the Italian Renaissance, including Domenico Ghirlandaio, Perugino, Botticelli, and Lorenzo di Credi. This gave Leonardo an unparalleled artistic education. In 1472, his apprenticeship culminated in his membership in the Guild of Saint Luke, certifying him as a master artist. Leonardo felt such an affinity for Verrocchio, however, that he continued to collaborate in his workshop until 1476.

Nothing definite is known of da Vinci's activity and work for the next two years, excepting a record showing that he was charged with, and ultimately acquitted of, the crime of sodomy. In 1478, he moved out of his father's house and was commissioned to paint an altarpiece for the Chapel of St. Bernard in Florence's Palazzo Vecchio. He was subsequently commissioned in March 1481 to paint *The Adoration of the Magi* for the monks of San Donato a Scopeto, also in Florence. But he left both works incomplete when Lorenzo de' Medici, in whose palace Leonardo may have lived, sent him to Milan. Lorenzo had commissioned him to create a silver lyre as a peace offering to the powerful and notoriously combative Ludovico Sforza, Duke of Milan.

Leonardo did more than make the delivery. He promoted his services to Ludovico—less as a painter (a competence he barely mentioned) than military engineer, which suggests much about how the artist thought of himself. He worked in Milan from 1482 to 1499, creating in this city the *Virgin of the Rocks* (for the Confraternity of the Immaculate Conception) and *The Last Supper* (for the monastery of Santa Maria delle Grazie). The latter was commissioned by Ludovico about 1495 and took some three years to complete. The humanity of Leonardo's depiction of the moment when Jesus informs the twelve apostles gathered for the Passover seder dinner that one would soon betray him was a breakthrough, unprecedented in its dramatic vividness. Tragically, however, the artist's impulse to innovate doomed the masterpiece to early decay. He tried a new technique for the mural, painting with tempera and oil on dried plaster instead of painting a genuine fresco, a work on fresh plaster. He lived to see the beginning of the severe flaking that, despite modern restoration, severely mars the painting today.

• • •

Ludovico Sforza was a great patron of the arts, best known for commissioning *The Last Supper.* But this was an epoch in which Renaissance men dealt with other Renaissance men, and so Sforza called on Leonardo to design the dome for Milan Cathedral and create a giant bronze monument showing Ludovico's predecessor, Francesco Sforza, astride his horse. When Sforza was overthrown and imprisoned by French forces during the Second Italian War (1499–1504), Leonardo lit out for Venice, whose doge employed him not as an artist but as a military architect and engineer. The onetime sculptor and painter set to work designing innovative fortifications to defend the city from seaborne attack.

Returning to Florence in 1500, Leonardo was housed by Servite monks at the monastery of Santissima Annunziata, where a workshop was set up for him. He created the cartoon—the full-size stencil used to lay out a fresco—for *The Virgin and Child with St. Anne and St. John the Baptist.* The work drew crowds of admirers to the monastery. But like so much else that Leonardo started, the work, now housed in London's National Gallery, was left unfinished.

The peripatetic Leonardo moved on to Cesena in 1502, seeking employment with Cesare Borgia, cardinal, military commander, bastard son of Pope Alexander VI, and the ruthless inspiration for Niccolo Machiavelli's *The Prince.* Determined to secure Borgia's patronage, Leonardo created a map of Imola, Cesare's stronghold, showing how to defend it. At the time, almost any map was an innovation—as mapmaking was largely a mystery and maps very rare—but a map created specifically for strategic military purposes was all but unknown. Leonardo gave Borgia a secret weapon—and Cesare Borgia hired the artist as his chief military engineer and architect. On his orders, Leonardo next created a map of the Chiana Valley in Tuscany, which Borgia used as a guide in planning the formidable defenses of his territories.

In 1503, Leonardo was on the move again. Over the next two years, he worked on *The Battle of Anghiari* for the Signoria in Florence. The work itself is lost, known today only through a copy by Peter Paul Rubens, but widely believed to be hidden behind the wall bearing a fresco by Vasari. Judging from the Rubens copy, it was a fresco of intense energy and action, in which the anatomy of clashing men and their horses in the most violent conflict was portrayed with meticulous accuracy. After he completed the fresco, Leonardo returned to Milan in 1506, was back in Florence the following year, and then again in 1508. His old age was spent, in part, living in the Vatican, under the patronage of Pope Leo X from 1513 to 1516. After King Francis I of France recaptured Milan in 1515, he commissioned Leonardo to make a mechanical lion that walked forward and opened its chest to reveal a cluster of lilies—*fleurs-de-lis* being the French heraldic emblem. King Francis's mechanical lion, though designed, was never constructed.

In 1516, the artist, now in the service of Francis, moved to a manor house, Clos Lucé, near the royal Château d'Amboise, in the Loire town of Amboise. Here he lived out the final three years of his life. He died at Clos Lucé on May 2, 1519. He was sixty-seven.

• • •

Leonardo's artistic legacy is relatively small, just two dozen works—though the authorship of some additional paintings and drawings is disputed and at least seven major works are known to be lost. During the nineteenth and twentieth centuries, much of the fascination with Leonardo turned from his paintings to his inventions. This fixation culminated in 1994 when Microsoft founder Bill Gates purchased the *Codex Leicester*, a 72-page notebook that is just one small part of the roughly 13,000 known pages of Leonardo's visionary journals. At $30.8 million, the highest price ever paid for a book, Gates believed he had acquired a bargain.

The *Codex* focuses on Leonardo's musings about water—about tides, eddies, and dams, about engineering water, and about the relationship among water, the moon, and the sun. In other manuscripts, Leonardo delved deeply into the nature of light, of anatomy—both human and animal—geology, botany, map-making (which he pioneered to an astounding degree), astronomy, alchemy, mathematics, and geometry.

It is, however, the inventions, the acts of pure innovation drawn and written about in his journals, that most excite our imagination. In his *Lives of the Artists* (1550 and 1568), the painter, architect, and biographer Giorgio Vasari mentioned Leonardo's "designs for mills, fulling machines and engines that could be driven by water-power." Vasari cited in particular his "models and plans showing how to excavate and tunnel through mountains without difficulty, so as to pass from one level to another; and he demonstrated how to lift and draw great weights by means of levers, hoists and winches, and ways of cleansing harbours and using pumps to suck up water from great depths." Writing years after Leonardo's death, Vasari was most interested in the mechanical ideas in the notebooks. Then and now, others were attracted by the array of war machines, which included assault vehicles, antipersonnel cannons that could shower the enemy with stones, a giant crossbow, breech-loading artillery capable of continuous fire, a multi-barrel precursor of the late nineteenth-century Gatling gun, and a diving suit to be used by a man to sabotage ships below the waterline. These designs had been commissioned by warlike princes and kings. Closer to our own time, the main attraction has been Leonardo's futuristic visions of flight. He designed a parachute that was never made, let alone tested, but that would almost certainly have worked, and a hang glider, based on his careful studies of bird and bat wings. This design also seems airworthy. More radical, because it departed from nature, was Leonardo's human-powered "aerial screw," a helicopter design based on a principle at least as old as Archimedes.

In his notebook, da Vinci captioned his drawing for the aerial screw with this comment: "If this instrument made with a screw be well made—that is to say, made of linen of which the pores are stopped up with starch and be turned swiftly, the said screw will make its spiral in the air and it will rise high." The far-seeing aerodynamic theory behind the design was sound. Leonardo's sketch was for a machine that compressed air to obtain flight, which is the principle by which modern helicopters fly. His comment shows that he also understood that the practicality of his invention depended on the material used and the energy available. This observation, alas, also identifies the two reasons why his disruptive dreams were so rarely translated into full-scale three-dimensional reality during his lifetime. The materials available in the sixteenth century did not combine the lightness of weight and the durability necessary to achieve flight. Not only were the available materials limiting, so were the available forms of energy. For some inventions, wind, water, or animal power could be harnessed. But for flight, the only available energy was human, and it was woefully insufficient.

In the end, Leonardo da Vinci's disruptive vision was a focused dream, a pattern for innovation, a way of imagining. It supplied pieces of a future—pieces, however, insufficient in themselves to build that future.

Hundreds of years later, machine guns, diving suits, helicopters, and much of the rest were invented. Leonardo did not inspire these, but, in hindsight, we recognize today that he *could* have, had his notebooks become known earlier and more widely. No matter. Leonardo's greatest innovation was himself as a presentation to the world—and, to the eye of history, the archetype of the Renaissance man, one who can indeed "do all things if he will."

WALT WHITMAN

(1819–1892)

"Our poets are men of talents who sing, and not the children of music," Ralph Waldo Emerson complained in an 1840 essay titled "The Poet." He criticized modern poets, especially American poets, for focusing primarily on "the finish of the verses," rather than the "argument"—the subject, the original insight, what the poet wanted to *reveal* to the world. "For it is not metres, but a metre-making argument, that makes a poem,—a thought so passionate and alive, that, like the spirit of a plant or an animal, it has an architecture of its own, and adorns nature with a new thing. . . . The poet has a new thought: he has a whole new experience to unfold; he will tell us how it was with him, and all men will be the richer in his fortune. For, the experience of each new age requires a new confession, and the world seems always waiting for its poet. . . ."

For Emerson, the waiting ended fifteen years after he wrote "The Poet." One day in July 1855, he walked into his Concord, Massachusetts, post office and was handed a package containing a book called *Leaves of Grass*. In it were a dozen poems, including the long first one, titled "Song of Myself":

> *I celebrate myself,*
> *And what I assume you shall assume,*
> *For every atom belonging to me as good belongs to you.*
> *I loafe and invite my soul,*
> *I lean and loafe at my ease . . . . observing a spear of summer grass.*

And it went on . . . and on:

> *Stop this day and night with me and you shall possess the origin of all*
> *   poems,*
> *You shall possess the good of the earth and sun . . . there are millions*
> *   of suns left,*
> *You shall no longer take things at second or third hand . . . nor look*
> *   through the eyes of the dead . . . nor feed on the spectres in books,*
> *You shall not look through my eyes either, nor take things from me,*
> *You shall listen to all sides and filter them from yourself.*
> *I have heard what the talkers were talking . . . the talk of the*
> *   beginning and the end,*
> *But I do not talk of the beginning or the end.*
> *There was never any more inception than there is now,*
> *Nor any more youth or age than there is now;*
> *And will never be any more perfection than there is now,*
> *Nor any more heaven or hell than there is now.*
> *Urge and urge and urge,*
> *Always the procreant urge of the world.*
> *Out of the dimness opposite equals advance. . . . Always substance*
> *   and increase,*
> *Always a knit of identity . . . always distinction . . . always a breed*
> *   of life.*

A poet singing of himself and thereby singing of everyone and everything that ever was or ever will be. A poet who had a "metre-making argument" that required unrhymed lines of varying length that sang out as if in a great operatic aria using the language of the American streets.

Here at last was the poet Emerson had hoped and pined for.

Whitman had not signed his name to the volume he sent or thought to include a return address. Emerson hunted it all up himself and wrote the poet a letter: "I greet you at the beginning of a great career," he began, "which yet must have had a long foreground somewhere for such a start."

• • •

That long foreground began with Walt Whitman's birth on May 31, 1819, the second son of Walter Whitman, a carpenter and house builder, and Louisa Van Velsor. There were nine children in the family, and they lived variously in Brooklyn and then farther out on Long Island through the 1820s and 1830s. When he was twelve, Whitman became apprenticed to a printer. He took to it instantly—though it was never merely a trade for him, but rather an introduction to the glories of the printed word. He gravitated not toward the works of the present day, but back to epic times: Homer, the Bible, Dante, and Shakespeare. His apprenticeship complete, Whitman became a journeyman printer in lower Manhattan, the heart of the printing district. He had hardly begun, however, when a great fire swept through the neighborhood and essentially wiped out the industry.

After a few years as a schoolteacher, Whitman took to journalism in 1841. He started his own weekly newspaper, *The Long-Islander*, and then took editorial posts at a succession of Brooklyn and Manhattan papers. He left a position at the *Brooklyn Daily Eagle* in 1848 to become editor of the New Orleans *Crescent*. But he did not last long there. The sight of slavery—the first time Whitman had seen slaves and masters in person—was overwhelming, the slave market physically and emotionally revolting. In the autumn of 1848, he rushed back to Brooklyn, where he started up an abolitionist newspaper he called the *Brooklyn Freeman*.

And he started to write poetry.

Unlike many budding poets, who imitate this or that conventional master, from the very beginning Whitman wrote work that was unlike any other. It was both epic in scope and bardic in the tradition of Homer, and yet it was intensely spontaneous, contemporary, and personal. It was alive and breathing—literally—the meter of the varied lines seemingly measured by breath and punctuated by ecstasy. The subject matter? It was everything the poet saw, heard, smelled, and felt.

By 1855, he had what he believed was sufficient material to publish, at his own expense, a volume he titled *Leaves of Grass*. Not *blades*, but *leaves*, like the pages of a book, so that the pages of his book were as leaves of grass, natural, organic, plentiful—"passionate and alive," as Emerson wrote years earlier, "like the spirit of a plant or an animal"—and intended to be trod by everyone in the world, now, in the past, and in the future. Whitman was the ultimate democrat, accepting of all people, high, low, free, slave, American, or of any nationality—and ancient, modern, living, dead, or as yet unborn.

When Whitman published again the next year, it was a new edition of the same book. The original twelve poems, passionate and alive, had grown to thirty-three, and the volume now opened with Emerson's letter to him and his own open letter to Emerson in response. (For all his artistic integrity, Whitman was also a shrewd marketer.) Depending on how you count them, there would be six or nine editions of *Leaves of Grass* published between 1855 and 1891–1892. By the end, in the so-called Deathbed Edition, *Leaves of Grass* comprised nearly four hundred poems, sprouted and matured as if by nature. New poems were added on to the older poems, which were changed, modified, elaborated, or simplified. It was less a book than an organism.

• • •

"Urge and urge and urge," Whitman had written. "Always the procreant urge of the world." That was the creative energy of his life's work, an urge, as it were, to "merge," to cross all boundaries—moral, political, religious, emotional.

The greatest challenge to this urge to merge was the Civil War, which tore the nation apart, asserting all the divisions Whitman had dedicated himself to overcoming. His response to the war was, in part, to write about

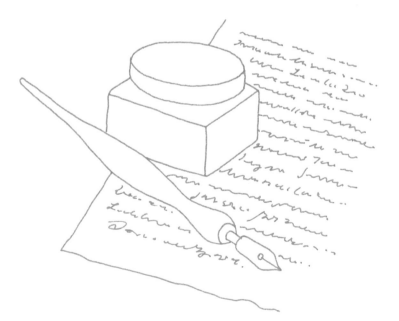

it, but, even more, to do all he could to actually heal it. He volunteered as a nurse, visiting the wounded in hospitals in and around New York City and then, in December 1862, moving to Washington, D.C., to care for his wounded brother. He ended up also caring for the wounded in the city's hospitals and then secured a position as a clerk for the Department of the Interior. This engagement lasted for eleven years until Secretary of the Interior James Harlan found out that Whitman was the author of *Leaves of Grass*, which he considered obscene. It was a charge later generations, inspired by him, would face and, like Whitman, overcome. They ranged from the likes of D. H. Lawrence in England to William Carlos Williams, Jack Kerouac, and Allen Ginsberg in America.

Fired from the federal bureaucracy, Whitman had a hard struggle to support himself, to continue to buy the supplies for the hospital patients he cared for, and to send money to his widowed mother and another brother, who had been an invalid from birth. Fellow writers who admired his poetry sometimes sent him money. These included American as well as British authors—for the English loved this poet. He liberated subject matter from outworn convention and verse from the necessity of rhyme and mechanical meter. For him, the purpose of poetry was to give voice—to anyone who wanted to claim that voice. America had claimed its political independence in 1776. Its intellectual and aesthetic independence came with the 1855 debut of *Leaves of Grass*.

Walt Whitman died on March 26, 1892, of pneumonia and the effects of long-untreated tuberculosis. He had prepared for his passing by editing the "Deathbed Edition" of *Leaves of Grass*. This was intended as his monument, but he also invested $4,000 (a fortune for him) to build a granite mausoleum as his resting place in Camden's Harleigh Cemetery. He was not shy about wanting to be embraced by his countrymen as a national legacy. "The proof of a poet," he had written in 1855, "is that his country absorbs him as affectionately as he absorbed it."

DISRUPTION:
CREATING ORGANIC
ARCHITECTURE, IN
WHICH STRUCTURES
ROSE IN HARMONY WITH
THE ENVIRONMENT AND
HUMANITY

FRANK LLOYD WRIGHT

(1867–1959)

In an era when the aggressive and defiant skyscraper was regarded as America's greatest contribution to the history of architecture, the most celebrated architect of the early twentieth century was Frank Lloyd Wright, best known not for soaring towers—though he designed one a mile high—but modest homes. During his lifetime, Wright became so famous that he was the inevitable answer if the proverbial man or woman on the street were asked to name an architect. In contrast to most of his colleagues, he was less interested in making a distinctive mark on the landscape than in creating structures that seemed at once to grow organically out of their environment and yet also to announce themselves not as creatures of nature but of a human heart and mind.

Frank Lloyd Wright was born on June 8, 1867, in Richland Center, Wisconsin. His mother, Anna Lloyd Jones, was a teacher, and his father, William Carey Wright, a preacher and musician. His family moved frequently around the Midwest and East Coast until Wright was twelve. It was Wisconsin, a place of lush green rolling hills, many rivers and streams, and lakes great and small, that drew out Wright's youthful passion. "The modeling of the hills, the weaving and fabric that clings to them, the look of it all in tender green or covered with snow or in full glow of summer that bursts into the glorious blaze of autumn," this, he wrote in "Taliesin," an article published in *The Architectural Record* in May 1914, is what he felt a part of—and always would.

Wright enrolled in the civil engineering program at the University of Wisconsin at Madison in 1886, earning his tuition as assistant to the dean of the engineering department. He also assisted the prominent architect Joseph Silsbee (1848–1913), who was overseeing construction of his Unity Chapel. Instantly convinced that he wanted to be an architect, Wright left the university in 1887 and went to work for Silsbee in Chicago. One year later, he embarked on an apprenticeship with Chicago's most innovative architectural firm, the partnership of Dankmar Adler (1844–1900) and Louis Sullivan (1856–1924).

A great architect and profound thinker about design, Sullivan believed that the form of a building should follow its function. He shunned ornament for the sake of ornament, but embraced ornamentation that grew out of the overall form of the building, which, in turn, expressed its function. Sullivan aspired to a style that expressed the democratic values of America. Wright became something of an apostle of his, but one who was determined to surpass his master in actually realizing the ambition of creating a uniquely American style of architecture. Indeed, Wright aspired to create an architecture suited to the diversity of the entire American continent. More than form following function, Wright believed that architectural form should follow its site.

Wright worked for Sullivan until 1893, when he casually breached his contract with Adler and Sullivan by taking on private commissions to design homes. This followed a lifelong pattern of unapologetic narcissism. Wright had, in 1889, at age 22, married nineteen-year-old Catherine "Kitty" Tobin, with whom he had six children. He would leave her—and their children—in 1909, six years after he began an affair with Mamah Cheney, the wife of a client. But in 1889, when the marriage was brand-new, he built a home for the family, which would also serve as his studio, in the Chicago suburb of Oak Park. His first architectural masterpiece, it is a precursor to the distinctive Wright style called the Prairie School, which came into full flower with the Winslow House in River Forest (1893–1894)—horizontal, open, and, in a word, organic.

More commissions came to Wright, as the single-story homes, with low, pitched roofs and expansive rows of casement windows made the Prairie School popular among those few Americans who could afford to hire an architect. The natural beauty of local materials, including wood that was often neither stained nor painted, distinguish such Chicago-area landmarks as the Robie House (1909–1910) and the Unity Temple (1905–1908).

Wright's buildings, especially his houses, seemed not so much constructed as composed. By the time he was forty, he was not only in demand in the United States, but had achieved international fame, especially in Germany and Holland and, later, in Japan, where he designed the Imperial Hotel in Tokyo in 1916–1922. While discerning American clients commissioned homes from him, commissions for banks, office buildings, and factories were rare—a fact that the ambitious architect resented. We can never know what Wright would have designed in the way of numerous large commercial structures—although his 1957 book, *A Testament*, includes a visionary design for a 528-story mile-high skyscraper, to be called *Illinois*—but his concentration on domestic architecture, even if forced on him by the marketplace, resulted in brilliant work that is always unmistakably his.

From the beginning of his career, Wright's houses revel in the cubic masses that are the elements of architecture. Upon these broad shapes, he deployed stone, brick, copper, and wood in ways that celebrate the very nature of the materials. Nothing was hidden, and nothing was superfluous. Moreover, windows and doors were, on the exterior, unornamented. Space was generous inside—and outside as well, with roofs and cantilevered eaves hanging over terraces and courts, leading to the landscape beyond. Space and light were used in the same way as any other building material, so that the built environment and the natural environment interlocked and interacted.

The best of the Prairie School houses, such as Chicago's Robie house, owed something to Japanese domestic architecture, but very little to anything else that came before, either in America or Europe—unless you include possible inspiration from the cubism that was being developed in modern European painting. Although Sullivan's form-follows-function dictum was subordinated to form-following-landscape, there was a secondary logic. The exterior of Wright's houses evolved, both visually and in the process of design, from the interior spaces. There was also, finally, a wild card behind the design. Wright's primary education had been influenced by the progressive ideas of educator Friedrich Fröbel (1782–1852), the originator of the concept and the word kindergarten, who encouraged teachers to provide young children with building blocks. The playhouse and school of Wright's Avery Coonley house (1908–1912) in Riverside,

Illinois, was directly inspired by children's blocks, but a block-like disposition of masses is evident in virtually all of Wright's work.

The relatively rare Wright commissions that were not houses show that he was more than a fine artist. His 1904 Larkin Administration Building (demolished in 1950), built in Buffalo, New York, for a soap manufacturer, was unprecedented in its integration of circulation, structure, ventilation, plumbing, furniture, office equipment, and lighting. Nothing was hidden, nothing left to chance, all was coordinated. His Imperial Hotel in Tokyo (1916–1922) incorporated construction designed to be resilient in earthquakes—perhaps the first public building so constructed. In 1895, Wright was commissioned to design row apartments, an assignment that compelled him to deal with a tight urban space and the social problems often associated with overcrowding. In 1929, he designed the St. Mark's Tower, a high-rise structure cantilevered from a central shaft, which Wright integrated into Broadacre City, a coherent, self-sufficient community Wright designed as a visionary project in 1931–1935 but was never built.

Wright differentiated himself from other cutting-edge architects when it came to solving practical engineering problems and pressing urban problems. Charles-Édouard Jeanneret, known as Le Corbusier (1887–1965) famously called the house "a machine for living in"; the great German architect founder of the Bauhaus, Walter Gropius (1883–1969), was aggressively mechanistic in his designs; and Philip Johnson (1906–2005) elegantly stripped away every vestige of ornament in his modernist approach. Wright, however, tried other ways.

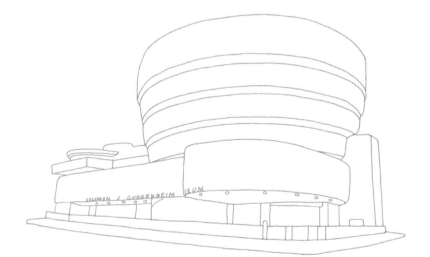

In buildings like the Barnsdall house (Hollywood, 1920), he drew inspiration from the way Mayan builders massed and ornamented their structures. But in the Millard house (Pasadena, 1923), he cast ornament into the structure's concrete blocks, making it integral with the masses of the building. His later work, such as his 1936–1937 masterpiece Falling Water (Bear Run, Pennsylvania), looks more modernist but also engages with the landscape even more than his earlier work does. The wonder of Falling Water is how such modern material as reinforced concrete is cantilevered and interlocked to poise dynamically over the waterfall that is very much a part of the house. In Phoenix, the Rose Pauson house (1940; destroyed by fire in 1943) used battered ashlar masonry and bare wooden walls to reflect the mountains and the desert, much as Taliesin West (1937), his own home on Maricopa Mesa, near Phoenix, does.

• • •

For many people, Frank Lloyd Wright is best known as the architect of the Solomon R. Guggenheim Museum in New York City. He worked on it for sixteen years, from 1943 to his death at the age of 92 in 1959. Unique among Wright's work and among museums, its sculptural spiral mass rises like a seashell from a deck-like horizontal mass. The viewer of the artworks inside is intended to ascend to the top level in an elevator and then descend—on foot—a long spiral ramp, leisurely viewing the works on the curved walls. If there is one problem with the museum, it is that the will of the architect seems constantly to assert itself in both the sculptural structure and the downwardly spiraling main gallery. The building threatens to overwhelm the art inside. It is Wright's valediction, proclaiming that the presence of this architect will not be subdued. Yet while the Guggenheim draws attention to its architect's vision, that vision is an homage to nature at its most organic. Gone are the blocks of Wright's domestic architecture. Here the shape evokes the shell of a conch or a snail, a shape at once supremely organic, spacious, and hard. As Walt Whitman created a poetic form expressly for celebrating the self, yet open to everyone and everything, so Wright had devised a signature architecture that gave human beings natural places in which to live their lives. His legacy was to encourage artists to claim a place for themselves in the landscape.

JACKSON POLLOCK

(1912–1956)

Long recognized as a radical innovator in government—the first nation found-ed on a set of concepts (liberty and equality foremost among them), not race, royal line, creation myth, or nationalist tradition—and a consistent innovator in science, industry, and commerce, the United States nevertheless suffered long from a collective inferiority complex when it came to the arts. In the nineteenth century, American authors such as Washington Irving, James Fenimore Cooper, Ralph Waldo Emerson, Nathaniel Hawthorne, Walt Whitman, and Harriet Beecher Stowe began to earn international fame. Early in the twentieth century, the Amer-ican movie industry quickly dominated world cinema, and American jazz gained listeners around the world. But fine art, especially painting, remained largely the province of the Old World, with Paris as its epicenter.

eyond question, the United States produced many extraordinary visual artists: John Singleton Copley (1738–1815), James McNeill Whistler (1834–1905), Winslow Homer (1836–1910), Mary Cassatt (1844–1926), John Singer Sargent (1856–1925), and Georgia O'Keefe (1887–1986) all achieved global recognition before the mid-twentieth century.

And yet, Americans persisted in deferring to Old World traditions and arbiters of taste in matters of "fine art" and "high culture." But after the Nazi threat sent many European intellectuals and artists fleeing to safer countries like the United States, and World War II left the continent in shambles, the Old World was no longer the sole arbiter of culture. After the war, Europe and the rest of the world increasingly looked to America for direction in the arts.

As it happened, in the postwar years, the art scene in New York City was developing a challenging, exciting school of art that was dramatic and disruptive enough to command the attention of the world. The artists who would come to be known as the "New York School" or, more generally, as abstract expressionists developed an approach to painting that broke dramatically with the artistic traditions of the past, not only in terms of subject and technique, but in the ways in which art was conceived and thought about.

The group was surprisingly diverse, as the works of its most famous exponents—Willem de Kooning, Robert Motherwell, Franz Kline, Mark Rothko, Barnett Newman, Adolph Gottlieb, Arshile Gorky, and Jackson Pollock—attest. But the artists were all united by the intensity of their lofty metaphysical ambition. In the middle of a century in which two world wars had already discredited traditions, torn down myths, shattered illusions, and left behind cruel and heartbreaking images of a grim new reality, they intended to find a fresh and redemptive truth in art. Rather than attempt to imitate—to represent—in painting the world beyond the canvas, these artists used the elements of art itself—form, line, and color—to both purely and directly convey emotion, myth, and symbol, ultimately to convey the very act of living. With the shell of life shattered, they sought a return to the varied energies of life itself.

The task, then, was to connect these raw energies without mediation, other than the mind and hand of the artist, with the canvas or the panel. Foremost among the artists of this movement was Jackson Pollock. It was he who first broke through the screen of outworn culture.

• • •

He was far from being a product of New York or of any other part of the long-settled East Coast. Pollock was born in Cody, Wyoming, in 1912, still very much a frontier town at the time. Before Jackson was a year old, his mother, Stella

May (McClure) Pollock, left her husband, LeRoy, an itinerant government land surveyor, and moved Jackson and his four brothers to San Diego. Jackson grew up there and in Arizona, where his mother briefly reunited with his father. By the time Jackson was eight, his father lived with his family only very intermittently. When the Pollocks moved to the Echo Park neighborhood of Los Angeles, it was without LeRoy. Essentially fatherless, Jackson, restless and ungovernable, was expelled from two high schools.

The young man did remain in touch with his father and, as a teenager, left his mother and brothers to tramp with him on surveying jobs. These were happy excursions for Jackson, and, among other things, introduced him to the art and culture of Native Americans in the Southwest.

Still, he had a vague sense that his future lay elsewhere. In 1930, he followed his older brother Charles to New York City, where they both enrolled at the Art Students League. They studied under the great Regionalist painter Thomas Hart Benton. It was a critical connection for Jackson. Although he had little feeling for Benton's Midwestern rural subjects, he was intensely attracted to the painter's brushwork. It was far from conventionally or straightforwardly "realistic," but, rather, rhythmical, primal, swirling. Benton's work pulsated with a living energy. What may have impressed Pollock even more strongly was the example Benton presented as an artist: impatient, gruff, and aloof, yet hard working and, most of all, uncompromising in his independence from the ebb and flow of aesthetic fashions around him. With Benton and fellow Art Students League pupil Glen Rounds, Pollock devoted one summer touring the West, both observing and painting.

Benton was crucial to Pollock's early development, but he was an artist with whom Pollock identified as much in opposition as inspiration. It was in 1936, while participating in an experimental workshop conducted in New York City by the radical Mexican political muralist David Alfaro Siqueiros (1896–1974), that he found the catalyst for the approach that would make him world famous. Siqueiros introduced Pollock to the technique of applying paint not with a brush, but by pouring. What appealed to Pollock about this was the direct linkage of action and the artwork.

He did not immediately exploit the technique, however. From 1938 to 1942, Pollock worked for the Depression-era WPA Federal Art Project, creating work that owed much more to Benton than Siqueiros or anyone else. It was also during this period that Pollock recognized that he was heavily dependent on alcohol, an addiction he endeavored to overcome by consulting two Jungian psychoanalysts. One, Dr. Joseph Henderson, encouraged him to attempt to surface his unconscious mind through drawing and painting. In works of the first two or three years of the 1940s, Jungian "archetypes"—graphic elements of the human collective unconscious—figure prominently in his work. The paintings gained notice from Peggy Guggenheim, the eminent and very forward-looking New York collector and gallerist. In 1943, she signed a gallery contract with Pollock and commissioned him to create *Mural* (1943), a vast canvas eight feet high by twenty feet long, which she hung in the entryway of her new townhouse.

An extraordinary "early" work, *Mural* hangs today in the University of Iowa Museum of Art. It is a hybrid of non-representative abstraction and shorthand Jungian-inspired images, but what stands out most clearly are the fluid rhythms, which mark it as a work driven by the *action* of painting, the artist's living, breathing engagement with the canvas. Clement Greenberg, the most influential art critic of the period—and a man to whom Pollock would owe much of his breakthrough recognition—declared that he "took one look at it and . . . thought, 'Now that's great art.'" He said that, from this first contact, he "knew Jackson was the greatest painter this country had produced."

Through the 1940s, Jackson turned to paint-pouring. But in 1947, he began using paint brushes and, sometimes, stirring sticks to drip rather than pour paint. This was what Greenberg and others began to call "action painting," and by the end of the 1940s and beginning of the 1950s, Pollock set aside palette, brushes, and easel altogether. Working in a barn on farmland he bought on Long Island, he laid large, raw, unprimed canvases flat on the floor, and dripped and splattered paint on them without ever directly contacting the surface. ("Jack the Dripper," the newspapers and magazines would call him.) Although this would seem a random method, it was anything but. Instead, it was a graphic record of human action, of movement, emotion, passion, and rhythm, unfettered by externally imposed regulations, including "regulation" by conscious thought and plan.

It was also connected to the venerable American tradition of men and women who challenged the status quo, often at their peril. Pollock was in a long line that had begun with early American religious reformers like Roger Williams and Anne Hutchinson, who elevated individual spiritual freedom over orthodox theology. His challenge to earlier artistic assumptions and rules is part of the same tradition in which Herman Melville, Walt Whitman, and Emily Dickinson challenged concepts of conventional literature, philosophers like Charles Sanders Peirce and William James challenged outworn intellectual systems, and architects like Louis Sullivan and Frank Lloyd Wright challenged sacrosanct historical precedents in building.

Pollock and the other members of the New York School—including his brilliant wife, the abstract expressionist painter Lee Krasner—absorbed all that had come before them, but only to interrogate and challenge it the more thoroughly. Neither "abstraction" nor "expressionism" was new. The combination—abstract expressionism—was radical in that it freed expression from abstraction, and what was "expressed" was nothing more or less than the artist's engagement with the surface of the canvas. It was the equivalent of modern jazz in paint. It was a record of the *action* of expression. It was the liberation of art from the world of non-art in which it was created.

The work he and the other abstract expressionists created became itself a benchmark that those who followed have embraced, used, transformed, and, in some cases, angrily renounced as a dead end unconnected to the world.

The August 8, 1949, issue of *Life Magazine* featured a profile of Pollock under the headline "Is he the greatest living painter in the United States?" For some, the answer was simple and obvious: *No.* As some found modern music so much noise, some thought Pollock and his colleagues were creators of so much paint. Nevertheless, this maverick painter received a level of popular recognition accorded very few American artists.

For Pollock, his genius and fame came with a heavy cost. He never outran his alcoholic demons. His drinking may have been a symptom of bipolar disease— or, perhaps, a self-medicating attempt to hold the disease at bay. All that is known for certain is that his behavior by the mid-1950s—the height of his commercial success and international acclaim—grew increasingly erratic, even violent. On August 11, 1956, at 10:15 in the evening, he was driving—very drunk— with his mistress, the painter Ruth Kligman, and her friend Edith Metzger. His Oldsmobile convertible veered off a Long Island country road less than a mile from his home. He was killed, along with Metzger; Kligman survived. His estranged wife, Lee Krasner, devoted much of her own life thereafter to administering her husband's estate and considerable artistic legacy.

3
SCIENCE

DISRUPTION:
USING SCIENCE AND
MATHEMATICS TO
DISCOVER TRUTHS
BEYOND HUMAN BELIEF
OR PERCEPTION

ARCHIMEDES

(C. 287 BCE–C. 212 BCE)

Archimedes has been called the greatest scientist of antiquity and, perhaps, the greatest scientist who ever lived. He lived, and he died, in Syracuse, Sicily, where it is said (*said*, because no one has ever found it) that his tomb was decorated with a sculpture of a sphere and a cylinder.

Perhaps this seems a ludicrously modest monument to the father of physics. We do know that Archimedes's own favorite among his many discoveries and inventions was his elegant mathematical proof that the volume and surface area of a sphere is two-thirds that of a cylinder of the same height and diameter. But, favorite or not, does such a mundane mathematical proof support the lofty appraisal of history—that Archimedes was the progenitor of modern science? Yes.

Consider the most celebrated story about Archimedes, which comes down to us from the great Roman architect Vitruvius (c. 80–70 BCE–after 15 BCE). It seems that King Hiero II of Syracuse had paid a certain goldsmith to fashion a votive crown for a temple. The king, who had personally supplied the required gold, was concerned that the goldsmith might have purloined some of the precious metal and melted in silver to make up the volume. He asked Archimedes to determine if the golden crown had been adulterated with silver.

In the ancient world, merchants and bankers knew the weight per volume of pure gold. The standard method of solving the problem, therefore, would have been to melt down the crown and pour the metal into a mold, so that the volume could be measured precisely, and the density of metal could then be calculated. But King Hiero II insisted that Archimedes solve the problem without destroying the crown. At the time, there was simply no known way to do this. No one could imagine how to calculate the volume of an irregular object. In fact, it seemed impossible because, as everyone knew, numbers were about regular shapes and could not be applied to irregular ones.

Apparently, Archimedes had something in common with at least two other famous men, men from the future. The late nineteenth- and early twentieth-century composer Gustav Mahler and the World War II prime minister of Great Britain Winston Churchill habitually settled into a nice hot bath when they needed to think through an intractable problem. Archimedes did the same thing. This time, while taking his bath, he noticed that the water level in the tub rose as he got in. Archimedes looked at the water rise, and he suddenly realized that this effect—the volume of water displaced by the volume of his body—could be used to calculate the volume and therefore the density of the crown. He understood that water, unlike air, cannot be compressed. Because of its incompressibility, a volume of water equal to the mass of his body was displaced by his presence in that tub. Put the crown in a known volume of water, measure the volume of water displaced by the crown, and you could determine the *mass* of the crown. Divide this figure by the volume of water displaced, and

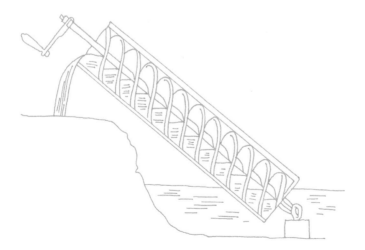

the *density* of the crown would be obtained. Since pure gold is of greater density than gold alloyed with cheaper metals, the displacement would solve the problem without harming the crown.

So thrilled was Archimedes by this scientific epiphany that he leaped out of the tub, neglected to dress, and ran out into the streets shouting "Eureka!" ("I've found it!"). As Vitruvius relates the conclusion of the anecdote, the measurement of displaced water proved that the gold used in the crown had been, in fact, adulterated. (What consequences the larcenous goldsmith suffered as a result of this scientific discovery, we do not know.)

The *Eureka!* story is a good one, though we cannot know whether it is true or not. We do have a treatise by Archimedes titled "On Floating Bodies," which describes the principle that a body immersed in a fluid experiences a buoyant force equal to the weight of the fluid it displaces, and no less a scientist—and disruptor—than Galileo believed it probable that Archimedes was able to compare the density of the crown to the density of a known sample of pure gold of equal weight. Archimedes would have balanced the two on a scale and then lowered the scale, with the two samples, into water. Any difference in density would have caused the balanced scale to tip.

Fact or fiction, the *Eureka!* anecdote is one of only two fragments of anecdotal biography that have come down to us concerning history's greatest scientist. The other concerns the manner of his death. About 212 BCE, during the Second Punic War, the city of Syracuse finally fell to Roman legions after a two-year siege. A Roman legionnaire approached Archimedes, who (according to the historian Plutarch) was "working out some problem with the aid of a diagram, and having fixed his thoughts and his eyes as well upon the matter of his study, he was not aware of the incursion of the Romans or of the capture of the city." The legionnaire demanded that he go with him to his commander, Marcellus. "This Archimedes refused to do until he had worked out his problem and established his demonstration, whereupon the soldier flew into a passion, drew his sword, and dispatched him."

Plutarch noted that there was an alternative version of this account, which said "that the Roman came upon him with drawn sword threatening to kill him at once, and that Archimedes, when he saw him, earnestly besought him to wait a little while, that he might not leave the result that he was seeking incomplete . . . but the soldier paid no heed to him and made an end of him."

The generations that followed Plutarch eagerly adopted both of these possible accounts as stories worthy of Archimedes's end, for both depict him as having, in effect, died nobly for science. Sometime after Plutarch, last words were even ascribed to Archimedes. They were in Latin, because Roman authors put them into the scientist's mouth: "*Noli turbare circulos meos*"—"Do not disturb my circles!"

Those "last words" make two good stories even better, but Plutarch mentions a third story, which is that Archimedes was simply robbed and killed. It is the most plausible of the tales, but the least popular, because it fails to support the same conclusion as the first two versions, that Archimedes died for science. Archimedes would have vehemently disapproved of the bias in favor of the first two versions. For the objective of science is to find truth, regardless of sentiment, rhetoric, or even the satisfaction of hearing a good story. Human beings believe or perceive many things to be true. Science and mathematics, Archimedes showed, can achieve a truth beyond human belief and perception.

• • •

What, then, do we know for certain? Archimedes was born in Syracuse in or about 287 BCE, the son of Phidias, an astronomer and mathematician. He may have been distantly related to the Syracusan king Hiero II. We also know that Syracuse at that time was a major trading town, as well as an intersection of art and science. It was a lively city, both commercially and intellectually, and therefore a wonderful place for the inquisitive son of an astronomer and mathematician to feed his hunger for problem-solving and insight. Nevertheless, it is reported that he very quickly exhausted the knowledge of the city's local teachers. He set off for Egypt to study in Alexandria, at that time the very zenith of learning in the Hellenistic world and home of the renowned library built by Alexander the Great himself. Euclid (born 300 BCE) had died years before Archimedes arrived in Alexandria, but his *Elements*, the great collation of the entire sum of Greek geometry, was available in the city, and Archimedes doubtless absorbed it all before he returned to Syracuse.

From his return to his native city until his death, all that we know of Archimedes was what he left the world in the form of eleven treatises, the most important of which are preserved in *The Archimedes Palimpsest*, a document discovered in Constantinople in 1906 by a Danish professor of philology, Johan Ludvig Heiberg (1854–1928). More precisely, it was not the *document* that he discovered, but an aspect of that document. The document was a 174-page goatskin parchment of prayers, which had been written in the 13th century CE. Over some seven centuries, many had read it before Heiberg got hold of it. But no one before him had realized that it was a *palimpsest*—a document on which the later text (those prayers) had been written over earlier writing, which had been erased. In an era when parchment, or vellum, was scarce and very valuable, it was common practice to scrape the ink away from existing works and write on the material again.

Heiberg could barely make out what lay beneath the prayers, but he recognized just enough to conclude that it contained mathematical works by Archimedes. A few years after Heiberg's discovery, in the 1920s, a private collector purchased the palimpsest, and on October 29, 1998, it was sold at a Christie's auction to an anonymous bidder for $2 million. Modern technologies, including the use of ultraviolet and other light sources as well as X-rays, have made the original overwritten text as clear as it must have been in the tenth century when a Byzantine Greek scribe, working from much earlier texts, copied it down. The seven foundational treatises are

* On the Equilibrium of Planes

* On Spirals

* Measurement of a Circle

* On the Sphere and Cylinder

* On Floating Bodies

* The Method of Mechanical Theorems

* The Ostomachion

Although most of what was discovered in the palimpsest had been known in less complete versions derived from Archimedes during Roman times and in the Renaissance, the original document contains the sum and substance of all that he introduced into the world:

> • *The laws of levers and pulleys, which proved fundamental to civilization as a means of moving heavy objects using small forces.* In these laws, Archimedes provided the key to multiplying human strength exponentially for the purposes of building and—in a military context—destroying. Archimedes's genius was in discovering and formulating the principles of physics and taking them from the realm of theory to application in a variety of machines. Although Plutarch and others make mention of numerous "engines" of war (catapults and the like), the most celebrated of Archimedes's machines is the Archimedean Screw, which enables water to be extracted from the ground. The principle and the device itself are still in use today.

- *The concept of the center of gravity.* Among the foundational concepts of physics, calculations employing the center of gravity are essential to engineering; the design of all kinds of vehicles; aeronautics and astronautics; and the study of astronomy and the solution to all problems relating to bodies in motion.

- *The most precise calculation of the value of* pi *prior to the invention of electronic calculators and digital computers.* Through the millennia, applications of *pi*—the ratio of a circle's circumference to its diameter—have emerged in every field of endeavor involving mathematics. It is among the numbers basic to civilization itself.

- *Mathematical proofs for formulas used to determine the volume and surface area of a sphere.* Archimedes made the connection between mathematics and the physical world seamless, thereby establishing that the universe is capable of being described mathematically. This is the foundation for classical physics and also, even more, for modern physics—the physics of Einstein, Planck, and Heisenberg, among numerous others.

- *The use of exponents to express numbers far greater than had ever been imagined before.* Archimedes gave untold generations of mathematicians, scientists, statisticians, engineers, and social and political leaders the tools to imagine, contemplate, and manipulate vast numerical values. He also provided the mathematical proof that to multiply numbers written as exponents, the exponents had to be added together, thereby greatly facilitating calculations using very large numbers. This is analogous in the realm of mathematics to his work with levers and pulleys in the physical world. As pulleys exponentially multiply the physical power of human beings, so exponents exponentially multiply their intellectual power.

Archimedes was the first physicist, in that he applied an advanced mathematics (largely of his own creation) to describe and manipulate the physical world. At the same time, he also reversed this process, becoming the first physicist to import lessons from physics—the law of leverage, for example—back into pure mathematics in order to solve problems in that intellectual realm. Thus, Archimedes effectively wedded the universe of mind to the physical universe of matter and energy. Without this union, our modern world and everything in it—virtually every invention, every item of technology—would be utterly unimaginable and therefore simply impossible.

This can be seen most explicitly in the achievements of Leonardo da Vinci, Galileo Galilei, and Isaac Newton, all of whom built key insights directly on the work of Archimedes. As Marshall Clagett (1916–2005), the foremost American historian of medieval science, wrote: "The importance of the role played by Archimedes in the history of science can scarcely be exaggerated. . . . His name appears on the pages of the works of the great figures that fashioned the beginnings of modern mechanics. . . . Galileo mentions Archimedes by actual count over one hundred times and in almost Homeric hyperbole. . . ."

Clagett credits Archimedes with having invented "a variety of machines and fields of science like statics, hydrostatics, combinatorics, and mathematical physics." In the "rebirth" of ancient learning that gave the Renaissance its name, Archimedes was not merely a *source* of knowledge, he was the *model* of a modern scientist—a human being who dares to challenge mere faith with mathematics, a symbolic logic that moves human expression beyond the limitations of language that relies on the distortions wrought by assertion, intuition, belief, faith, hope, desire, fear, religion, and political coercion.

GALILEO (1564–1642)
GALILEI

A man of deep religious faith, Galileo nevertheless defied the Catholic Inquisition to emerge as the archetype of the modern rational man of science. He was an adept experimentalist and observer as well as an incisive theorist, who used his telescope—which he himself built, improving on a Dutch original—to discover the moons of Jupiter and the mountains on Earth's moon. He made important observations of Kepler's supernova and of Venus, Saturn, and Neptune. His discovery of sunspots challenged religious-based theories of the literally spotless "perfection" of that heavenly body. He discovered that the Milky Way was not the nebulous cloud it was thought to be, but a multitude of stars. Using his telescope and his own development of mathematical physics, he supported and popularized the Copernican model of the solar system, in which the earth was but one of several planets orbiting a central sun. Turning from the heavens down to the earth, Galileo invented the compound microscope and made pioneering observations with it. He made discoveries foundational to mathematical physics, especially concerning the motions of bodies and the basic principle of relativity—by which the laws of motion are the same in any system moving at a constant speed in a straight line. This became the baseline assumption central to Albert Einstein's epoch-making special theory of relativity in the twentieth century.

G alileo Galilei was born on February 15, 1564 in Pisa, Italy. At the time of his birth, "science" did not exist. By the time of his death seventy-eight years later, science was a rapidly emerging discipline—thanks to him.

After moving with his parents and siblings to Florence in 1572, Galileo began studying to become a priest, but soon returned to Pisa and the university there to study medicine. Before completing the work for this degree, however, he changed focus yet again and embarked on the study of mathematics. In 1589, he obtained an appointment to the chair of mathematics at the University of Pisa. Just three years later, he accepted a more prestigious and remunerative professorship in mathematics at the University of Padua. In this city, he met Marina Gamba, whom he married. Together, they had three children, Virginia (1600), Livia (1601), and Vincenzo (1606).

In Padua, Galileo did much of his work in physical mechanics and commenced his observations with the telescope. In 1610, he published his *Sidereus Nuncius* (*The Starry Messenger*), product of the world's first telescopic observations of the heavenly bodies. Partly due to the fame generated by this publication, Galileo was offered a position as mathematician at the University of Pisa and the official post of philosopher to the Grand Duke of Tuscany, which ushered him into the powerful court of the Medici. (A scientist not above politics, Galileo named Jupiter's moons, which he had discovered, after the Medici.) In 1611, he was honored by membership in the Academia dei Lincei, generally recognized as the world's first scientific learned society.

In 1612, Galileo published *Discourse on Floating Bodies*, which, among other things, reported his discovery of sunspots and his observations on the phases of Venus, the strange shape of Saturn (his telescope lacked sufficient resolution to reveal the planet's rings; Galileo saw them as "ears"), and the periods of the orbit of Jupiter's moons. A year later, he published his *Letters on the Sunspots*, in which he presented his support for the bold assertion of the Polish astronomer Nicolaus Copernicus (1473–1543) that the planets, including the earth, orbit the centrally located sun.

During 1613–1614, Galileo further developed his thoughts on the heliocentric Copernican solar system, and in 1616 expressed these in his *Letter to the*

Grand Duchess Christina. At this time, the Sacred Congregation of the Index, an arm of the Grand Inquisition of the Catholic Church, condemned Copernicus's book *On the Revolution of the Heavenly Orbs.* Galileo was summoned to an audience with Cardinal Robert Bellarmine, who warned him neither to teach nor further defend Copernican theory, which the Church believed challenged scripture.

Galileo did not publish again until 1623's *The Assayer* (*Il Saggiatore*), which argued that comets were sublunary phenomena. He also asserted the basis for mathematical physics with the claim that "the book of nature is written in the language of mathematics." Historically, *The Assayer* is considered the first developed statement of the scientific method of empirical inquiry. Although the Church never condemned this work, it was actually Galileo's most powerful challenge to faith-based knowledge.

The year 1623 also saw the election of Maffeo Barberini—whom Galileo considered a great friend and was a longtime supporter of Galileo—as Pope Urban VIII. This encouraged the scientist to resume his work in support of Copernican theory. Titled *Dialogues Concerning the Two Great World Systems*, the geocentric universe and the heliocentric universe, it was not published until 1632. Galileo presented further proof that Copernicus was correct: the sun, not the earth, was the center of the known universe.

Very soon after the publication of *Dialogues*, the Inquisition banned its sale and summoned Galileo to Rome for an ecclesiastical trial. He was condemned as a heretic the following year and held under house arrest. He used this enforced seclusion as an opportunity to write his final work, *Discourses and Mathematical Demonstrations concerning Two New Sciences*, which was smuggled out of Italy and published in Protestant Holland. The "new sciences" that are the subject of the book concern the strength of materials and the motion of objects—predecessors of the foundational modern fields of material engineering and kinematics, the study of points, objects, and bodies in motion.

Galileo died on January 8, 1642. Because he was still under condemnation as a heretic, he was buried in an obscure corner of Florence's Basilica of Santa Croce, only to be reinterred in the main portion of that Basilica, under a magnificent monument to him, in 1737.

Galileo was posthumously rehabilitated by the Church, signified by his reburial and by Pope John Paul II's official expression of regret on behalf of the Church on October 31, 1992. This was a long-overdue resolution to a dispute between the Church and a man of sincere faith (Galileo's two daughters had, with his enthusiastic blessing, become nuns) who nevertheless could not deny the truth as his new scientific method delivered it to him. He had been summoned by the Inquisitors to four hearings during 1633, at the last of which, on June 21, he was compelled to recite and to sign a written "abjuration" for "having held and believed that the sun [is] in the center of the universe and immoveable, and that the earth is not at the center of same, and that it does move."

Popular legend has long held that, after uttering this abjuration, denying that the earth moves, Galileo muttered under his breath "And yet it moves." He almost certainly said no such thing, but his work spoke for him and for the enduring triumph of rational inquiry as systematized by the scientific method despite subsequent assault by religious zealots and political deceivers and tyrants.

DISRUPTION:
CREATING CLASSICAL
PHYSICS BY ACCOUNTING
FOR THE PHENOMENA OF
THE PHYSICAL WORLD
THROUGH MATHEMATICS

ISAAC NEWTON
(1642–1727)

The two bombshells dropped by Albert Einstein—the Special Theory of Relativity in 1905 and the General Theory of Relativity in 1915—disrupted classical physics by showing that Newton's Three Laws of Motion, which had been accepted as absolute truth since 1687, when they were published in his *Philosophiae Naturalis Principia Mathematica* (*Mathematical Principles of Natural Philosophy*), were only approximately correct. According to Einstein, Newton's Laws of Motion broke down when the velocities in question approached the speed of light. Later in the twentieth century, the emergence of quantum mechanics showed that the laws also broke down at the micro level.

Why, then, do we still study Newton if modern physics has effectively repealed his "laws"? The answer is very simple. While the mechanics of Newton do not apply near or at the speed of light or in the unimaginably small spaces of atomic-particle physics, none of us lives near or at the speed of light or within the spaces defined by particle physics. Light speed is real, and the behavior of atomic particles is real. But, day to day, neither of these much matters to us. We live in a reality that is both much slower than the speed of light and much bigger than the dimensions of atomic particles. In our reality, everything Newton revealed to us remains of great use and is absolutely fundamental.

No theorist of physics is more important or more original—and therefore more disruptive of all that went before him—than Newton. His laws of motion and his law of universal gravitation explained all that moves on earth or in heaven. He invented the calculus, giving human beings a method for calculating continuous change, which, until calculus, was essentially incalculable. He explained the nature both of light and of color. He both enabled and triggered the great scientific revolution of the seventeenth century. Since we cannot travel at light speed or live within an atom, we cannot get away from Isaac Newton.

● ● ●

According to the Julian calendar then in use, Isaac Newton was born on Christmas Day 1642, in Woolsthorpe, near Grantham, Lincolnshire. It was an auspicious day on which to be born—unless, like Newton, you were premature, tiny, frail, and fatherless—the illiterate yeoman farmer who sired him having died before his son entered the world. Newton's widowed and impoverished mother entrusted his care to his grandmother by the time he was three. She remarried a wealthy rector who would take Hannah Newton as his wife only if she were free to raise *his* family, not hers. As fate would have it, he was not long-lived, and Hannah returned to Woolsthorpe in 1653 after his death.

She returned to an unhappy, lonely boy, whom she took out of school so that he could work the farm. To the immeasurable benefit of science, he was a miserable farmer, and he resumed his schooling in Grantham, preparing to enter Trinity College, Cambridge. When he left Woolsthorpe in June 1661, it was without regret. At Cambridge, he found the home he had never really had.

Cambridge was highly respected in the seventeenth century; but, like other universities of the era, it was still largely dedicated to an early Renaissance curriculum. Aristotle and a handful of other classical authors were the basis of education. Though he reveled in his books, Newton was by no means a standout undergraduate—at least not in class. Much of his education during his Cambridge years was self-administered. He read contemporary thinkers, such as Descartes and Hobbes. In preference to Euclid's *Elements*, cornerstone of the Cambridge mathematics curriculum, he embraced Descartes's *Géométrie*, which was far more advanced and complex. Although he was awarded his degree in 1665, it was without honors or distinction of any kind.

Newton would have nevertheless preferred to stay on at Cambridge for graduate study, but 1665 was the first of two straight plague years, and the university was forced to shut its doors. For the next two years, Newton was compelled to wait out the plague in Woolsthorpe.

He did not idle there. He later commented that in those days of plague, he was in his "prime of age for invention, and minded mathematics and philosophy more than at any time since." It was in the solitude of Woolsthorpe that he began the invention of what he called his mathematical "method of fluxions," the calculus, a method that the German polymath Gottfried Wilhelm Leibniz (1646–1716) would independently invent a decade later. Calculus gave Newton and physics a mathematical procedure for calculating continuous change—rates of change and slopes of curves in the case of differential calculus, and the accumulation of quantities and the areas under or between curves in the case of integral calculus. Calculus would become the language through which the physics of a dynamic universe could be created and communicated. As if this were not sufficient achievement, during his eighteen months of enforced exile from Cambridge Newton also outlined his breakthrough theory of light and color and began to work out the mechanics of planetary motion—the problem that would result in his mature masterpiece, *Philosophiae Naturalis Principia Mathematica* (1687).

● ● ●

In April 1667, Cambridge reopened and Newton returned. Despite his lack of official academic distinction, he gained election as a minor fellow at Trinity College. In 1668 he was awarded a master's degree and made a Trinity senior fellow. Stunningly, in 1669, though he was yet to reach his twenty-seventh birthday, Newton was named to succeed the distinguished Isaac Barrow (1630–1677) as Lucasian Professor of Mathematics. From this new office, he set about ordering and analyzing his research into optics.

Elected to the Royal Society in 1672, he presented his first public paper, on the nature of color, demonstrating by experiment that "the colours of all natural bodies have no other origin than this, that they are variously qualified to reflect one sort of light in greater plenty than another." In other words, white light is composed of the colors of the spectrum and color is a property of light. Objects interact with the colors of light rather than generating color themselves.

For ages before Newton, the proposition that color is intrinsic to light was subject to debate. Newton ended the dispute—almost. The prickly natural philosopher and early microscopist Robert Hooke (1635–1703), curator of experiments at the Royal Society, persisted in attacking this explanation, and so the argument over various aspects of Newton's experimental methods roiled until 1675, when Newton published another paper, which Hooke did not disagree with but attacked as a plagiarism of his own work. Deeply wounded, Newton withdrew from public and, in 1678, suffered a nervous collapse. This was intensified the next year by the death of his mother, which caused him to withdraw even deeper.

Newton began secretly studying alchemy, accumulating and devouring books on the subject, and conducting many elaborate experiments. Until recently, modern scholars believed that Newton's clandestine approach to alchemy was the futile pursuit of an irrational superstition. They lamented the waste of a genius's time. This interpretation, however, reveals more about modern scholarly prejudices than it does about Newton.

Close study of Newton's alchemical notes reveals that his experiments were quite serious and meticulously executed. He hoped to find in alchemy an insight into nature that could not be found through mathematics, mechanics, and optics. Newton saw in alchemy an assertion that hidden forces of attraction and repulsion were critical at the infinitesimal particulate level. In a sense, Newton's alchemical insights anticipated, however vaguely, the much later insights of atomic and particle physics. More immediately, however, alchemy shaped his view of celestial mechanics, including the mysterious force he would call gravity.

• • •

Everyone knows the story of what happened when Newton observed the fall of an apple in his Woolsthorpe garden one day in 1666. Some versions of the story portray him as dozing under an apple tree and being rudely awakened when an apple hit him on the head. In fact, his own recollection makes no mention of being apple-struck, but he did remark that in this year he "began to think of gravity extending to the orb of the Moon."

Newton scholars today believe he had a slip of memory. The concept of gravity did not come to him suddenly with the fall of an apple, but worked its way through his mind over some twenty years. Surprisingly, it was the disputatious Hooke who spurred his thought. Hooke began corresponding with Newton in November 1679 on the subject of planetary motion. Newton replied, only to soon break off the exchange. But he did not stop thinking. Early in 1680, he began formulating the relationship between central attraction and a force, gravity, that fell off with the square of distance. He did not participate directly in the London conversations among Hooke, the astronomer Edmund Halley (1656–1742), and the architect Christopher Wren (1632–1723) concerning the problem of planetary motion—that is, what drives the planets to move, and why is that movement orbital? It was Halley who, in August 1684, left London to visit Newton in Cambridge and pose to him the question: What type of curve does a planet describe in its orbit around the sun, assuming an inverse square law of attraction?

Newton was prepared with an answer: It was an ellipse. Surprised, Halley asked him how he knew.

Newton responded that he had calculated it—but, having mislaid the calculation, he promised to do the mathematical work again and send the result to Halley.

What he sent to Halley in November 1684 was a manuscript titled *De motu corporum in gyrum* (*On the Motion of Bodies in an Orbit*). Over the next three years, his calculations explaining the motion of orbiting bodies grew into *Philosophiae Naturalis Principia Mathematica*. Published in 1687, this may be the single most important book in the history of science. The book is best known for its three laws of motion and the law of universal gravity. These alone explained not only planetary orbits, but the physical nature of all things that moved anywhere in the universe. The fact that someone had finally explained something so basic as why a thing fell and why a thing had weight was disruptive. But the very title of the book got to the heart of the disruption: *Mathematical Principles of Natural Philosophy*. Newton proved that mathematics could account for the phenomena of nature. In this, he connected the human intellect directly to the world outside the mind.

● ● ●

Principia revealed something else—the basic emotional fragility of Isaac Newton. Ever the troublemaker, Hooke wanted a share of the credit for Newton's book, and, as his dispute with Newton dragged on, Newton threatened to withhold Book III of the *Principia* from publication—just to spite him. When others persuaded him to proceed, Newton did so, but not before removing every mention of his enemy's name. (Indeed, when he finally assembled and distilled all his work on light in his *Opticks*, he delayed publication and stopped attending meetings of the Royal Society until Hooke, ailing, finally died in 1703.

Principia made Newton famous. In 1689 he was even elected to Parliament. In 1693 he suffered another nervous collapse. After some three years, he recovered and, in need of financial support, was appointed Warden of the Mint in 1696. Ensconced in London, he basked in fame and accolades. The self-imposed delay in the publication of *Opticks* turned out to be fortunate, because it added to his glory at a time when he had largely ended his scientific and mathematical work. In 1705, the year after the publication of *Opticks*, this impoverished half-orphan from Woolsthorpe was knighted. He lorded over the Royal Society as its president and used his position to outmaneuver Leibniz to gain for himself the lion's share of credit for calculus. He died, in London, on March 20, 1727.

DISRUPTION:
FORMULATING THE
FOUNDATIONAL
PRINCIPLES OF
HEREDITY—BY
EXPERIMENTING IN A
MONASTERY GARDEN

GREGOR (1822–1884)
MENDEL

The pious do not become monks to disrupt the world, and neither do gardeners. Yet Gregor Mendel was both a monk and a gardener—albeit with scientific training—whose patient experiments with the humble pea plants in the garden of his monastery allowed him to outline the basis of heredity. With Mendel, the study of genetics began.

He was born Johann Mendel on July 22, 1822, to a farming couple, Anton and Rosine Mendel, in what was called at the time Heinzendorf, Austria. He would surely have become a farmer had not the local schoolmaster appreciated the eleven-year-old boy's zeal for learning and depth of understanding. He recommended that the youngster progress to a secondary school in Troppau. Despite the high financial cost of the move, Mendel's parents journeyed to Troppau and enrolled Johann. Shy and timid, Johann had a great deal of trouble adjusting to life in the larger town—and yet he was anxious to justify his parents' sacrifice. He worked hard, graduating with honors in 1840.

From the school at Troppau, young Mendel enrolled in a two-year course of study at the Philosophical Institute of the University of Olmütz. He excelled again, especially in mathematics and physics, and found work as a tutor, which defrayed both tuition and living costs. Yet the emotional toll on him was heavy. Seriously depressed, he was forced at one point to suspend his studies, but recovered sufficiently to continue, and in 1843 he completed the program.

But Mendel then took a turn that pleased neither his professors, who expected him to continue on to a scientific career, nor his father, who expected him to take over the family farm. Instead, he embarked upon the rigorous course of study and devotion necessary to prepare for life as a monk. In quiet and solitude, perhaps he hoped to find the peace that evaded him in other pursuits. He was embraced by the Augustinians at the St. Thomas Monastery in Brno and took, upon his ordination, the name Gregor.

While he had expected to live a retired and contemplative life, Gregor Mendel found himself in a monastery that was the region's center of culture and learning. Many of his fellow monks were engaged in research and teaching. The monastery had a large modern library, which was not restricted to works of religion but also contained the latest scientific publications. There were also well-equipped laboratories.

Mendel threw himself into study and research to the point of debilitation and serious illness. Concerned for him, his superiors sent him off in 1849 to teach in the Moravian town of Znaim (modern Znojmo, Czech Republic). When he failed to pass the examination for his teaching certificate in 1850, the monastery paid for his enrollment at the University of Vienna, where he studied mathematics and physics under the eminent Christian Doppler (for whom the Doppler effect is named) and botany under Franz Unger, a forward-looking scientist who was an accomplished microscopist and a prescient exponent of biological evolution—some eight or nine years before Charles Darwin published his *On the Origin of Species* (1859).

Completing his university studies in 1853, Mendel returned to the monastery in Brno, where he was assigned to teach at a secondary school associated with the order. His career here spanned a decade, during which he began conducting, in 1854, the experiments that constituted his research in the transmission of hereditary traits in plant hybrids.

The prevailing theory during this period—a theory so pervasive as to be accepted as self-evident fact—was that the hereditary traits of the offspring of any species were nothing less than the diluted blending of traits present in the parents, as if genetic material were some homogenous brew capable of dilution down through the generations. It was further assumed that, given a sufficient number of generations, any hybrid would revert to its original form, the variations having been sufficiently diluted. Thus, a hybrid could never create new permanent forms. Both of these commonly accepted assumptions were dubiously confirmed by a handful of desultory observations. Mendel noted, however, that no scientist had ever devoted sufficient time to confirm these observations over many generations. As a monk, time was one commodity he possessed in abundance. A godly, patient man, he was in no hurry. Between 1856 and 1863, Mendel conducted his quiet experiments on tens of thousands of individual plants, each of which he meticulously observed and notated.

His choice of experimental subject was very deliberate. He chose peas. They were rich in their highly distinctive varieties, and their offspring were quickly and readily produced. Mendel concentrated on cross-fertilizing plants with the most distinctly opposite characteristics. He crossed short with tall, wrinkled with smooth, those producing green seeds with those producing yellow. His purpose was to reduce the subjective factors of observation to a minimum. And, after years of observation, he was prepared to formulate two breakthrough conclusions.

First was the Law of Segregation, which demonstrated that some traits are dominant and others recessive. These traits are passed down randomly from parents to offspring. The concept of dominant and recessive traits disproved the universally accepted notion that inheritance is a matter of simply blending traits. Second was the Law of Independent Assortment, in which each trait was passed down independently of other traits. Beyond these two conclusions, Mendel, well trained in mathematics, theorized that heredity follows the basic laws of statistics. Boldly, he claimed that his experiments on pea plants applied to all organisms with identifiable traits. In other words, he had discovered basic and universal principles of heredity.

• • •

Mendel presented his findings in two 1865 lectures before the Natural Science Society in Brno. The society also published his studies in its journal in 1866 under the misleadingly modest title "Experiments on Plant Hybrids." This generic, noncommittal title, together with Mendel's own constitutional disinclination to promote his own work, meant that its disruptive impact was hardly appreciated at the time. Those relatively few who read his study assumed that Mendel was merely reaffirming what had already been generally observed. This is understandable due to the simple reason that Mendel failed to underscore the differences and refused to tout the magnitude of his breakthrough. Worst of all, many readers of his study took the work as confirmation—not refutation—of the simple assumption that all hybrids revert eventually to their original form.

The fact is that even Mendel himself seems to have failed to appreciate the magnitude of what he had observed. He did not pursue his observations on variability to their full significance for evolution. Moreover, he retreated from his original claim that his findings applied to all species and all types of traits. Thus, Mendel's work was not seen as essentially disruptive until years later, when it was rediscovered and interpreted in the context of Darwin.

If Gregor Mendel felt any disappointment, none was apparent. He seemed quite content to be elected, in 1868, abbot of the school in which he had taught for fourteen years. This position, however, required him to do a good deal of administrative work. For these reasons, his career as an experimental scientist was effectively at an end, which may have been just as well since his eyesight, so essential to observational work, had dimmed with the passing years.

Mendel died on January 6, 1884, a respected religious figure within his small circle, but little known as a scientist. Years would pass before his fundamental work was rediscovered and recognized for what it was. In 1900, three botanists, Hugo de Vries, Carl Correns, and Erich von Tschermak-Seysenegg, together duplicated Mendel's experiments and results. They claimed their results as having been independently reached. They said that they published before they became aware of Mendel's 1866 paper. Not everyone believed them. Accused by some of plagiarizing Mendel and taking credit for his work, the trio scrambled to give the monk credit for what he had done. Thus, in this backhanded way, Mendel was brought posthumously into the limelight.

Even so, his work met with resistance from some Darwinians, who discounted its relevance to the theory of evolution. Only by the second quarter of the twentieth century were the observations of this modest man recognized as absolutely essential to understanding the field of genetics. They were seen as what they had been: the first major insights into the process of hereditary transmission before the discovery of the visualization of the DNA double-helix model by Francis Crick and James Watson in 1953.

LOUIS PASTEUR

(1822–1895)

Louis Pasteur came from an age of heroic science, created by the scientists Paul de Kruif profiled in his 1926 classic *The Microbe Hunters*—which included Pasteur among eleven others. They were explorers who dared confront the threats posed by an indifferent nature, an ignorant society, and, all too often, their own hidebound colleagues. Reading such a celebratory author like de Kruif today is to feel we are reading popular mythology rather than objective history. But the likes of Pasteur were in fact the knights of science, and the discoveries they made disrupted long-held beliefs, changed civilization, and struck a selfless blow for the value of fact-based enterprise and action in the service of saving and improving life. In the case of Louis Pasteur, by discovering that microorganisms cause both fermentation (vital to the wine industry, which was in turn vital to France) and disease (a threat to life), he advanced the science of vaccination in a world-changing way and closed the gap between the theorist and the experimentalist in science.

Louis Pasteur was born on December 27, 1822, in Dole, France, the middle child of five in a family of leather tanners. As a child, there was no hint of the scientist he would become. He was a passable student in elementary school, but his passion was not in his textbooks. He was an avid fisherman who also enjoyed drawing—a talent his neighbors and friends appreciated, since he gave away the many portraits he sketched. He earned a degree in philosophy and another in science and mathematics. The latter proved tough going for him, and he failed his first examination. Persevering, he went on to earn a degree in general science in 1842 and decided to venture the entrance exam for the École Normale Supérieure, the prestigious Parisian teachers' college. Only through very hard work did he pass the entrance exam—and with a very high ranking. In 1845, Pasteur earned his master's degree in science and, two years later, a doctorate, writing not one but two theses, in physics and in chemistry. He taught as a professor at the Dijon Lycée in 1848 and was subsequently appointed professor of chemistry at the University of Strasbourg. There he met, courted, and, in 1849, married Marie Laurent, daughter of the university rector. The marriage was fruitful, producing five children—but in an age in which bacterial disease was a poorly understood scourge, three of the Pasteur children would die of typhoid before reaching adulthood.

While waiting to find a full-time academic position, Pasteur had supported himself as a laboratory assistant at the École Normale. He used the laboratory there to pursue the research he had begun for his doctoral dissertation in chemistry, studying the property of "optical activity" exhibited by certain crystals or solutions, which rotate plane-polarized light clockwise or counterclockwise. Through exquisitely acute observation—perhaps his single greatest strength as a scientist—Pasteur showed that such optical activity was most often related to the shape of the crystals of a compound. From this, he concluded that it was the internal arrangement within the molecules themselves that twisted the light. This is a foundational hypothesis in the early development of structural chemistry, the study of molecules in three dimensions.

In 1852, Pasteur was promoted to chairman of the chemistry department at the University of Strasbourg and, two years later in 1854, accepted appointment as the first dean of the newly created faculty of sciences at Lille University. Here he began a long research project into the nature of fermentation, an important natural process, of course, but one of special concern to the French, whose lifestyle and economy were closely bound up with the making and consuming of wine.

The prevailing belief was that fermentation was a spontaneous process created by chemical reactions involving enzymes, which, at the time, were not yet directly associated with living organisms. Pasteur took the view of a small minority of scientists, that all fermentation is carried out by living microorganisms. By 1858, he was ready to publish his proofs, which were based on extremely precise observation and a well-informed idea of what to look for. "In the field of observation," he told an audience at a ceremony marking his inauguration to the Faculty of Letters of Douai and the Faculty of Sciences of Lille, "chance favors only the prepared mind."

Pasteur not only showed that fermentation was a biological process produced by the action of microorganisms, but that when the "wrong" microorganism contaminated wine, lactic acid, not just alcohol, was created, making the wine sour and spoiling it. Armed with this knowledge, Pasteur went on to create his "pasteurization" process in 1865. He found that when "raw" wine was heated to between 60°C and 100°C, the microorganisms that fermented the wine as lactic acid were killed, leaving only those that fermented it to alcohol. This process was a boon to the French wine industry. Pasteurization was later extended to many other spoilable substances and foodstuffs, most notably milk. Pasteur was not practicing "pure" theoretical science, but science in the service of life and livelihood.

● ● ●

Pasteur was capable of intense focus, yet his vision was never monolithic. His studies of fermentation led him to believe that many diseases were, like fermentation, caused by microorganisms. This so-called germ theory was not Pasteur's discovery: it had been adumbrated as early as the 1670s by Anton van Leeuwenhoek (1632–1723), the early pioneer of microscopy and microbiology. Between 1808 and 1813, the Italian entomologist Agostino Bassi (1773–1856) demonstrated that a microscopic "vegetable parasite" caused a costly disease of silkworms. Other scientists had their suspicions as well, but, even as late as the 1860s, the vast majority of physicians rejected the germ theory, arguing that the chief factor in any disease was some flaw, weakness, or imbalance within the body of the victim.

To Pasteur, this was a non-answer. In the 1860s, he took up where Bassi had left off, looking for the precise cause of pébrine, a silkworm disease wreaking havoc on the French silk industry. He isolated the microorganism associated with the disease (*Nosema bombycis*—the name supplied by another researcher in 1870) and created a method by which silkworm eggs could be screened for infection, and the infected eggs discarded and destroyed. As he had done for wine, so Pasteur did for silk: he saved an industry.

● ● ●

In 1868, while he was engaged in his silkworm studies, Pasteur suffered a stroke, which left him partially paralyzed on the left side. Two years later, France was defeated in the Franco-Prussian War (1870–1871). In the aftermath of the war, Emperor Louis-Napoléon, with whom Pasteur had entered into negotiations for a new state-of-the-art laboratory, was overthrown. Such was Pasteur's hard-won prestige, however, that the new republican government did not hesitate to agree to fund a new laboratory and to award Pasteur a salary sufficient to free him from his academic and administrative duties so that he could devote himself exclusively to the study of disease.

His first target was anthrax, a costly scourge of livestock. In the course of studying this disease, however, one of those happy accidents that bring a break-through to the "prepared mind" drew Pasteur to make a detour into the study of fowl (or chicken) cholera. From an eminent veterinarian, he received cultures of fowl cholera, which he cultivated using chicken broth. Some of the culture was spoiled, however, and failed to infect Pasteur's experimental chickens. Not wanting to waste the still-healthy birds, he attempted to infect them with a fresh culture—only to discover that they would not get sick. His conclusion was that the bacteria in the spoiled culture were not dead, just weakened, or attenuated. Infecting the chickens with attenuated bacteria produced no disease or very mild disease—but it did leave the chickens immune to the disease.

Using a weak strain of a disease to immunize against its virulent form was not new. It had been used against smallpox in the eighteenth century. What Pasteur discovered was that one could artificially attenuate disease organisms by treat-ing them with heat or chemicals or a combination of the two. He applied what he had accidentally discovered with fowl cholera to anthrax, producing vaccines from weakened anthrax bacteria. He proved the effectiveness of his vaccines in public demonstrations at Pouilly-le-Fort in 1881.

Pasteur also discovered the truth behind what farmers believed were "cursed fields"—plots of pasturage that seemed to infect all the animals who grazed them. When Pasteur learned that farmers buried in these fields animals that had died of anthrax, he theorized that earthworms brought the bacteria from the decay-ing carcasses to the surface of the soil. To prove this, he examined earthworm excrement microscopically and discovered the anthrax bacillus in the material. Prevention of such infection was simple, he declared: do not bury dead animals in the grazing fields.

• • •

Pasteur decided that it was time to move his work into the prevention of human disease, but he was faced with ethical problems in how to conduct his experiments and also with a more specific problem: he was a chemist, not a physician. He decided to research a disease that afflicted both animals and human beings, so that he could focus at least his initial investigation on the animals. The most obvious and urgent among such diseases was rabies, which infects animals and can be transmitted to human beings via a bite. In fact, human beings rarely contracted the disease; but, when they did, the symptoms were horrific and almost invariably fatal. For this reason, rabies created disproportionate terror. The treatment commonly used after a person had been bitten by a rabid animal—cauterization of the bite with a red-hot iron—was not only brutal but ineffective.

Pasteur faced other problems in researching the disease, especially with regard to finding a vaccine. The microorganism that caused rabies had so far defied identification, and all efforts to culture it *in vitro*—in a culture dish—had failed. Pasteur discovered that rabies could, however, be injected into other species and attenuated. He used rabies attenuated in monkeys and, later, in rabbits to inoculate dogs. This protected healthy dogs as well as animals already bitten by another rabid animal. He was, however, reluctant to make any kind of trial on a human being—until July 6, 1885, when a nine-year-old boy named Joseph Meister was brought to him. The sick child had been bitten by a rabid dog and was almost certainly doomed to a terrible death. Believing he had nothing to lose, Pasteur inoculated Joseph with attenuated rabies, even though he could not identify the microorganism. (In the days before the scanning electron microscope, no one could have. The disease was caused not by a bacterial organism, but by a virus, not large enough to be visible to nineteenth-century optical technology.)

The result was historically momentous. Meister recovered, showing that a cure for rabies had been found, along with a preventative vaccine for animals. Vaccination, which had been limited mainly to smallpox, now became a widely accepted form of prophylaxis as well as a treatment for active disease. Medical scientists became interested in developing attenuated vaccines for a wide variety of diseases. Before Pasteur's work with the rabies vaccination, physicians could do little for patients afflicted with major infectious diseases, except to give palliative and supportive care. Pasteur's work began a movement, at long last, to arm physicians with effective medicines.

People from all over the world made cash contributions to the Institut Pasteur, which Louis Pasteur founded on June 4, 1887 to study biology, microorganisms, diseases, and vaccines. Officially opened in Paris in 1888, the Institut is now a global network with some thirty branches and is a living monument to the scientist, who died on September 28, 1895.

SIGMUND FREUD

(1856–1939)

When his eighty-one-year-old father, a wool merchant named Jacob, died in 1896, Sigmund Freud suffered an emotional crisis that brought the forty-year-old physician, an associate professor (docent) on his way up at the University of Vienna, to the verge of nervous collapse. His early work had been as a researcher in cerebral anatomy, but he soon became interested in "neuropathology" (diseases of the nervous system) and then psychiatry. The year before his father died, Freud had published *Studies in Hysteria* as coauthor with his mentor and friend, Dr. Josef Breuer.

A t the time, mental illness, of which hysteria—a cluster of debilitating psychosomatic ailments—was one form, had few significantly effective medical treatments. Breuer, however, discovered that when he encouraged his "hysterical" patients to talk to him, their symptoms improved as they expressed emotional traumas and the feelings related to them. Often, memories of the traumas had been long suppressed but were recalled by talking. Once resurfaced, they could be analyzed further—often with curative results. Breuer called this method the "talking cure," and now a near-prostrate Freud tried it on himself. He essentially allowed his thoughts to flow freely, and then he analyzed the product of this stream of consciousness. He also paid close attention to the dreams that he was having at this time, convinced that they brought to consciousness thoughts that had been repressed.

Freud's self-analytical process during his emotional crisis was complex, but its main contours were something like this: His deceased father had two grown sons by a previous marriage, Emmanuel and Philip. The young Freud grew close to Philip's son John, who was his own age. Freud began to remember that, as he approached puberty, he frequently fantasized that John's father, Philip, was actually his own real father. Along with other memories, this fantasy convinced Freud that he unconsciously wished his biological father, Jacob, were dead because he was a rival for his mother's affection. Freud came to understand that he had deep love and admiration for his father, yet these feelings were also entangled with those of shame and hate. The latter, Freud concluded, were bound up with his own sexual feelings toward his mother—what Freud later called "the Oedipus complex."

To Freud's great relief, the fruits of his self-analysis relieved and resolved the emotional crisis following his father's death. Based on this result, he became convinced of the efficacy of the "talking cure," which he would go on to develop as what he called the science of psychoanalysis. He was also persuaded that sexuality, long assumed to be nonexistent in preadolescent children, was merely latent in them. Moreover, he concluded, the child's early sexual feelings were fixated on the parents—the mother in the case of the male child, the father in the case of the female. The result was what he later called the "family romance," in which a son commonly develops ambivalent feelings toward his father, who figures as a rival for the romantic love of his mother, and a daughter harbors a similar ambivalence toward her mother, who is her rival for her father's love.

According to Freud, psychopathology, capable of producing great suffering, might emerge in adult life if these early ambivalences are not resolved. Moreover, while sufferers are certainly aware of their suffering, they often have no idea of what underlies it. The sources are unconscious, which meant, Freud decided, that human beings were aware of only a small portion of their own thoughts and memories and impressions. The vast portion of mental life formed what he called the unconscious mind. To the degree that a person suffering from mental illness could raise the content of the unconscious mind to consciousness, he or she might be cured.

This was a breakthrough. It was also a profound disruption of the prevailing picture of human behavior. In the West especially, morality and society had been founded on the principles of free will and responsibility for one's actions. To entertain sexual thoughts about one's parents and to violate the Sixth

Commandment by failing to "honor" one's father and mother were regarded as not only grave sins, but sick and sickening abominations. Freud's mission was to overcome multiple universally prevailing prejudices to gain acceptance for his new science of the mind.

• • •

Sigmund Freud was born Sigismund Schlomo Freud in Freiberg, Moravia, on May 6, 1856, but moved with his family to Vienna when he was just four years old. The Freuds were Jews living in an Austrian empire in which anti-Semitism was endemic, part of the very fabric of society. In a sense, Freud was a born outsider, prepared to expect objection from the civilization of which he and his kind had never been wholly a part. Yet it would be in a semi-hostile Vienna that Freud would develop psychoanalysis.

When he was nine, Freud enrolled in the Leopoldstädter Kommunal-Realgymnasium, a prestigious high school. Here he developed a deep love for literature in an array of languages—German, French, Italian, Spanish, English, Hebrew, Latin, and Greek. Before he finished at this institution, he considered becoming a philologist, a classical scholar or a student of literature and languages. But when he enrolled at the University of Vienna in 1873, he was determined to study law. Instead, he soon switched to medicine, initially concentrating on biology and physiology under the most eminent physiologist of his time, Ernst Brücke. Freud went on to specialize in neurology, receiving his MD in 1881.

Freud's chief interest was in research and experimentation. But his engagement to Martha Bernays and the necessity of providing for a family (the couple would have six children, the youngest of whom, Anna, became a noted psychoanalyst) prompted him to work as a clinical physician at Vienna General Hospital. Having accumulated a nest egg by 1886, he married Martha and then opened a private practice for the treatment of psychological disorders. This proved remunerative and also furnished a wealth of clinical material on which he built a life's work that transformed not only the treatment of mental illness, but our picture of humanity itself.

During 1885 and part of 1886, Freud lived in Paris to study with the French neurologist Jean-Martin Charcot, who used hypnotism to treat hysteria and other forms of mental illness. At first, Freud believed Charcot had found a reliable portal into the unconscious; but when he returned to Vienna and began using hypnosis himself, he concluded that, while it often had beneficial effects, which were sometimes quite dramatic, they typically did not last. Patients relapsed.

Freud then returned to Breuer's "talking cure." In his 1895 book with Breuer, he formulated the concept that many neuroses—including phobias, hysterical paralysis and pains, and even some forms of paranoia—could be traced to traumatic childhood experiences that had been repressed and were now lodged deeply in the unconscious mind. Again, working with Breuer, Freud proposed the talking cure as a means of enabling the patient to recover the trauma and the emotions associated with it from the unconscious mind, so that they could be dealt with intellectually and emotionally. To describe the result of this, Freud borrowed a term from Aristotle's *Poetics*—"catharsis," the cleansing effect that great Greek tragedy exercised on the minds of an audience.

Although the collaboration of Breuer and Freud was highly productive, Breuer broke with Freud over what he believed was an overemphasis on the sexual origins—especially childhood sexual origins—of neuroses. Because of this, Freud continued to develop the theory of psychoanalysis by himself. In 1899, at the threshold of the new century, he published one of the most influential books of modern times, *The Interpretation of Dreams.* This masterpiece, based in large measure on Freud's own monumental self-analysis, introduced in full detail his theories of the unconscious and of the Oedipus conflict. It also postulated that dreams are the "Royal Road" into the world of the unconscious, that it is through dreams that the human mind endeavors to resolve psychological conflict within the unconscious, and that to the extent that one can consciously recall their dreams, they can peer into their unconscious and resolve emotional issues rationally and even curatively.

Freud's tremendously fertile mind resulted in another major book two years later. *The Psychopathology of Everyday Life* took his psychoanalytic concepts—especially the operation of the unconscious—beyond abnormal psychology,

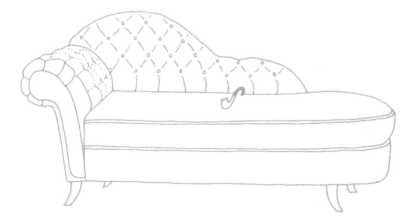

the realm of mental disease, and into "normal" everyday life. If *The Interpretation of Dreams* is Freud's masterpiece, *The Psychopathology of Everyday Life* is his most widely read book. In it, Freud explores what he calls "parapraxes," the errors in speech, memory, or even physical action that became popularly known as "Freudian slips." These "errors," Freud wrote, often have their origin in the unconscious; and their nature, therefore, is another window into that dark realm. When, for example, a man answered a woman's question, "What would you like—bread and butter, or cake?" with "Bed and butter," the parapraxis *bed* for *bread* indicated a sexual feeling that he may have wished to hide from her but, unconsciously, also wished to express to her.

The disruptive implication of Freud's books of 1899 and 1901 may be compared to Galileo's espousal and empirical proofs of the Copernican solar system, in which the earth is revealed as just one of several planets that orbit a central sun and not the unmoving, perfect center point in a universe created by God, who has also created man to live at this center of everything. As Galileo dethroned the position of humankind in the universe, so Freud dethroned humankind's conscious will, forcing that faculty to share control over thought, feeling, and action with the unconscious mind.

While both the 1899 and 1901 books provoked controversy, they also created converts and followers. Freud's 1905 *Three Essays on the Theory of Sexuality*, in which he most fully developed his psychoanalytic theory, was not so kindly received. It provoked more outrage and revulsion than acceptance. But by 1908, when, at Freud's instigation, the first International Psychoanalytical Congress was held at Salzburg, the resistance had clearly been outweighed by wider acceptance. The acceptance of psychoanalytic theory increased the following year when Freud was invited to the United States to give a course of lectures in his new science. These served as the basis of his *Five Lectures on Psycho-Analysis*, published in 1916. It was the work that catalyzed his international reputation and fame.

Freud continued to work as a clinician and to publish and lecture prolifically. His collected works comprise more than twenty book-length volumes. He labored relentlessly to refine and revise his theories. He also became the nucleus of a school of psychoanalysis, training physicians and others in his methods, always with an eye toward establishing psychoanalysis as an enduring approach to both the scientific understanding of human behavior and the treatment of mental illness.

In 1923, his aggressive approach to self-imposed revision resulted in the publication of *The Ego and the Id*, which presented his new tripartite model of the mind as composed of the id, super-ego, and ego. The id—Latin for *it*—consists mainly of instinct that bubbles up from the unconscious; the super-ego, which draws on parental and social rules and norms, is the critical and moralizing component of the mind; and the ego—Latin for *I*, or *self*—is the conscious self-identity, organized and realistic, that presents the person to the world and struggles to mediate between the impulses of the id and the repressive forces of the superego.

Freud's work attracted a small but growing legion of psychoanalysts, not just in Austria but worldwide, especially in the United States. Some who gravitated toward Freud, most notably the Austrian physician Alfred Adler (1870–1937) and the Swiss physician, anthropologist, and philosopher Carl Gustav Jung (1875–1961), broke with Freud to found their own "schools" of psychoanalysis, which took the science in new directions. In some ways, these breaks resembled the schisms that typically occur in new religious movements. Freud did his best to resist or overcome the impulse to lash out against what he sometimes felt were betrayals by disciples, reminding himself that disagreement over basic principles was an important feature of the scientific method and therefore indicated that psychoanalysis was a genuine science and a living body of thought.

● ● ●

Freud lived to see what may be interpreted as the mass effect of human psychopathology in the rise of Nazism in Germany and Austria. When, in 1933, Freud's books were among those burned by the Nazis, Freud attempted to make a joke: "What progress we are making. In the Middle Ages they would have burned me. Now, they are content with burning my books." It was a symptom of his inability—a blindness that afflicted many—to recognize the peril that was overtaking Western civilization in general and menacing Jews in particular. At last, following the *Anschluss*, the German annexation of Austria, on March 13, 1938, Dr. Ernest Jones, the British psychoanalyst who served as president of the International Psychoanalytical Association, facilitated the emigration of Freud, his daughter Anna, and others of his family to England. (Freud had finally seen the handwriting on the wall when the Gestapo—the German secret police—detained and interrogated Anna.) The exodus took place on June 4, 1938, when the Freuds took the Orient Express to Paris. From Paris, they traveled to London, arriving on June 6.

Freud was safe from the Nazis, but by this time he was suffering from advanced cancer of the jaw, probably caused by his lifelong tobacco habit. By the middle of September 1939, he was in steep physical decline, always in great pain. On September 22, at his request, his physician began administering doses of morphine intended to induce unconsciousness and bring a peaceful death. He died early in the morning of September 23. His work, despite many controversies, continues as a pillar of the modern view of humanity and society.

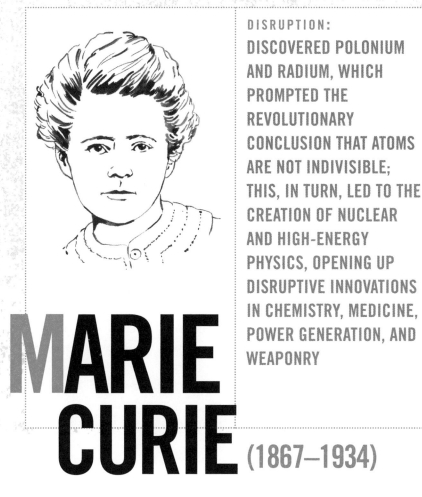

MARIE CURIE (1867–1934)

Born November 7, 1867 into a Warsaw family, highly educated but impoverished by government confiscation of property during their involvement in uprisings aimed at Polish independence, Maria Skłodowska struggled to attain her own education. She attended local public schools while also studying at home with her father, a secondary-school teacher whose political activism had cost him his job. Maria's oldest sibling, Zofia, had succumbed in 1874 to typhus, which she contracted from one of the boarders her mother and father took in to help make ends meet. Three years later, Maria's mother, Bronisława, died of tuberculosis, and ten-year-old Maria grew closer to her teacher-father, who gave her a thorough grounding in the sciences—and who inspired her involvement in a Warsaw students' revolutionary group.

With Polish universities open only to male students, Maria and her sister Bronisława (named for their mother) became active in an underground "Flying University" (Uniwersytet Latajacy), which was not only covert, but a hotbed of nationalist revolutionary activity. Feeling the authorities breathing down her neck, Maria fled Russian-dominated Warsaw for Cracow, which was then part of the Austro-Hungarian Empire. After further struggle in that city, she went to Paris, to which Bronisława had moved earlier with her physician husband. Maria enrolled at the Sorbonne, from which she obtained licentiateships (the equivalent of master's degrees) in physics and mathematics.

While studying at the university in 1894, she met Pierre Curie, professor in the school of physics. The two married in 1895. That same year, the German physicist Wilhelm Röntgen discovered X-rays. The following year, the French scientist Henri Becquerel discovered that uranium salts emitted rays he concluded were similar to X-rays because, like them, they had the power to penetrate solid matter. When Becquerel demonstrated that the energy radiated from the uranium salts was a property of the salts and not derived from any external source, Marie Curie, in search of a subject for a doctoral thesis, decided to study these "uranium rays." She made use of a modified electrometer Pierre Curie had developed years earlier. With it, she demonstrated that the uranium rays caused the air around a sample to conduct electricity. Using the electrometer, she was able to measure the degree of activity of uranium salts and showed that the amount of activity depended on nothing other than the quantity of uranium present. This led her to propose that the activity—the radiation—came not from molecules in the impure uranium compound but from the atoms of the underlying element. In other words, contrary to untold centuries of atomic theory, atoms were divisible into smaller particles, which, in this case, were highly energetic.

The birth of the Curies' daughter Irène in 1897 prompted Marie to accept a teaching post at the École Normale Supérieure to help support the child. Nevertheless, she and Pierre made time to research two uranium minerals, pitchblende and torbernite, in an effort to refine them to their constituent elements. The only space available to them was a wretched shed, which had served as a medical school dissecting room. They labored here, quite unaware that their continuous close work with radioactive substances was harmful and, ultimately, lethal. Finding that both pitchblende and torbernite were more radioactive than uranium alone, Marie Curie concluded that the minerals must contain another substance far more radioactive than uranium. By 1898, Pierre Curie abandoned his own research to collaborate with his wife on hers. In April and July of that year, the Curies announced the existence of two previously undiscovered elements, polonium (which Marie named in honor of her native country) and radium (Latin for *ray*).

They were now faced with the task of isolating the actual elements. The elements existed in such small quantities in pitchblende that it required years of work to isolate them. From one ton of pitchblende ore, a mere tenth of a gram of radium chloride was finally separated in 1902. It took another eight years to isolate a trace amount of the pure radium metal. By that time, Marie was working alone, her husband having been killed on April 19, 1906, when he slipped on a rainy Paris street and was run over by a horse-drawn wagon. (Madame Curie never succeeded in isolating polonium, an element with a fugitive 138-day half-life, compared to radium's 1600-*year* half-life.)

Pure radium is an element. An element is an atom, not a molecule. The fact that radium, an atom, emitted radiation meant that energized particles were being thrown off by the radium atoms. This, in turn, meant that the atom—assumed since ancient times to be the final, indivisible building block of matter—was capable of being divided into smaller particles. By itself, this discovery was tremendously disruptive, forever changing a basic assumption about the nature of the physical world.

But there was more. Curie had discovered an elemental source of energy. Among the thirty-two papers she and her husband had published (separately or jointly) between 1898 and 1902, one revealed the extraordinary result of exposing tumor cells to radium: the diseased cells died before the healthy ones. Radiation, it seemed, might be a cure for cancer. Who knew what other miracles the new energy source would be capable of creating?

• • •

During the long period of her work with radium, Marie Curie rose rapidly in French intellectual and academic circles. In 1900, she was appointed the first woman on the faculty of the École Normale Supérieure. In 1903, she was awarded a doctorate from the University of Paris. Also in 1903, Marie and Pierre Curie shared with Henri Becquerel the Nobel Prize in Physics for their research into the "radiation phenomena" that Becquerel was credited with having discovered. Marie Curie was the first woman to be awarded a Nobel Prize.

Following Pierre's death in 1906, Marie Curie was given his place as professor of general physics on the faculty of sciences at the University of Paris, the first woman to hold that position. In 1911, she was awarded a second Nobel Prize, this time not in physics but in chemistry, for her discovery of polonium and radium and her isolation of radium. This made her not only the first woman to receive two Nobel Prizes (at the time of this writing, she is still the only woman to have done this), but the first person, man or woman, to be awarded prizes in two different scientific fields.

In 1914, Madame Curie was appointed director of the Curie Laboratory in the brand-new Radium Institute of the University of Paris. In addition, she received many honorary science, medicine, and law degrees, as well as honorary memberships in learned societies worldwide. With Pierre Curie, she received the Davy Medal of the Royal Society in 1903, and, in 1921, U.S. President Warren G. Harding, "on behalf of the women of America," presented her with a highly valuable gram of radium in recognition of her service to science.

The honors were great and many. Having disrupted physics and chemistry, having disrupted an ancient and, it had seemed, eternal principle of physical reality—the indivisibility of the atom—and having blurred the absolute distinction between matter and energy by her work with *atomic* radiation, Marie Curie also upended equally entrenched concepts of gender roles by achieving in rapid succession so many lofty firsts for women. Her daughter Irène would go on in 1935 to share a Nobel Prize for Chemistry with her husband, Frédéric Joliot.

Yet there was also a terrible price to pay for all this. On July 4, 1934, while visiting her native Poland, a now sickly Marie Curie died from the effects of aplastic anemia. Almost certainly, her illness was related to her frequent and long-term exposure to radiation—not only in the laboratory, but during her voluntary service as a radiologist operating a mobile X-ray truck with primitive and totally unshielded equipment in French field hospitals during World War I. Indeed, both she and her husband had suffered from various chronic and increasingly debilitating ailments—in her case, including cataracts that nearly blinded her. All were almost certainly caused by radiation exposure.

Even Curie's legacy is radioactive. To this day, her personal papers are stored in lead-lined boxes and can be handled only by scholars who are willing to don protective clothing and limit their exposure. Irène Joliot-Curie, the daughter who, as a young woman, often assisted her mother in the laboratory, died of leukemia in 1956 at the age of fifty-eight. Her name is commemorated with that of her mother and 357 other researchers on the Monument to the X-ray and Radium Martyrs of All Nations, in Hamburg, Germany.

DISRUPTION:
REWRITING THE "LAWS"
OF PHYSICS, ENABLING
RADICAL NEW VISIONS
OF THE UNIVERSE, AND
POINTING TOWARD NEW
SOURCES OF ENERGY AND
MASS DESTRUCTION

ALBERT EINSTEIN
(1879–1955)

Some years in history stand out for just about everybody: 1066 saw the Battle of Hastings, which brought the Norman Conquest of England. In "fourteen hundred and ninety-two, Columbus sailed the ocean blue"—and "discovered" America. The year 1945 marked the end of World War II. And then there is 1905. The year probably appears on few popular lists of historical standouts, but physicists call it the Annus Mirabilis, the "Miraculous Year." It was the year that Albert Einstein, a twenty-six-year-old assistant patent examiner working at the Swiss Patent Office in Bern, published four articles in the internationally prestigious *Annalen der Physik* (Annals of Physics) scientific journal. That publication record alone would make a Miraculous Year for any aspiring scientist. But these particular four articles were far more than personal triumphs. They transformed classical physics into modern physics and thereby disrupted humankind's vision of reality.

To a non-scientist, the titles of the four papers do not seem like breakthroughs. In fact, they may be barely comprehensible. The first paper, published on June 9, 1905, was "On a Heuristic Viewpoint Concerning the Production and Transformation of Light." It focused on the "photoelectric effect," the emission of electrons when light shines on a material. Einstein did not discover this effect, but he addressed a bewildering disconnect between theory and observation and, in so doing, began the disruption of classical physics into quantum mechanics.

Classical physics theory said that changing the intensity of light falling on a material would induce changes in the kinetic energy of the electrons emitted from that material. Moreover, exposing a material to a sufficiently dim light would create a time lag between the initial shining of the light and the emission of an electron. That was the *theory*, and it made good common sense. *Observation*, however, revealed something very different—which fit neither the theory nor common sense. Observation revealed that electrons are emitted only when the light reaches or exceeds a certain threshold frequency (energy). Below this threshold, no electrons are emitted, regardless of the intensity of the light. Einstein resolved the disconnect between theory and observation by postulating that energy is exchanged not in continuous amounts, but in discrete packets. Discrete wave packets of light—called photons—released a discrete packet of energy, called a quantum. Classical physics theorized that energy is exchanged in continuous amounts. Based on the photoelectric effect, Einstein postulated that energy is exchanged only in packets, or quanta. In 1921, Einstein received the Nobel Prize for what the prize citation called the "law of the photoelectric effect," which laid the foundation for quantum mechanics, the basis for today's physics.

The second 1905 paper, published on July 18, was "On the Motion of Small Particles Suspended in a Stationary Liquid, as Required by the Molecular Kinetic Theory of Heat." It was based on Einstein's interpretation of Brownian motion, the microscopic observation made by botanist Robert Brown in 1827 that particles trapped in cavities within pollen grains moved through water—*for no apparent reason*. What made them move? In his paper, Einstein explained that the pollen was moved by individual water molecules. Stunningly, this explanation was the first *empirical* evidence of the existence of molecules and, therefore, also the first empirical evidence of the existence of atoms.

On September 26, 1905, Einstein's "On the Electrodynamics of Moving Bodies" laid the foundation for his most famous equation and the theory that accompanied it, the Special Theory of Relativity. The September 26 paper reconciled with the classical laws of mechanics the equations that the great British physicist James Clerk Maxwell (1831–1879) had created for electricity and mechanics.

Einstein did this by introducing major changes to those laws at speeds close to that of light. Einstein showed that the laws of physics are identical in all non-accelerating frames of reference and that the speed of light is the same for all observers, regardless of the motion of the light source. Motion is relative to a frame of reference, except when it is near or at the speed of light. At or near light speed, the differences between Maxwell's equations for electricity and mechanics, which conflict with the classical laws of mechanics below light speed, are reconciled. This showed that Newton's laws of motion, basic to classical physics, do not apply as one approaches light speed.

The September 26 paper prepared the way for the paper Einstein published on November 21, the title of which asked the question "Does the Inertia of a Body Depend Upon Its Energy Content?" The answer was the principle of mass-energy equivalence, which is, as Einstein stated in the most famous equation of the modern world, $E = mc^2$, anything with mass has an equivalent amount of energy—and vice versa. Energy (E) may be calculated as mass (m) multiplied by the speed of light squared (c^2). Conversely, anything that has energy has a corresponding mass (m) given by its energy (E) divided by the speed of light squared (c^2). Mass and energy are equivalent.

All of the *Annus Mirabilis* papers are foundational to modern physics. This means that they are basic to the modern understanding of the universe, to how we understand reality. What is more, each of the 1905 papers profoundly disrupted our previous understanding. In a practical, existential sense, the mathematical proof of mass-energy equivalence can be seen as the seed from which atomic energy—energy released by nuclear fission, the splitting apart of particles forming the nucleus of an atom—was explored and exploited, both as a source of energy for such things as the propulsion of ships and the generation of electricity, and as the heart of nuclear and thermonuclear weapons capable of destroying all life on earth.

• • •

The *Annus Mirabilis* papers were just four of the more than 300 scientific papers Einstein published in his intensely creative lifetime. This most productive and celebrated of twentieth-century scientists was born in Ulm, in Württemberg, Germany, on March 14, 1879. His father, Hermann, was a salesman and engineer, and his mother, Pauline Koch, was a homemaker. The family moved to Munich six weeks after Albert was born, and it was here that Hermann and his brother Jacob founded a company that made electrical equipment. Although the Einsteins were Jews, they were non-observant, and Albert was enrolled in a Catholic elementary school from ages five to eight, when he entered the Luitpold Gymnasium, which is now named for him.

The products the Einstein company manufactured were designed to work with direct current (DC) electrical systems. By 1894, when the company made a make-or-break bid on supplying electric street and outdoor lighting for all of Munich, the city, like many others worldwide at this time, had chosen to electrify with the more innovative and efficient alternating current (AC) system. The Einstein brothers could not raise sufficient capital to convert their own factory to make products compatible with AC, lost the bid, and were forced to shutter and sell their factory. Einstein's parents moved to Italy to start anew, leaving Albert in Munich to finish his gymnasium studies. He rebelled against the strict rote-learning regimen there and, in December 1894, feigned illness and left school to join his parents in Pavia. While waiting to take examinations required to enroll in the Swiss Federal Polytechnic Institute in Zurich, he wrote his first scientific paper, "On the Investigation of the State of the Ether in a Magnetic Field." He was sixteen.

Although young Einstein failed the general examination, he excelled in mathematics and physics, which prompted the Polytechnic's sympathetic principal to recommend that he enroll in the Argovian cantonal school in Aarau, Switzerland, address his knowledge gaps there, and then reapply to the Institute. He did well in Aarau, adroitly renounced his German citizenship to avoid compulsory service in the Kaiser's army, and, at seventeen, was admitted to the Polytechnic. Here he met his future first wife, Mileva Marić—who may (although no evidence has ever been found) have contributed to his *Annus Mirabilis* papers.

In 1901, Einstein graduated from the Polytechnic Institute certified as a teacher in physics and mathematics. That year, he also received Swiss citizenship. Despite his credentials, he was unable to find a teaching position. He went to work instead as "technical assistant" in the Swiss Patent Office while also attending the University of Zurich, from which he received his doctorate during that Miraculous Year of 1905. Between 1908 and 1913 he held professorships at universities in Bern, Zurich, and Prague. In 1914, he once again took out German citizenship and moved to Berlin, taking a position at the University of Berlin, and lived in that city until 1933.

• • •

The disruptive impact and breadth of his theoretical work, together with the clarity of his expression and his irrepressible personal charm and charisma, not only provoked and electrified the rarefied world of advanced physics, but made Albert Einstein the most famous scientist in the world by the early 1930s. His name became a household word, and he was widely sought as a lecturer and visiting professor. In 1930–1931, he traveled to the United States as a research fellow at the California Institute of Technology. On both the Pacific and Atlantic coasts, he was fêted as a celebrity. New York's colorful mayor Jimmy Walker presented him with a key to the city, and the president of Columbia University hailed him as "the ruling monarch of the mind."

Einstein returned to Germany just as the rise of Hitler and the Nazi regime made it increasingly clear to him that life in his homeland would soon be impossible for any Jew. He embarked on another trip to the United States at the start of 1933 for his third two-month visiting professorship at Caltech. He and his second wife, Elsa, set off on a return to Europe in March. During their voyage from America, they learned that their summer cottage had been raided by the Nazis. They were told that, among other things, their small personal sailboat had been confiscated for use at a Hitler Youth camp.

When the Einsteins landed at Antwerp, Belgium, on March 28, they went directly to the local consulate, surrendered their passports, and renounced their German citizenship. They rented a house in Belgium, where they lived before accepting the invitation of Commander Oliver Locker-Lampson of the British Royal Navy, to come to England and live in his cottage outside London. Concerned that German agents might abduct or kill the great scientist, Locker-Lampson provided armed guards to protect the cottage and its inhabitants. He also attempted to secure a Parliamentary act granting the Einsteins British citizenship. When this effort failed, the Einsteins left for the United States, where he accepted a position as resident scholar at Princeton University's Institute for Advanced Study—a place already well known as a haven for scientists (many of them Jews) in flight from Nazi Germany. Einstein became a U.S. citizen in 1940.

On the eve of World War II in August 1939, the Jewish Hungarian refugee physicist Leó Szilárd asked Einstein to endorse a letter to President Franklin Roosevelt warning him about German experimentation in the field of atomic weapons and urging the United States to begin its own research program.

Although Szilárd had originated the letter, he recognized that no scientist was held in higher esteem in the United States than Einstein. He was less interested in taking credit for the letter than in having it read and acted upon. He was right. FDR read the "Einstein letter" and immediately authorized what became in 1942 the Manhattan Project, the vast secret program that created the two atomic bombs dropped on Hiroshima and Nagasaki in 1945.

• • •

After World War II, Einstein turned away from physics—except for work on formulating a unified field theory, a single grand theory intended to explain all of physics—and became increasingly active in the World Government Movement. In the U.S., he was a passionate supporter of civil rights, joining the NAACP and pronouncing racism the "worst disease" afflicting the U.S. When the African American scholar and civil rights activist W.E.B. Du Bois was tried in 1951 for failing to register as a foreign agent when he accepted the chairmanship of the Peace Information Center (which had some affiliation with foreign nationals), the trial judge summarily dismissed all charges when Du Bois's attorney informed him that Einstein had offered himself as a character witness. *That* was the scientist's social authority.

Einstein was long active in Zionist causes and had been instrumental in establishing the Hebrew University in Jerusalem in 1925. In 1952, he was invited to become president of Israel, but declined with an expression of gratitude and humility. An avid amateur violinist, Einstein occasionally played with the likes of the Zoellner and Juilliard string quartets. Although he was a critic of capitalism and inclined toward socialism, he reserved his political advocacy for the so-called global-government movement, which advocated a central governing body for the world's nations. He was convinced that nuclear weaponry, in the creation of which his own work had played a part, posed a grave danger to humankind that only a global government could mitigate.

At the time of his death—on April 18, 1955, caused by the rupture of an abdominal aortic aneurysm—Einstein had left unfinished the search he had begun after working on his General Theory of Relativity. He was groping toward what he called a "unified field theory," a way to generalize his geometric theory of gravitation to encompass electromagnetism, thereby creating a unified theory to explain all the fundamental forces of the universe. It is this quest—to unify with gravitation the principal laws of physics—that drives much of modern physics today.

RICHARD FEYNMAN (1918–1988)

Richard Feynman was among the most famous scientists of his time, in part because of his disarming personality and his ability to popularize the most difficult of concepts. Once asked to explain quantum mechanics, he replied, "I think I can safely say that nobody understands quantum mechanics." The response was more than witty, since it conveyed the very core of quantum theory, which is, in fact, beyond easy human understanding yet quite capable of mathematical expression. Thus, Feynman's quip expressed the essence of modern physics.

I f one asks physicists today to name Feynman's greatest breakthroughs, the answers give bewildered non-scientists precious little satisfaction:

- The Feynman path integral, a breakthrough in quantum field theory, which seeks to unite and reconcile modern concepts of fields, Einstein's theory of special relativity, and quantum mechanics in an effort to create a coherent physics.

• Feynman diagrams, which facilitate calculations in quantum mechanics—calculations that would otherwise be too technically difficult to carry out.

• Quantum electrodynamics, a quantum field theory of the interaction of light and matter, which won Feynman and his two co-creators the 1965 Nobel Prize for Physics.

• The parton model of hadrons, a breakthrough in understanding the complexity of the proton and thereby understanding particle physics, which is ultimately essential to understanding nature itself.

Quantum mechanics is a branch of physics that strikes not only non-scientists as alien, but was even too much for Albert Einstein to accept. It explores nature at its most fundamental levels, levels at which subatomic particles behave in very strange ways. They take on more than one state at the same time. They interact with other particles that are far away and seemingly unrelated and unconnected. This led Einstein to mockingly say that quantum mechanics dealt with "spooky action at a distance." And yet, thanks in large part to Feynman's work, today's physicists see quantum mechanics as the royal road to an understanding of the universe. Computer scientists see it as a means of computing the most complex problems imaginable or, indeed, unimaginable. Nanotechnologists see it as a means of hitherto unimaginable innovation.

● ● ●

The man destined to venture into territory that even Einstein shunned was not raised in exotic, other-worldly circumstances and surroundings. He was born on May 11, 1918, in the borough of Queens, New York, to Jewish immigrants from Russia and Poland. Where many parents are annoyed by their children's incessant questions, Melville Feynman encouraged his son to ask and ask more and, in particular, to challenge what most people accept as self-evident and beyond question. His mother, Lucille, instilled in him a sense of humor, which he carried throughout his life. This humble, ordinary family actually produced two world-class physicists, Richard and his sister, Joan.

Feynman's habit of questioning everything led him to atheism early in life. He threw himself into engineering and science, winning the New York University Math Championship in high school. Atheist though he was, he found himself confronted by anti-Semitism when his first-choice school, Columbia University, refused to enroll him because the institution had already met its "Jewish quota." He enrolled instead at the Massachusetts Institute of Technology (MIT), graduating in 1939 and then entering Princeton University, where he studied mathematics and physics under the likes of Albert Einstein, Wolfgang Pauli, and John von Neumann. His doctorate was awarded in 1942, with a dissertation that presented a novel approach to quantum mechanics. The prevailing picture of what was at the time an emerging field had been developed by the great British physicist James Clerk Maxwell (1831–1879) in terms of electromagnetic waves. Feynman rejected the wave approach and instead based his descriptive theory entirely on the interaction of particles in space and time.

During World War II, Feynman worked on the Manhattan Project. Although already beginning to make his mark as a theorist, he was also an exceedingly practical scientific "engineer." It was Feynman who developed the computational systems for calculating neutron equations for nuclear reactors, an important aspect of the Manhattan Project's early work. He also developed safety procedures for storing radioactive materials at the Army's facility in Oak Ridge, Tennessee, one of two sprawling plants that produced the fissionable material for the first atomic bombs. In addition, Feynman developed theoretical background for a proposed uranium hydride bomb which, however, proved impractical.

Whatever else the Manhattan Project was, its Los Alamos, New Mexico, laboratory served as a forum and arena in which the era's foremost physicists interacted. Feynman became a close friend of Niels Bohr, a giant of atomic theory, and of Robert Oppenheimer, the scientific director of the entire project. While Feynman found the Manhattan Project experience intellectually exhilarating, he was afflicted with depression and guilt after the atomic bombing of Hiroshima and Nagasaki. Nevertheless, he emerged from World War II as a hot commodity in American science. He stunned colleagues by turning down an offer from the Institute for Advanced Study in Princeton, academic home of Einstein and the mathematicians Kurt Gödel and John von Neumann. Instead, he joined Hans Bethe at Cornell University, where he was a professor of theoretical physics from 1945 to 1950. From here, he moved to the California Institute of Technology (Caltech) as professor of theoretical physics, where he taught for the rest of his career.

Feynman proved himself to be a great teacher, and, as his lectures were widely published in a series of popular books for a broad readership, he was nicknamed "The Great Explainer." His December 1959 presentation at a meeting of the American Physical Society, "There's Plenty of Room at the Bottom," unfolded the feasibility of building structures atom by atom or molecule by molecule. At the time, this seemed the stuff of science fiction, but it soon became the basis of nanotechnology. His pioneering work in quantum computing produced similarly practical results, as Feynman became involved in building the first massively parallel computer—work that was continued by his son, Carl, a computer scientist. Richard Feynman envisioned applying quantum computing to the building of neural networks and elaborate physical simulations using cellular automata.

Feynman's Caltech years saw groundbreaking work in quantum electrodynamics, which resulted in his sharing the 1965 Nobel Prize for Physics; the quantum behavior of superfluidity in supercooled liquid helium; a model of weak radioactive decay, which was crucial to the study of certain subatomic particles; and the parton model for analyzing high-energy hadron collisions. The quantum electrodynamics work, which involved the interaction of light and matter, prompted him to develop his Feynman diagrams, which he and others have used to calculate interactions between particles in space-time, especially between electrons and their antimatter counterparts, positrons. The diagrams presented an alternative to otherwise prohibitively complex calculations and have been applied by many other physicists to a wide range of problems, including theories of quantum gravity, string theory, and membrane theory (M-theory).

Feynman earned new public notice when he was appointed to the Rogers Commission, formed to investigate the causes of the 1986 *Challenger* Space Shuttle disaster. The booster exploded moments after it was launched from Cape Kennedy on January 28, 1986. By the time the commission was created, Feynman was already critically ill with two very rare forms of cancer (liposarcoma and Waldenström's macroglobulinemia), and his physicians advised him not to undertake the arduous task of the investigation. Feynman, however, felt that it was his duty. He followed up on a suggestion from Dr. Sally Ride (an astronaut herself) that O-rings, which served as sealing gaskets between segments of the launch vehicle's solid rocket boosters (SRBs), had not been tested at temperatures below 50°F. The morning of the launch was freezing—rare frigid conditions for central Florida, even in winter. Feynman concluded that the O-rings lost resilience in the unusual cold, a theory he dramatically demonstrated on live television by simply immersing O-ring material in a glass of ice water. The sample became visibly brittle. Feynman went on to point out flaws in NASA's safety culture, arguing that agency leaders had failed to recognize that, for "a successful technology, reality must take precedence over public relations, for nature cannot be fooled." Always the disruptor, Feynman was unafraid of stepping on institutional toes, even if some of those belonged to fellow scientists.

Richard Feynman died on February 15, 1988, after a failed attempt to treat his cancer surgically.

4

TECHNOLOGY

JAMES WATT
(1736–1819)

In the International System of Units (SI), the watt is a unit of power commonly used to quantify the rate of energy transfer. If you are an engineer, you know that 1 watt is the transfer of 1 joule (a unit of energy) per second. If you are anyone else, you know that a 100-watt lightbulb is brighter than a 60-watt lightbulb or that a 100-watt amplifier makes music louder than a 30-watt amp. This most basic unit of power is named after James Watt, the Scottish engineer, chemist, and inventor who was asked to fix a 1712 Newcomen steam engine and ended up transforming it into the 1781 Watt steam engine, thereby creating the machine that powered the Industrial Revolution.

This alone is ample reason to name the watt in his honor. But there is more. Having transformed Thomas Newcomen's engine into something sufficiently practical and efficient to disrupt civilization, Watt borrowed a concept introduced by another early steam-engine tinkerer, Thomas Savery, to market his innovation. Before the *watt* was accepted as a universally understood unit of power, the unit Watt devised, *horsepower*, had already become a standard unit for measuring the rate at which work is done. Moreover, if Watt's steam engine required mechanical genius to create, the concept of horsepower required a combination of philosophical and marketing genius. Having created a profoundly transformative technology, Watt sold it to the world by presenting its value in terms of the very technology—animal power—he had transformed.

The Watt steam engine would fundamentally disrupt human society. Horse-power made the value of that disruption comprehensible to anyone who had ever used a horse to pull a wagon or a plow or turn a grinding wheel in a mill—or who had even *watched* a horse perform any of these tasks. Watt defined the shockingly new in the language of the comfortably familiar, even as his breakthrough set the universe of the horse on an inexorable course of obsolescence as a work engine.

● ● ●

James Watt was born in 1736 in the Firth of Clyde seaport of Greenock, Scotland, the son of a shipwright and the grandson of a mathematician. Raised a Presbyterian, Watt grew up into a deist. There was a God, he argued, but it was man who had to get things done on earth. The deity of the deist offers no guid-ance and no help, but doesn't interfere either.

Watt struggled through early life, puny, sickly, continually assailed by migraines and toothaches. He was home-schooled early on and then enrolled in Greenock Grammar School, where he excelled at mathematics but had no interest in Greek and Latin. Carpentry he learned from his father—and he took naturally to working with his head and hands. As his father applied his wood-working skills to building ships in the busy seaport town, Watt became interested in their navigation instruments: quadrants, compasses, telescopes, and the like. In his teens, Watt decided he wanted to become an instrument-maker. The deci-sion came none too soon. His father suffered a serious financial loss when a ship he owned was wrecked, his wife died suddenly, and his own health went into freefall. He was pleased that his mechanically inclined son was eager to learn a lucrative trade.

But Watt couldn't learn it in Greenock. Now eighteen, he went off to Glasgow in 1754, where he called on a relative, who introduced him to Robert Dick, a scientist working at the University of Glasgow. Dick was instantly impressed by the instrument-making skills Watt already possessed, but he also recognized that the young man had a great deal yet to learn, and he counseled him to go to London for training. Watt set off, spending two weeks in the capital seeking an apprenticeship opportunity. He repeatedly ran up against the rules of the instrument-makers' guild known as the Worshipful Company of Clock-makers: the only apprenticeships offered under the Worshipful Company's rules lasted seven long—and impoverished—years. At last, however, Watt found John Morgan, whose workshop was in the center of the city and whose attitude toward the rules was highly pliable. He would take Watt on as an apprentice and, what is more, cram into a single year everything he needed to know about the trade of instrument-maker. In return, Watt would serve him during that year for almost no salary at all. He snapped up the offer.

Watt began his accelerated apprenticeship in 1755 and learned fast. Morgan was astounded to see Watt quickly surpass the level of skill of his official apprentice, who had been employed in Morgan's shop for two years. Watt drove himself hard, working ten hours a day in training and then many additional hours doing minor repair work for slim compensation. Though pressed for cash, his father sent him what little he could when he could, but young Watt began to buckle under the combination of short rations and long hours. Add to this the outbreak of the Seven Years' War, during which agents of the Royal Navy and British Army were prowling the streets of London looking to "impress" (draft) young men into naval or military service. Fearful of being caught in the dragnet, Watt spent even more time cloistered in the shop to avoid exposure on the streets. After his year was up, he had completed the apprenticeship with flying colors—only to fall dangerously ill.

Sick though he was, Watt felt he had no time to convalesce. Instead, he returned to Glasgow in 1756 and, through his few connections at the university, got some work for the institution. He used the meager proceeds to set up his own shop, only to find that other instrument-makers refused to accept him as one of their profession. They did not complain about the brevity of his apprenticeship, but were outraged that it had been served in London. The truly fine instrument-makers, they declared, were those trained in Glasgow! Fortunately for Watt, however, his work for the university impressed the professors, who prevailed on the institution to provide space for him to set up shop on campus with the official title of "Mathematical Instrument Maker to the University."

It was a fine position, but the volume of work was still too small to make a decent living. With the town's instrument-makers against him, Watt looked for related additional employment and began making musical instruments—something in which the other members of his trade had no interest and therefore did not regard him as an unqualified competitor. What gave Watt an edge was that he looked at existing instruments critically, and he identified aspects of their design that could use improvement. He not only repaired or made instruments, he made them better—and this began to draw customers. In 1758, a local architect invested in his business, which enabled him to open a shop in the heart of Glasgow. By 1763, he was well established as a maker of a variety of mechanical products, ranging from musical instruments to toys to the kinds of "mathematical instruments" he made for the university, for whose scientific faculty he continued to work from the small shop on campus.

• • •

Among the luminaries with whom Watt made friends at the university were the physicist and chemist Joseph Black, who made important discoveries concerning the evolving science of thermodynamics, and Adam Smith, whose 1776 *An Inquiry into the Nature and Causes of the Wealth of Nations* would make him the father of political economy, precursor to modern economics. Another Glasgow professor, John Anderson, was less famous than either Black or Smith, but nevertheless instrumental in applying science to the creation of the technology that enabled the Industrial Revolution, and he was dedicated to the education of the working man. He was also the older brother of one of Watt's grammar school classmates. In 1763, Anderson came to Watt with a problem. He had a small laboratory model of a Newcomen pump, the first practical steam engine, invented in 1712 by Thomas Newcomen and used chiefly to pump out water from coal mines. Anderson was using the model engine to investigate why the full-size mine pumps were so inefficient, requiring a huge amount of steam to function even minimally. Anderson's small machine would start up, pump a few strokes, and then stall out. *What was wrong*, the professor wanted to know.

Watt could tell just by looking at the machine. The boiler was too small to furnish sufficient steam to reheat the cylinder after just a few strokes. But he did not stop with this simple diagnosis. He decided to observe the failure closely. In doing so, he discovered more than a problem with Anderson's particular Newcomen pump: he discovered why all Newcomen engines, including the full-size pumps, were so inefficient. With each stroke, the cylinder in which the piston moved cooled and had to be reheated. That continual reheating process consumed a great deal of heat—energy that was therefore unavailable to do useful work. Watt understood that what was needed was a means of condensing the steam without cooling the cylinder, and he pondered how to do it. The pondering extended over months and then years of experimentation.

While working on the problem, Watt made himself an expert on the properties and physical dynamics of steam. He discovered something that his friend Professor Black had earlier found out independently, namely what Black called the *latent heat* of vaporization: the amount of energy that had to be added to a liquid to transform it into a gas or vapor (such as steam). The key, Watt realized, was that the quantity of energy for vaporization, called the enthalpy, was a function of the pressure at which the transformation from liquid to vapor took place. Watt discovered this key in May 1765, fully two years after Anderson had brought him the ailing Newcomen model.

After a moment of inspiration that happened during "a walk on a fine Sabbath afternoon, early in 1765," as he later wrote, Watt imagined an engine with a separate condenser, in which condensation could take place continually, so that the steam cylinder could be evacuated without cooling in the process. The vapor would rush into the condenser, in which the pressure was approximately equal to the vapor pressure of water. In the meantime, steam would be injected into what Watt later called a "steam jacket" surrounding the cylinder. In this way, the cylinder was kept at or close to the high temperature of the steam that was injected into it from the condenser. The loss of heat was thus minimized, which meant that more of the energy provided by the steam was available for useful work.

Work. That was one thing Watt felt he could not do on the Sabbath. Deist though he was, he observed prevailing custom and, itching to get into his workshop, he nevertheless agonized patiently until Monday morning. Come the dawn, he went to work with great speed. For purposes of an expeditious experiment, he improvised a cylinder and condenser by using a large brass surgeon's syringe, four inches in diameter and ten inches long. American engineer and professor of mechanical engineering at the Stevens Institute of Technology Robert Henry Thurston described the experiment in his 1878 *History of the Growth of the Steam Engine*:

> At each end [of the syringe] was a pipe leading steam from the boiler, and fitted with a cock to act as a steam-valve. A pipe led also from the top of the cylinder [that is, the syringe] to the condenser, the syringe being inverted and the piston-rod hanging downward for convenience. The condenser was made of two pipes of thin tin plate, 10 or 12 inches long, and about one-sixth of an inch in diameter, standing vertically, and having a connection at the top with a horizontal pipe of larger size, and fitted with a "snifting-valve." Another vertical pipe, about an inch in diameter, was connected to the condenser, and was fitted with a piston, with a view to using it as an "air-pump." The whole was set in a cistern of cold water. The piston-rod of the little steam-cylinder was drilled from end to end to permit the water to be removed from the cylinder.

It worked "very satisfactorily, and the perfection of the vacuum was such that the machine lifted a weight of 18 pounds hung upon the piston-rod." Watt quickly went on to construct a bigger model, which also worked.

The breakthrough had come. Watt was just twenty-nine years old. Nevertheless, his steam engine was not commercialized until eleven years later, as the inventor labored over the details of perfecting a full-scale version. The main problem was that the metalworkers of the day could not machine the piston and cylinder with sufficient precision to create an efficient engine. While Watt struggled trying to solve this problem and secure a patent, his principal backer, an industrialist named John Roebuck, went bankrupt, and Watt himself had to take day jobs as a surveyor and civil engineer to put food on the table. He labored in this way for eight years, during which time another industrialist, Matthew Boulton, purchased Watt's patent rights, but worked closely with the inventor. He saw what Watt apparently did not see—that the machine under development was much more than an improved water pump: it was a source of energy capable of driving any type of machine that could be attached to it. So Boulton backed Watt financially and, most important, secured for him the services of John "Iron Mad" Wilkinson, who had developed precision boring techniques for making cannons. A cannon was essentially a bored-out cylinder. If Wilkinson could make this, Boulton figured he could make a cylinder precise enough for Watt's engine.

Boulton was right, Watt perfected the piston and cylinder, and the two men discovered that they made very good business partners. Boulton provided the capital and management expertise, while Watt provided the genius. The first commercial Boulton-Watt engine was purchased in March 1776 by the Bentley Mining Company. It performed astoundingly well, making some fourteen to fifteen strokes per minute and emptying in less than an hour a coal pit 90 feet deep and filled with 57 feet of water.

By the early 1780s, Boulton was urging Watt to develop designs to enable the "Watt-Boulton Steam Pump" to be used in other applications. He wrote to his partner in 1781: "The people in London, Manchester and Birmingham are steam mill mad. I don't mean to hurry you, but I think in the course of a month or two, we should determine to take out a patent for certain methods of producing rotative motion. . . ." This led to Watt's invention of a mechanical linkage that converted the reciprocating motion of a rising and falling piston to a rotating motion that could drive anything with a shaft. In addition, Watt continually improved the steam engine itself, always with an eye toward increasing efficiency.

● ● ●

In 1782, a large sawmill placed an order for a massive Watt-Boulton engine. It had to replace and do the work of a dozen mill horses. Watt therefore set out to quantify how much work a single horse could do. He set up an experiment in which he proved that one horse could lift 33,000 pounds the distance of 1 foot in 1 minute. With this calculation, he now knew how to calculate the required specifications for the new engine: just multiply everything by twelve to get the equivalent of the work of twelve horses.

But Watt also realized that he had found something else. In 1702, Thomas Savery, another early steam-engine inventor, wrote a book called *The Miner's Friend; or, an Engine to Raise Water by Fire, Described.* In it, he compared the work his primitive steam pump could do with what horses could do: "So that an engine which will raise as much water as two horses, working together at one time in such a work, can do, and for which there must be constantly kept ten or twelve horses for doing the same. Then I say, such an engine may be made large enough to do the work required in employing eight, ten, fifteen, or twenty horses to be constantly maintained and kept for doing such a work." Reading this description, Watt formalized *horsepower* as a unit for measuring the rate at which work is done. He intended it as a tool to promote his engines by quantifying the value they offered in terms familiar to almost everyone living in a century run on horse power. But he succeeded in doing something more: he transformed energy into a commodity. The business in which Watt and Boulton were engaged became, in effect, an energy business—or, more precisely, a work business, since *work* is the word used to describe the useful application of energy.

From this point forward, the Industrial Revolution was not only driven by steam, but was conceptualized, promoted, and managed in terms of energy and work produced, the cost to produce it, and the profit to be made from it. Civilization hereafter had a new system of value and values, a relentlessly precise combination of physics and economics.

SAMUEL COLT
(1814–1862)

In 1992, historian of American literature and culture Richard Slotkin published a book he subtitled "The Myth of the Frontier in Twentieth-Century America." Its main title was *Gunfighter Nation*. Everybody knew what he meant by this juxtaposition. As a cultural equation, title and subtitle just made sense. The western frontier had long loomed large in American identity, and that frontier had long been intimately connected with guns and men who sling them: the gunfighters.

Somewhere in the back of America's collective memory is a phrase associated with a "six-shooter" revolver that was manufactured as the Colt Single Action Army and even better known as the "Colt .45" or "The Peacemaker." The weapon was introduced in 1872 and adopted by the U.S. Army the following year, remaining in service with the U.S. military through 1892. Between 1873 and 1941, the military model gave rise to a variety of civilian models, including the Colt Frontier Six-Shooter, the Bisley Model, and the Buntline Special, and it went through two more generations of modifications, from 1856 to 1974, and from 1976 to the present.

The original Peacemaker was dubbed "The Gun that Won the West." And the name has stuck to the Colt revolver ever since, making it an emblem of a "gunfighter nation." Samuel Colt, its inventor, preferred another name for what he termed the "revolving-chamber pistol." He called it the "equalizer," implying that it would even the odds in any hostile encounter; that it instantly made one man the equal of any who opposed him; that it was, in fact, a weapon eminently suited to the values of an egalitarian democracy.

● ● ●

Born in Hartford, Connecticut, on July 19, 1814, Colt was the son of a well-to-do textile manufacturer and the grandson of Major John Caldwell, an early American businessman active in Connecticut state politics. The family fortunes suffered badly in the economically ruinous War of 1812, however, and the effects on the Colts lingered for years after the war itself ended in 1815. This meant that Samuel was obliged to go to work at a very early age. After helping out at the Hartford textile mill and studying briefly at a school in Amherst, Massachusetts, he shipped out as an ordinary seaman when he was only thirteen.

During a long voyage to Calcutta aboard the ship *Corvo*, Colt whiled away his downtime by carving a rough wooden model of a new sort of pistol he had envisioned. The idea came to him as he had watched the helmsmen steer the ship. He saw that, no matter which way he spun the wheel, each spoke always came in direct line with a clutch that could be set to hold it. This set the wheels of young Colt's mind spinning and led to his concept for a firearm with a multiple-cylinder revolving chamber that aligned each cylinder, in succession, with a single barrel. The multiple-cylinder chamber meant that the weapon could hold several bullets—not just a single shot in a single-cylinder chamber. Colt's idea was to create a mechanical system that would advance each cylinder in the chamber to align it with the firing mechanism and the barrel each time the trigger was pulled. Thus, in a "single action"—the pulling of the trigger—the hammer would be cocked, the projectile fired, and the cylinder rotated to align the next round. This allowed rapid fire.

When he returned to the States, he again joined the family mill, learned some chemistry pertinent to its affairs, but also persuaded his father to finance the production of two working prototypes of his innovative weapon, one rifle, one pistol. The rifle performed quite well. The pistol? It blew to pieces the first time it was fired. Colt's father took little note of the success of the rifle and instead focused on the catastrophic failure of the pistol. He told his son that he would finance no further development.

Undaunted, Colt persisted, laboring to refine his design. By the time he believed he had it right, he was eighteen years old and, eager to raise on his own the capital he needed to make new prototypes, he took to the road as an itinerant showman. Billing himself as the "Celebrated Doctor Coult of New-York, London, and Calcutta," he gave public demonstrations of a newly developed anesthetic, nitrous oxide, better known as laughing gas. He discovered that he had a natural flair for promotion and spent three years traveling nationwide with his nitrous demonstration. Having amassed a handsome sum from his long tour, he built his new prototypes and traveled with them to Britain and France where, in 1835, he successfully obtained patents. He returned to the United States and, in 1836, the U.S. Patent Office also granted him a patent for the multi-chamber, rotating cylinder that discharged through a single barrel.

Colt formed the Arms Company in Paterson, New Jersey, to manufacture what he called his "revolver." By the end of 1837, he had an inventory of more than a thousand weapons—none of which had been sold. Worse, a national financial downturn, the Panic of 1837, made it nearly impossible to obtain needed funding to build needed manufacturing machinery. Colt packed up his inventory and traveled to general stores across a wide region of the country, hand-selling his guns.

What he desperately craved were very big customers, even just one or two. He demonstrated the weapon to the U.S. Army, but two different army boards recommended against adopting the handgun. At last, the Texas Rangers bought the weapons to use in their territorial campaigns. It was a solid sale, though the Rangers were not a large agency.

Decades before Henry Ford developed his famed assembly line to build his Model T automobile, Colt streamlined production in his factory, aiming to create maximum efficiency and a high degree of precision. He built most of the machine tools required for manufacture on site, and he designed an early version of a formal assembly line, by which different workers were assigned to create the different sub-assemblies that made up the finished weapon. Colt used only interchangeable parts, which not only sped up the work, but ensured that customers' weapons could be serviced in the Colt plant or by any gunsmith who purchased official Colt spare parts. Thus, repairs on any Colt revolver could be made virtually anywhere in the world.

Having had a gun blow up on him taught Samuel Colt great respect for the reliability of a firearm. He wanted to employ a workforce that was both skilled and seriously committed to creating quality. To ensure this, he applied something highly unusual in nineteenth-century America: an enlightened management style. "Workers who have good pay, steady employment, comfortable housing, and plenty of good entertainment and recreation," he declared, "are more profitable than underpaid, ill-housed, disgruntled wage-slaves whose only diversion is getting drunk on Saturday night." He promoted his best men to the post of supervisor-inspector, with responsibility for closely overseeing all output.

In the winter of 1837, Colt traveled to Florida and sold enough revolvers to local citizens, militiamen, and soldiers fighting the Seminoles to briefly save his company. Based in part on the experience of the Texas Rangers and the Indian fighters, a new army board examined the Colt pistol in 1840. This time, the board endorsed the weapon—unanimously.

The army purchase was too little, too late. Sales continued to lag behind expenses, prompting Colt to close his factory in 1842. He set the revolver aside and turned to another innovative technology. He began tinkering with the burgeoning business of telegraphy, which had been launched by Samuel F. B. Morse's patent of 1837. In 1843, Colt invented the first waterproof electric cable, which he used to connect Manhattan telegraphers with stations on Fire Island and Coney Island. He also developed an underwater explosive mine to be used for harbor defense; designed a forerunner of the modern torpedo; and, using electric batteries and explosive charges, invented an explosive weapon that could sink ships via remote control. He presented all of these marvels to the U.S. Navy, which promptly rejected each.

Then came the United States-Mexican War of 1846–1848. In the war's second year, General Zachary Taylor persuaded the U.S. Army to purchase a thousand Colt revolvers for use in combat. Having closed his plant, the inventor rushed to improvise production facilities in Eli Whitney's firearms factory near New Haven, Connecticut. Together, Samuel Colt and the successors to Whitney (who had died in 1825) filled the army's order with the latest, upgraded model of the revolver. It performed so well that in 1848, Colt was again able to establish his own plant, this time in Hartford, Connecticut.

Purveying what was now an amply proved product, Colt attracted customers from all over the world, and in a remarkably short time Colt's Patent Fire-Arms Manufacturing Company became the largest private armory on the planet. Colt sold to the armies of several nations, and he had no compunction about selling weapons to all sides of a given conflict. When the American Civil War broke out in 1861, he furnished firearms to both the Union and Confederate forces. He himself, however, died early in the war, succumbing to gout on January 10, 1862. His widow, Elizabeth (née Jarvis) Colt, successfully assumed leadership of the firm.

Colt pistols were the dominant handgun throughout the Civil War. They were, in effect, the brand to beat. And in 1873, when it was released to the public, the Peacemaker revolver model gained instant acceptance, becoming the weapon of choice throughout the American West—among settlers, townsmen, cowboys, sheriffs, marshals, and the outlaws they pursued. In this way, the ubiquitous weapon emerged as an American icon.

For more than two centuries, the time-consuming process of reloading and cocking a single-shot firearm had greatly limited the usefulness of the weapon. In military applications, deficiency in the rate of fire could be compensated for by deploying large numbers of riflemen, some of whom fired while others reloaded. For individual use, however, the necessity of reloading after a single shot made the shooter vulnerable to his armed enemy. The ability to fire six shots rapidly not only multiplied the lethality of the handgun, it encouraged the owner to be more aggressive. In civilian life, Colt's revolver made handguns seem a viable way to settle disputes. This, of course, remains an issue that has become ever more acute in modern America.

DISRUPTION:
INSPIRING, IF NOT
ACHIEVING, CONTROLLED
MANNED FLIGHT IN
HEAVIER-THAN-AIR
VEHICLES

OTTO LILIENTHAL
(1848–1896)

You know the story: at about 10:35 on the morning of December 17, 1903, at Kill Devil Hills in Kitty Hawk, North Carolina, Orville Wright made the first sustained powered flight in an aircraft heavier than air. The flight was in part the product of two events, one that took place in 1878 and the other in 1896. The first was the day Milton Wright, father of Wilbur and Orville, gave the boys a gift he believed was educational. It was a toy helicopter designed by an early French aeronautical experimenter named Alphonse Pénaud. In 1912, during testimony in one of many patent suits he and his brother initiated, Orville described the toy as "actuated by a rubber spring which would [drive a four-bladed rotor and] lift itself into the air." Orville went on to say that "Our interest [in flight] began when we were children," when "Father brought home to us [this] small toy." In fact, the brothers were inspired to build "a number of copies of this toy, which flew successfully," but when they "undertook to build the toy on a much larger scale, . . . it failed to work so well."

They wanted to make a helicopter sufficiently large and powerful to enable them to fly. They could not do this, and yet they never forgot their dream of flight. Beginning in 1890, the pair avidly followed reports in the fledgling aviation press about the work of Otto Lilienthal, a German experimenter with gliders. Then, in 1896, they read that Lilienthal had been killed on August 10 as a result of injuries sustained when one of his gliders crashed.

"The brief notice of his death," Wilbur later recalled in an essay titled "Some Aeronautical Experiments," reawakened "a passive interest which had existed from my childhood." Otto Lilienthal—and, in particular, the failure that caused his death—disrupted the lives of two bicycle shop owners in Dayton, Ohio: from 1896 on, Wilbur and Orville Wright could hardly think of anything other than manned flight.

• • •

Otto Lilienthal was born on May 23, 1848, in Anklam, Prussia. His father, Carl Gustav, was a merchant, but neither Otto nor his brother Gustav had much interest in pursuing a mercantile life. They attended a grammar school associated with their parents' church, St. Nikolai, where a schoolmaster's lessons included material covering the flight of birds. The boys were fascinated. If birds could fly, why couldn't they?

Together, the brothers fashioned a pair of strap-on wings. When these, naturally, failed, Gustav lost interest in the project of manned flight, but Otto did not. After completing grammar school, he enrolled in a Prussian regional technical school at Potsdam. After completing the two-year course of study, he was hired by an industrial firm, which gave him on-the-job training as a design engineer. The experience left him wanting even more, and he soon enrolled at the Royal Technical Academy in Berlin.

In 1867, Lilienthal began systematically conducting experiments dealing with what he called "the force of air." These were interrupted when he was commissioned as an engineer in the Prussian Army during the Franco-Prussian War (1870–1871). After his release from the army, he found employment with a succession of engineering companies. He designed and patented a mining machine in 1871, and in 1876 started his own company, making boilers and steam engines. He quickly grew prosperous, and in 1878 he married Agnes Fischer, a young woman with whom he shared a passion for music. She was a gifted amateur pianist and singer, he a French-hornist with a pleasant tenor voice. They married and made their home in Berlin, where they raised a family of four children.

While he continued to develop his engineering company, Lilienthal made a systematic study of bird flight, which he embodied in an 1889 book titled

Der Vogelflug als Grundlage der Fliegekunst (*Bird Flight as the Basis of Aviation*). He studied most closely the flight of storks, creating polar diagrams, which plotted the sink rate of the bird against its horizontal speed. Using these diagrams, he analyzed the aerodynamics of the bird's wings, and then, beginning in 1891, he started emulating the structure of these wings in manned gliders. His first glider version was called the *Derwitzer* (after the nearby village of Derwitz), which he flew from an artificial hill he built near Berlin. Later glider iterations were flown from artificial as well as various natural hills—most of the latter in the Rhinow region.

Lilienthal was obsessive in his work, making more than 2,000 manned flights and meticulously recording and evaluating the results. He tirelessly experimented, struggling to achieve better, more sustained, and, above all, more controlled flights. At first, he managed to make jumps and flights as long as eighty-two feet. He typically worked with a photographer to capture each flight for later study. He discovered that he could take advantage of the updraft of a 10 meter-per-second wind against a hill, which was sufficient to hold the glider stationary, so that he could shout to his photographer to find the best position for the photograph.

His brother Gustav rejoined him for many of his experiments, as Otto refined the design of the glider's wings and patented various features of his aircraft, which were, in fact, early forms of hang gliders. Lilienthal built twelve distinct monoplane glider designs in addition to some wing-flapping aircraft and two biplane gliders. Control of flight was achieved by changing the center of gravity simply by the pilot shifting his body, as in today's hang gliders. Control and stability, however, remained problematic. The gliders were airworthy, but difficult to maneuver. Lilienthal introduced various design features aimed at increasing stability and control, but his success was always limited. He envisioned creating an engine-powered aircraft—in which the engine would flap the wings in the manner of a bird.

By 1892, Lilienthal was flying from a hilly area called Maihöhe, in Steglitz, near Berlin. On this hilly ridge, he built a shed thirteen feet high, the top of which served as a jumping-off platform. The following year, he made use of a higher set of hills, called the Rhinower Berge, and, in 1896, the Gollenberg, which was close to the village of Stölln. He also built an artificial hill near his house in Lichterfelde, which he called *Fliegeberg* ("Flight Hill"). Perfectly conical, 49 feet high, with a flat top, *Fliegeberg* allowed him to launch his gliders into the wind, whatever its direction.

Lilienthal's experiments always drew a fascinated crowd of spectators, and reports of his work spread far beyond Germany—certainly reaching the Wright brothers. Visitors included many luminaries of the early days of manned flight, among them Samuel Pierpont Langley from the United States, Nikolai Zhukovsky from Russia, Percy Pilcher from England, and the Austrian Wilhelm Kress. Zhukovsky called Lilienthal's gliders the most important inventions in aviation.

On August 9, 1896, Lilienthal flew, as he often did, from the Rhinow Hills. One of his first three flights was a new record for him—or for any other attempt at heavier-than-air flight—820 feet. It was during the fourth flight, however, that Lilienthal's craft suddenly pitched forward. This was an aerodynamic weakness of his gliders, and one that was difficult to correct using the body-shifting technique. Lilienthal worked to shift his weight, but could not correct the dive. He and his machine plummeted some fifty feet to the ground.

At first, he did not seem badly injured, but his mechanic, Paul Beylich, laid him down in a horse-drawn carriage and drove him to Stölln, where a physician examined him. He diagnosed a fracture of the third cervical vertebra. Shortly after this determination, Lilienthal lost consciousness and was transported by train to Lehrter station in Berlin. The next morning, he was carried to the clinic of Dr. Ernst von Bergmann, an eminent surgeon. It was, however, too late. Some thirty-six hours after the crash, Lilienthal, who drifted in and out of consciousness, uttered to his brother Gustav his last words, "*Opfer müssen gebracht werden!—Sacrifices must be made!*"

* * *

The death of Otto Lilienthal made a powerful impression on the Wrights of Dayton, Ohio. Wilbur understood that, flying as he did in this hang glider, with his only means of control the shifting weight of his body, Lilienthal had been, sooner or later, doomed. He pronounced the aviator's "apparatus" for achieving equilibrium in flight "inadequate."

Importantly, Wilbur Wright did not base his conclusion solely on "the fact that [the glider eventually] failed," but on his own firsthand observations of bird flight. These had convinced him "that birds use more positive and energetic methods of regaining equilibrium than that of shifting the center of gravity." They achieved control and maintained equilibrium not by merely shifting their body weight, Wilbur reasoned, but by turning the leading edge of one wingtip up and the other down.

This was the disruptive revelation of Lilienthal's death: control was everything. Lilienthal died because he failed to achieve sufficient control. Wilbur believed he had a way to achieve it. Control would make all the difference—if, *if* he and his brother could devise a way to imitate in an artificial wing the opposed twisting of the leading edges of birds' wings.

Wilbur was working in the Wright Cycle Shop one July afternoon in 1899 when the rectangular cardboard box in which an inner tube had been packed caught his eye. The end tabs of the box had been ripped off. He reached out, picked up the empty box, and twisted it in his hands. It hit him: design a wing that could be twisted in a controlled fashion. The design and method the Wrights came up with would be called "wing warping," and although it would later be replaced (through the work of other aviation pioneers) with flaplike panels called ailerons, it worked. Lilienthal's death revealed to the Wrights that the single most important aspect of manned flight was not power or even the shape of the wing: it was control. Now, thanks to Lilienthal's insights, data, designs, and ultimate failure, the boys from Dayton had it. The German had been correct: sacrifices had to be made.

FREDERICK (1856–1915)
WINSLOW TAYLOR

Something went wrong with Frederick Taylor's eyes. At least that was the reason the young Philadelphian gave for not going to Harvard, even after he passed the entrance exams with honors, and he followed his father into the practice of law. His eyesight had gone bad, he said. Yet Taylor soon turned from both Harvard and the law to a far less prestigious industrial trade that depended even more on having good vision: he apprenticed as a foundry patternmaker and machinist while earning an engineering degree from the night school of Stevens Institute of Technology in Hoboken, New Jersey. From here, he went on to disrupt the industrial workplace—indeed, the very nature of modern work. And, unlike many of the business consultants who would work to enact his principles in later years (for a price, of course), all of it was the product of close observation, the results of which he published in the unlikely 1911 blockbuster with the off-putting title *Principles of Scientific Management.*

B y the 1880s, Taylor had worked his way up to machine shop foreman at Philadelphia's Midvale Steel Company. He watched his men, very closely, and concluded that many were "soldiering"—that is, not just slacking off, but working at the slowest rate possible without incurring punishment. Even more striking was his observation that, despite the growing mechanization throughout the plant, the rate of production still depended largely on the pace set by the least productive workers. As Taylor saw it, both the "soldiers" and the most highly skilled employees were equally unproductive.

This was a breakthrough insight: according to Taylor's research, the workers most highly valued (and therefore most highly paid) for their skills had precisely the same negative impact on productivity as the least valued, most incorrigible loafers.

Taylor continued to observe his workers, analyzing the human aspects of productivity—what people did, how they moved when they did it, and in what order they performed each step of a given process. He saw over and over again that "excessive idiosyncrasy" (the trait of the skilled worker, the true craftsman) had the same effect as laziness (the trait of the "soldier"). Both retarded the rate of production. For productivity to be maximized, Taylor concluded, managers, not the workers, had to be given full control of all manufacturing processes. Managers had to prescribe methods, and managers had to set the required pace.

Power was to be taken from the worker and transferred to the manager; however, Taylor did not propose giving managers *absolute* power. He believed that it was the responsibility of managers to apply *science* to regulating their workers for maximum productivity. Each manufacturing operation was to be observed, analyzed, and broken down into discrete steps. Then, each step needed to be evaluated as to the nature and number of every movement made by each worker. Once a manager had accurately collated these observations, Taylor believed they would have a blueprint that revealed the correct human role for getting a given industrial process done in the best—that is, most highly productive—way possible.

Taylor quickly ascended to the upper levels of engineering and management. In 1893, after his know-it-all ways had made him an unpopular executive at Bethlehem Steel, he left to set up as the world's first professional management consultant. His brand-new business card announced himself as "Consulting Engineer—Systematizing Shop Management and Manufacturing Costs a Specialty." This profession, which he invented, was the culmination of an evolution that had begun in the eighteenth century with the introduction of textile-manufacturing machinery driven by steam or water power. This had marked the beginning of a long—often unhappy—working relationship between human workers and machines.

By the late nineteenth century, it was clear to factory and workshop managers that machines were inherently more efficient than human workers, who increasingly either tended the machines or performed portions of production processes that had yet to be mechanized. Taylor's idea was to design standardized procedures that would bring human workers closer to the efficiency of machines. He believed that every job had "One Best Way" to do it. But he never asked workers themselves about their jobs. Instead, he watched them.

Taylor performed what he called "time-and-motion studies," breaking down even the simplest jobs into their component parts and measuring each part to the hundredth of a minute. Often, his object was to show managers how to precisely prescribe required procedures and methods. But at his best, Taylor also sought to marry the human and mechanical components of any given job. For instance, while working at Bethlehem Steel, he noticed that workers used the same shovel for all materials. He calculated that the most efficient shovelful was 21.5 pounds. So, he had the workers issued specialized shovels that would scoop up 21.5 pounds of whatever material they were intended for. The result was a three- to four-fold increase in productivity, which was rewarded with pay increases for the workers.

Taylor's "scientific management"—or "Taylorism"—roiled the American workplace. There was no question that his methods increased productivity. But while Taylor sometimes advocated for workers, calling for frequent breaks and good pay for good work, he also compared unskilled laborers to beasts of burden, labeling both equally "stupid." Taylor was a strong advocate for the division of labor, assigning workers to various phases of production based on their suitability to the nature and demands of the work. This segmentation deprived workers of a vital sense of connection to what they produced. Industrial work became inherently fragmented, repetitive, unfulfilling, and meaningless. Reduced to being a cog in a machine, a worker could take little pride in what he did. Craftsmanship had become a quaint relic of an unproductive past. Anomie—the breakdown of social bonds between individual workers and the greater community—became a dreary hallmark of mass production.

As it reduced the satisfaction that workers took in their jobs, Taylorism intensified the demands placed on them. Taylor introduced the concept of "scaled piecework rates" as an incentive for workers to move faster and achieve higher output. The consultant promoted this as a fair method of compensation. But the workers perceived the system as dehumanizing, stripping away their autonomy and individuality.

While a gulf opened up between labor and craftsmanship, an even wider gulf yawned between labor and management. Strikes, often violent, were commonplace, and labor unions became a divisive subject in the national dialog. The House of Representatives was moved to investigate the human cost of Taylorism after a strike shut down the army's Watertown Arsenal in Massachusetts. A House committee concluded in 1912 that scientific management provided many benefits, including increased production at lower costs, but that it also handed management an unacceptably high level of unregulated power. In the end, the U.S. Senate banned the application of Taylorism from the Watertown Arsenal.

While Taylorism often made work miserable and thereby contributed to individual despair and social unrest, the increases in production and reductions in costs put an unprecedented variety and volume of consumer goods within reach of the average American family. At the same time, the "de-skilling" of many factory jobs allowed companies to first hire cheaper labor and then to phase out human workers altogether. As industrial processes were analyzed and broken down, it became increasingly feasible for machines to replicate what human workers had been doing.

Taylorism thus accelerated the progress from mechanization (machines tended or complemented by humans) to automation (machines requiring no human operators). The resulting lower or even non-existent wages meant that *fewer* consumers could afford to buy many of the products being produced in greater quantities at lower costs. In many cases, the unintended, highly disruptive consequence of increased industrial efficiency was a decline in product demand and therefore a decrease in corporate revenues. This was a vicious circle, the opposite of the intended "virtuous circle," in which highly paid workers would be enabled to purchase more goods and services, thereby driving the economy. This decline, in turn, reduced the demand for labor, which further decreased the number of consumers with sufficient means to buy the output of efficient industrial production. The Great Depression was the result of many causes, but chief among them was an imbalance of production and demand. Companies produced too much of what too few could afford to purchase.

The work of Frederick Taylor helped to make America an industrial giant. Capitalists the world over claimed that scientific management actually improved the lot of unskilled labor, since anyone, even those with no specific skills or training, could be trained to do repetitive tasks and thus get a job. For example, Taylor discovered that workers moving 12.5 tons of pig iron per day could be incentivized, through scaled piecework rates, to move 47.5 tons per day, provided that managers determined, through close observation and analysis, the optimal timing of lifting and resting. Left to their own devices, workers invariably tired and fell short of the 47.5-ton quota. Yet, Taylor concluded, even using the scientific approach, only an eighth of pig-iron handlers could regularly move 47.5 tons. He argued that this presented strong but unskilled laborers with a unique opportunity for well-paid work. Others argued that Taylor's demands meant that seven-eighths of weaker but equally unskilled laborers were disqualified from moving pig iron. In the end, many workers accepted Taylorism, especially if they believed the added efficiency was increasing their pay; yet many more found the close monitoring, especially the use of stopwatches, intolerable. This single issue was the complaint most often heard among the workers who struck the Watertown Arsenal.

In seeking to increase productivity and lower costs, Taylorism often abandoned the search for balance between people and technology. Overwhelmingly, efficiency of production outweighed the engagement and happiness of the workers. The result of the movement Taylor started was, therefore, ever-expanding automation, not only in industrial production, but in virtually every aspect of human activity, from driving a car to piloting an airplane. Today, industrial robots build other industrial robots, and the nature of work is changing yet more radically and rapidly, opening up new industries even as it threatens to diminish employment in the old.

DISRUPTION:
CREATING ALL THE KEY
TECHNOLOGIES FOR
ALTERNATING CURRENT,
WHICH MADE GLOBAL
ELECTRIFICATION
PRACTICAL, AND IMAGINING
SOME OF THE ESSENTIAL
INVENTIONS OF
TWENTIETH- AND TWENTY-
FIRST-CENTURY LIFE

NIKOLA TESLA

(1856–1943)

Nikola Tesla designed and built Wardenclyffe Tower at Shoreham, Long Island, during 1901–1902. It was billed as an experimental station for the wireless trans-Atlantic transmission of telegraph messages, telephone calls, and even images. His revolutionary theory was to dispense with "wires and all other artificial conductors" by using "the Earth itself as the medium for conducting the currents," as he explained in the February 1901 issue of *Collier's Weekly*. It made sense to his principal financial backer, the redoubtable J. P. Morgan, but when Tesla proposed two expensive changes, Morgan bowed out.

Tesla decided to scale up the facility from an experimental station to a fully operational transmitting station big enough to compete with the radio system Guglielmo Marconi had already successfully demonstrated. He also proposed using the station for something far more disruptive. As he explained in *Collier's*, what he was building at Shoreham was like "a pump in its action, drawing electricity from the Earth and driving it back into the same at an enormous rate, thus creating ripples or disturbances which, spreading through the Earth as through a wire, could be detected at great distances by carefully attuned receiving circuits." Now, here was the *really* wild part:

In this manner I was able to transmit to a distance, not only feeble effects [low currents] for the purposes of [wireless] signaling, but considerable amounts of energy, and later discoveries I made convinced me that I shall ultimately succeed in conveying power without wires, for industrial purposes, with high economy, and to any distance, however great.

J.P. Morgan was not a very imaginative man. And belief in what Tesla proposed called for enormous imagination. Thomas Edison had started the commercial transmission of conventionally generated electric power via wires in the 1870s. Tesla was proposing to "pump" electricity from the ground and transmit it through the ground wirelessly and for unlimited distances. After Morgan's withdrawal, Tesla was unable to win any other backer. He was forced to abandon Wardenclyffe in 1906, and the great steel tower, which housed the "apparatus for transmitting electrical energy," was demolished and sold for its scrap value—all of $1,750 in 1917. The property itself was foreclosed by the bank in 1922.

The failure of Wardenclyffe marked the beginning of the inventor's long financial decline. The year of the foreclosure, 1922, Tesla began living in a series of Manhattan hotels, leaving each when his unpaid bills had become too large for hotel management to ignore. He spent a good deal of time walking in Central Park, feeding pigeons, bringing injured pigeons back to his room to nurse them to health. "I have been feeding pigeons, thousands of them for years," he wrote. "But there was one, a beautiful bird, pure white with light grey tips on its wings; that one was different. It was a female. I had only to wish and call her and she would come flying to me. I loved that pigeon as a man loves a woman, and she loved me. As long as I had her, there was a purpose to my life." It is said that he spent more than $2,000 to hasten her recovery from a broken wing and leg.

And so, he moved from hotel to hotel until, in 1934, Westinghouse Electric and Manufacturing Company began sending him a modest $125 monthly stipend that paid his living expenses at the Hotel New Yorker. Tesla had worked with George Westinghouse himself on the development of alternating current (AC), and the company clearly felt it owed him a debt. It is in Room 3327 of that hotel that Nikola Tesla died on January 7, 1943, aged eighty-six, of "coronary thrombosis." As always, he had been alone in his room. His body was discovered by a maid who finally ignored the DO NOT DISTURB sign after it had remained on the door for two days.

His decline took place in obscurity, but his death brought some two thousand mourners, including a number of Nobel laureates, to what has been described as a "state funeral" at the Cathedral of St. John the Divine on January 12. Telegrams of condolence poured in from dignitaries such as First Lady Eleanor Roosevelt. Two days earlier, New York's Mayor Fiorello LaGuardia had broadcast over the radio a eulogy written by Louis Adamic, like Tesla a Croatian-American. Tesla was cremated, his ashes interred in a glimmering golden sphere—his favorite, perfect shape—which today is displayed at the Tesla Museum in Belgrade, Serbia, beside the inventor's death mask.

* * *

Nikola Tesla deserved more. His work on alternating current was critical to the creation of the modern electrical power grid. For that alone, he should have died a wealthy man. But his nearly 300 patents did not even begin to cover what he imagined:

- The wireless transfer of high-voltage electric power

- The "thought camera" (an imagined device to photograph the human mind)

- The AC motor (designed and built, even though many considered such a thing impossible)

- Hydroelectric power generation (he designed the plant at Niagara Falls, which provided Buffalo with electric power—but he envisioned even greater plants)

- X-ray research (eight years before Wilhelm Röntgen's 1895 "discovery" of the phenomenon)

- The "death ray" weapon (a particle beam device)

- Robotics (he actually built a radio-controlled boat, and he envisioned a world of autonomous devices and self-driving cars)

- An "earthquake machine" (an oscillator device that, tuned to the inherent vibrations of large structures, amplified them and was capable of shaking even massive buildings apart; in 1898, Tesla claimed to have built the machine, but destroyed it when he realized its dangerous potential)

In the end, he imagined far more than he invented, and while his imaginings may yet produce disruptive inventions by others, his only partially realized career defines the limits of pure genius to create and implement disruptive innovation.

• • •

Nikola Tesla was born on July 10, 1856, in Smiljan, Lika, Croatia, at the time part of the Austro-Hungarian Empire. His father, Milutin Tesla, was a Serbian Orthodox priest and his mother, Djuka Mandic, was an inventor of household appliances. His parents recognized Nikola's potential and sent him to study at the *Realschule* (Higher Real Gymnasium), in Karlovac, where he became interested in the physics of electricity. He graduated in 1873, evaded compulsory service in the Austro-Hungarian Army by running away to the mountains in 1874, and lived in the countryside until he enrolled in the Austrian Polytechnic Institute at Graz, Austria, in 1875. He dropped out at the end of 1878, and then severed relations with his family, perhaps out of shame for having failed to complete his degree. He suffered a nervous breakdown the following year, after refusing his father's plea to return home. He went to Prague in January 1880 to study at Charles-Ferdinand University, but left at the end of the year.

In 1881, Tesla went to work as chief electrician for the Budapest Telephone Exchange, for which he claimed to have invented a telephone amplifier, although no such device was patented. There is a story that, while strolling through a

Budapest park with a friend, Tesla suddenly stopped and, using his walking stick, drew a diagram in the dirt, explaining to his companion that this was an induction motor, an electric motor capable of running on alternating current. In 1882, he took a job in Paris for the Continental Edison Company, installing incandescent lighting throughout the city. While living in Strasbourg the next year, he cobbled together a prototype of his induction motor and demonstrated it, but was unable to interest investors. So, when Charles Batchelor, a co-worker of Tesla's from Paris who was also Edison's right-hand man, asked Tesla to join the Edison firm in the United States, he jumped at the chance. One of his childhood dreams, he told Batchelor, was to harness the force of the falling water of Niagara Falls to generate electricity.

Tesla showed up at Edison's office in 1884 with a letter from Batchelor addressed to his boss: "I know two great men," it said, "one is you and the other is this young man." Edison hired him on the spot, assigning him to find ways to improve the dynamos his factory was building. Tesla did as he was told, but he took a step beyond his brief and tried to persuade Edison to redesign his electrical generating and distribution system for alternating current (AC) instead of direct current (DC). Tesla pointed out that the DC system Edison was installing was inefficient, with voltage dropping off very quickly with distance. Indeed, current could not be transported more than two miles because it could not be stepped up to the high voltage levels that were needed to make efficient transmission possible. DC required building generating stations every two miles. In contrast to DC, which flows continuously in one direction, AC changes direction fifty or sixty times per second and can be stepped up to very high voltages, thereby minimizing power loss across even very considerable distances. While it was true that designing electrical appliances suitable for AC was more complicated, Tesla was convinced that the future belonged to alternating current.

Edison wanted to hear none of it. When George Westinghouse began building his AC electrical distribution system in direct competition, more and more utility companies joined the Westinghouse camp. Edison dug in and launched a public relations campaign beginning in 1888 to convince the public that his relatively low-voltage DC system was far safer than Westinghouse's high-voltage AC transmission system.

Tesla left Edison's Machine Works just six months after joining it, and he set about patenting an arc lighting system, based on an apparatus to produce a brilliant electric light by means of an electric arc—a kind of artificial lightning. After rounding up financial backers, he founded the Tesla Electric Light & Manufacturing Company. Setting himself up as Edison's competitor, Tesla quickly patented a significantly improved dynamo—as if to rub salt into Edison's wound, it was not an AC generator, which Edison's company did not offer, but a *direct current* dynamo, which was one of its major products. Tesla secured a lucrative contract to install the dynamo to supply electricity to Rahway, New Jersey.

Tesla was enjoying his triumph when, suddenly, his backers, having no interest in supporting Tesla's efforts to create AC motors and AC electrical transmission equipment, pulled out. They started up their own electric utility, leaving the inventor without a dime. He was forced to piece together a living as a ditch digger until he found new backers for a new Tesla Electric Company. By 1888, he had money in place and quickly developed a successful AC motor. George Westinghouse licensed the motor and also hired Tesla as a consultant. For Westinghouse, Tesla next developed a complete system of polyphase alternating current generators, motors, and transformers—the complete suite of technology necessary to create an AC-based electrical grid. He had now planted his flag firmly in one camp as Westinghouse and Edison went to war over which system would power America and the world.

* * *

Tesla's affiliation with Westinghouse put him on the right side of the history of innovation in electric power, and his public demonstrations of AC electricity at the 1893 World Columbian Exposition in Chicago were a spectacular success that made him world famous. Two years later, his design for the first hydroelectric power plant in Niagara Falls represented the decisive triumph for AC, and Tesla was hailed outright as a hero. King Nikola of Montenegro, a small nation allied with his native Serbia, even presented him with the Order of Danilo.

Tesla went on to pioneer in varied fields. His Tesla coil, invented in 1891, enabled him to conduct many experiments in lighting, X-ray generation, and high-frequency alternating current. The Tesla coil eventually found application in a wide array of electronic equipment throughout the twentieth century. He also made major discoveries that were commercialized by others, including fluorescent lighting, aspects of laser science, wireless communications, remote control, robotics, turbines, and even vertical-takeoff aircraft. As a committed futurist, Tesla predicted the emergence of solar power and energy generated from the wave motion of the sea. He predicted the use of satellites in global communication.

After his death, Tesla passed quickly into popular mythology as a kind of technological folk hero. His charismatic legacy spawned a legion of partisans, active even to this day. They claim on his behalf the inventor's precedence in radio and television technology, and they believe that his advocacy of the wireless transmission of electric power will someday be vindicated. The discovery of terrestrial stationary waves, which Tesla himself considered his most important breakthrough, did prove that the earth could be used as a conductor. In one demonstration, Tesla wirelessly illuminated 200 lamps from a power source located twenty-five miles away.

Yet it was his creation of the essential elements of AC technology that proved to be the high-water mark of Tesla's success as a practical creator of disruptive technology. The rest of his innovative legacy demonstrated the *potential* for disruption, which was realized, years later, by others or remained unrealized. In the end, Tesla may be seen as a martyr to the business of disruption. Innovators like Edison and Westinghouse lacked the *visionary* genius of Nikola Tesla, but they possessed in abundance a genius for *applying* innovation. They made disruption profitably transformative, not just potentially transformative. Tesla's career is proof that genius and audacity are useful, perhaps even necessary, to creating disruptive innovations, but they are not sufficient to doing so.

DISRUPTION:
TRANSFORMING
MATERIAL
CIVILIZATION INTO
A VAST SYNTHETIC
ENVIRONMENT

LEO BAEKELAND

(1863–1944)

Much of the long story of civilization, which occupies roughly the most recent 6,500 years, has been about making things; and for the first 6,391 years of that period, things were made out of materials that either grew from the ground (trees that were turned into timber), were pulled out of the ground (ore from which metals were refined), or were taken from animals (textiles, ivory, and the like). Then, in 1909, an accident occurred that disrupted the history of civilization.

We think of accidents as sudden events, but this one had a sixty-three-year backstory. In 1846, collodion, which is what you get when you mix nitrocellulose (also known as gun cotton or pyroxylin) with ether and alcohol, was invented by a French poet, painter, historian, and chemist named Louis-Nicolas Ménard (1822–1901). Collodion is a kind of syrupy substance that rapidly dries into a gluey gel film. In 1847, it found a practical use as a brush-on bandage to cover wounds, and in 1851 an English photographer, Frederick Scott Archer (1813–1857), discovered that collodion could be brushed onto glass plates to make a far better photographic film than the albumen (egg white) emulsion that was then in use.

Another Englishman, Alexander Parkes (1813–1890), a metallurgist by profession and an inventor by avocation, realized that collodion could be used not just to coat things, but as a substance for forming standalone objects. He called his version of collodion, patented in 1862, Parkesine.

A great many things were happening in the United States during the 1860s, paramount among them the Civil War. But war or no war, the decade saw a huge boom in the business of billiards. Americans' passion for the game created a huge demand for the requisite paraphernalia, including balls. And therein lay a problem. Billiard balls were made of ivory, always an expensive material. With the demand for billiard balls at an all-time high, expensive turned outrageous. The cost of ivory threatened the growth of the billiard industry, which, accordingly, offered a $10,000 prize to anyone who could come up with a viable substitute for the animal product.

The prospect of prize money jogged the memory of a young American chemist named John Wesley Hyatt, who recalled that Parkesine was often called "synthetic ivory." Spurred by the recollection, he quickly acquired the American rights to Parkes's patent and started tinkering with collodion as a means of making synthetic billiard balls. Surely, these would be much less costly than balls made of ivory. In 1869, Hyatt used a combination of cloth, genuine ivory dust, shellac, and collodion to make synthetic billiard balls. With a group of investors, Hyatt founded the Albany Billiard Ball Company, and in 1872 he and his brother Isaiah added camphor to the mix, which significantly improved the durability of the company's billiard balls. It was Isaiah who came up with "celluloid" as a distinctive name for what was, in effect, Parkesine 2.0.

In addition to cheap billiard balls, celluloid was used to make flexible photographic film (and was therefore essential to the invention of motion pictures), detachable shirt collars and cuffs, and household items like children's dolls, table tennis balls, and guitar picks. Except perhaps for flexible photographic film, none of these applications qualifies celluloid as a profoundly disruptive invention. Celluloid is known as a thermoplastic, meaning that it becomes pliable and capable of being molded when heated above a certain temperature. Below this temperature, it solidifies. If reheated, however, it again melts. Many thermoplastic products melt in the sun or even in summer temperatures. The low melting point greatly limits the usefulness of celluloid and other thermoplastics, because they are less durable than most natural materials.

That is where what we might call the pre-plastics industry stood as of the year 1909. It was a new year in a new century, and it ushered into prominence another chemist, Leo Baekeland (1863–1944). He worked a good deal with celluloid and similar materials, but he wasn't experimenting with the material, and he had no intention of looking for a way to make celluloid and its chemical brethren more commercially useful. Much less was he thinking about elevating celluloid from the realm of billiard balls to a material capable of disrupting the manufactured-and-built civilization of the planet.

No, he had a more immediate problem. It was how to remove the tarry, organic substance he disgustedly called "guck" that accumulated on his costly experimental apparatus whenever he worked with plastic-like substances. So, one day in 1909, he set out to finally clean up his lab. He approached his problem systematically by testing a variety of solvents. To ensure that his experimentation would produce measurable results, he first created a special test "guck" by combining phenol and formaldehyde. The substance that emerged from this unholy union was incredibly stubborn, thoroughly resistant to one solvent after another.

Initially frustrated, Baekeland soon found his frustration turning to inspiration. If the guck he had created was sufficiently durable to resist the attack of powerful solvents, it might well be a commercially valuable product. Setting aside his search for a solvent, he began looking for ways to make his *resin*—for he now thought of it as something more than *guck*—even tougher and harder, yet more easily worked. After much trial and error, he came up with a liquid that could be poured into a mold, from which it emerged as a dense, tough solid that could even be cut and machined further, like many natural materials. Baekeland perfected a complex process to produce a very hard material, which was not only insoluble, but *infusible*—that is, not capable of being remelted once it had hardened.

The trouble with celluloid was that it was thermoplastic. It could be melted and molded in manufacturing, but the finished product remelted at fairly low temperatures. Baekeland's material was not a thermoplastic, but a *thermosetting* plastic. The heating processes that created it and also allowed it to be poured into molds to make almost anything imaginable yielded a finished product with a molecular structure that even very high temperatures would not unlock and melt down. Moreover, despite the highly flammable chemicals used to create it, the finished material was itself non-flammable. Leo Baekeland named this synthetic wonder after himself, simplifying the spelling slightly. He called it Bakelite.

• • •

Bakelite was immediately used in a dazzling variety of products. Because Bakelite was a great electrical insulator, it was perfect for small electrical appliances. It was terrific for kitchenware, especially the handles of knives and other utensils, but also cups and saucers. Jewelers loved working with it—as did gunsmiths, who fashioned Bakelite handle grips for pistols and stocks for rifles. Smooth, good-looking, and highly tolerant of heat, Bakelite was wonderful for pipe stems and fancy cigarette holders. The toy industry was revolutionized by the material. Indeed, any manufactured product that needed small, precision-machined, and lightweight but strong components found a use for Bakelite.

For many years, telephones were made of the material. Indeed, during the 1910s through the 1940s, Bakelite was ubiquitous. It was the first synthetic material that could be made to look like any one of a vast number of natural materials—gems, marble, wood, and so on. Or it could be fashioned into something beautiful for itself. Even when it was not mimicking a natural substance, Bakelite was quite pretty. Little wonder that Baekeland made a fortune with it.

Not that he needed the money, for he was already a wealthy man. He had not been born that way. He was a native of Ghent, Belgium, born on November 14, 1863, into the family of a shoemaker and a house maid. He enrolled in the Ghent Municipal Technical School, from which he graduated with honors that earned him a scholarship awarded by the city. With this, he studied chemistry at the University of Ghent. He remained at that institution until he had earned a PhD maxima cum laude when he was only twenty-one. From 1887 to 1889, he was professor of physics and chemistry at the Government Higher Normal School in the lovely medieval town of Bruges. He was appointed associate professor of chemistry at the University of Ghent in 1889, and in the summer of that year married Céline Swarts, the daughter of his former professor Theodore Swarts and Celine (Platteau) Swarts. The marriage would produce three children, George, Nina, and Jenny.

By way of a honeymoon, Baekeland and his bride used a travel scholarship to visit universities in Britain and the United States. In New York City, Baekeland met Professor Charles F. Chandler of Columbia University and Mr. Richard Anthony, of E. and H. T. Anthony, America's largest maker of photographic supplies during the last half of the nineteenth century and the predecessor of Ansco, a Binghamton, New York firm active until the 1990s. Young Baekeland had already invented and patented (1887) a process for developing photographic plates with water and no other chemicals. Impressed, Anthony jumped at the chance to offer him a position with his company, and Professor Chandler piped up, urging him to immigrate and take the job.

Baekeland worked for Anthony just two years before going into business for himself in 1891 as a "consulting chemist." When this proved insufficiently profitable, he turned again to invention. He had earlier explored the possibility of producing a photographic paper for printing enlargements by artificial light. At this time, printing negatives on photographic paper required long exposure to sunlight, since the emulsions used on the paper were quite insensitive. The necessity of sunlight exposure greatly reduced the practical utility of photographic paper. By 1893, Baekeland had invented Velox (Latin for *swift*), the first commercially successful photographic paper, which could be used to print negatives using artificial light.

This was a great invention. The only thing wrong was Baekeland's timing. The United States was in the throes of the Panic of 1893, the worst American economic depression prior to the Great Depression of the 1930s. As important a breakthrough as Velox was, the inventor could not find investors—or even wholesalers—to finance mass production of the paper. Faced again with a personal economic crisis, Baekeland strove to make ends meet by partnering with a businessman named Leonard Jacobi, with whom he started the Nepera Chemical Company in the Nepera Park neighborhood of Yonkers, New York. Six years later, Jacobi, Baekeland, and another partner, Albert Hahn, sold the company to George Eastman of the Eastman Kodak Co. for $750,000. Baekeland's share of the sale was about $215,000, which he used to buy a large Yonkers house, Snug Rock, in which he established both his family home and a state-of-the-art chemical laboratory.

Free at last to experiment, Baekeland felt himself in heaven. His only constraint was the non-compete clause that barred him from doing photographic work for twenty years. But he soon turned this prohibition into a spur to research areas new to him. He sailed to Germany in 1900, where he took classes in electrochemistry at the Technical Institute at Charlottenburg, and then he returned to the United States to put his fresh education to profitable use by collaborating on the creation of a commercial electrolytic cell. He was hired as a consultant with carte blanche to design and operate a pilot plant for the cell. He went beyond this, creating a number of improvements to the cell, which led to the establishment of the Hooker Chemical Company in 1903 and the building of a massive electrochemical plant at Niagara Falls. Hooker was a great success through the late 1960s, but earned an unfortunate reputation for polluting the area around the Love Canal, which became the first EPA superfund site in 1983.

By the time his work leading up to Hooker Chemical had borne fruit, Velox (the rights to which he still owned) was finally selling very well, having gained preeminence among professional photographers and photofinishers. With steady revenue flowing in, he worked on a variety of commercial projects. The invention of Bakelite, therefore, was not a rags-to-riches story so much as a tale of riches to even greater riches. In addition, the chemist was showered with honors, including the Perkin Medal in 1916 and the Franklin Medal in 1940. By the year of his death in 1944, he held more than a hundred patents, many of which were very profitable—but none more than Bakelite, which reached a global production of 175,000 tons that year. The plastic was a principal material in some fifteen thousand distinct products by this time.

• • •

Unlike seminal innovators such as Ford, Edison, and Westinghouse, maturity of years did not treat Leo Baekeland kindly. As he aged, he steadily descended into madness. He fought fiercely with his son over issues of money and control over his company, General Bakelite. After selling the company to Union Carbide in 1939, he withdrew from commerce, chemistry, and eventually life itself. He became reclusive, a hermit who took his meals alone, usually eating canned goods directly out of the cans. His solitary passion became a tropical garden, which he developed on the grounds of his winter home in Coconut Grove, Florida. But he did not have long to enjoy this. His final years were spent in a Beacon, New York, sanatorium, where he died of a massive cerebral hemorrhage on February 23, 1944.

As for Bakelite, it began to decline in the 1940s due to competition from the growing array of new plastic products it had spawned, all of which were beginning to supplant their progenitor. By the 1950s, the accidental breakthrough sparked by the "guck" Baekeland had concocted was morphing into the dazzling variety of plastics that form so much of our world. As the first fully synthetic plastic, Bakelite introduced a whole new set of physical realities to our built-and-manufactured universe. Virtually everything we handle and use every day consists at least in part—and usually in very large part—of plastic. Almost any product that can be imagined can be made in plastic. Thanks to digital 3-D printing technology, designs can come into existence in plastic within minutes of their conception as bits and bytes. At the same time, the profusion of plastic products has had the unintended consequence of creating massive, non-biodegradable piles of global trash, both on land and in the world's oceans. In the long run, this may end up being the most consequential disruption wrought by Baekeland's invention.

TRANSFORMING THE AUTOMOBILE FROM A COSTLY LUXURY FOR THE ELITE INTO AN INDISPENSABLE COMPONENT OF MODERN SOCIETY AND CIVILIZATION

HENRY FORD
(1863–1947)

Henry Ford was a disruptive innovator, but not an inventor. Ask who invented the automobile, and "Ford" is likely to be the most frequent answer. Ask who invented the assembly line, and, among those who can come up with any answer, it will almost certainly be "Henry Ford." But Ford invented neither the car nor the assembly line. In fact, he invented nothing at all. Nevertheless, this captain of early twentieth-century American industry created more disruptions of the social, economic, technological, political, and material environment than any inventor ever did or (probably) ever could.

Ford was born on July 30, 1863, in Michigan's Greenfield Township. His father, William, was a farmer hailing from County Cork, Ireland, and his mother, Mary Litogot, was a born Michigander, the daughter of Belgian immigrants. Ford had four siblings, two boys and two girls.

There is a story about young Henry, one of those stories that seems so fitting as to be fiction. William gave his teenage son a pocket watch, which Henry took apart and—more importantly—reassembled repeatedly for the edification and entertainment of his friends and neighbors. True or not, Henry never seriously considered becoming a farmer like his father. Crops didn't interest him. Machinery did. And so, in 1879, he packed his things and set off for nearby Detroit, where he apprenticed to a machinist's firm, James F. Flower & Bros., and then moved on to the Detroit Dry Dock Co. He returned to Dearborn and the farm in 1882, but soon earned a local reputation for his ability to operate, adjust, maintain, and repair the Westinghouse portable steam engine, which was growing in popularity among farmers. The Westinghouse company hired Ford to service their steam engines.

But if young Henry did not see himself as a farmer, neither did he see himself as simply a mechanic. He took an accounting and bookkeeping course at Goldsmith, Bryant & Stratton Business College in Detroit. Clearly, he had a vision of someday running his own enterprise.

But not quite yet. In 1888, when he was twenty-five, Henry Ford married Clara Jane Bryant. He returned to farming to ensure that he could support his wife, and he made extra money operating a sawmill. In 1893, their one child, Edsel, was born. That was the same year Henry was promoted to chief engineer of the Edison Illuminating Company, a Detroit firm he had joined two years earlier. Being the chief had its perks, including the spare cash and time to invest in tinkering with a device Ford found fascinating: the gasoline-powered internal combustion engine. He did not invent that engine, but he did modify it for use in a small self-propelled vehicle he hand-built in 1896, the Quadricycle, which he took for its first spin on June 4. It was *his* first automobile—and it was a wonder. But it was not *the* first automobile. Carl Benz had patented the first vehicle powered by a gasoline engine ten years earlier, on January 29, 1886.

Eighteen ninety-six was also the year that Ford met his boss, Thomas Edison, at a meeting of Edison company executives. He told the inventor-industrialist about his automotive experiments. Had Edison been more of an industrialist and less of an inventor, he might have expressed some displeasure at his employee's extracurricular use of his time. Instead, Edison encouraged Ford and advised him to keep experimenting—Edison being the trial-and-error inventor who once declared "Genius is 1 percent inspiration and 99 percent perspiration."

Edison *was* enough of a businessman to recognize that Ford was far from alone in his automotive passion. A lot of young men in America were building cars in their barns and sheds, just like Henry Ford. Unlike him, however, most stopped after they had managed to get something to run. Ford, however, recognized that the Quadricycle, with its four wire-spoke bicycle-type wheels and its inability to travel in reverse, left room for a great deal of improvement. He did not want merely to build an automobile, he wanted to build and sell many automobiles.

In 1898, two years after the debut of the Quadricycle, Ford built his second vehicle. He designed it as a prototype to recruit investors in a company—*his* company—to manufacture what the world was calling horseless carriages. In two ways, Ford had achieved success: his second automobile was much better than his first, and he had demonstrated a genius for putting his vision into words sufficiently persuasive to attract investment. In a third way, however, Ford failed. He could not generate sufficient demand to make his new vehicle a commercial success. He tried again, with a second company. When it also failed, Ford decided that he had to do something to create public excitement about the automobile.

He realized that there was nothing all that exciting about a "horseless carriage"; but just as everyone loved a horse race, the prospect of racing cars was even more exciting. He recruited a former bicycle racer named Tom Cooper to work with him on a race car with a large, better-than-80-horsepower motor. He called it the 999 and paid America's first professional racecar driver, Barney Oldfield, to race it. In an October 1902 contest, the 999 beat all comers.

The 999 was an impressive vehicle and attracted to Ford the financial backing of a friend, Alexander Y. Malcomson, a prosperous Detroit-area coal dealer. Together, they started Ford & Malcomson, Ltd., to manufacture automobiles— inexpensive cars within reach of any reasonably well-off driver. With slow sales, Malcomson convinced Ford of the need to reincorporate with more investors, and on June 16, 1903, the Ford Motor Company was born. A second version of the 999 helped to publicize the new company when it achieved a record-breaking speed of 91.37 mph in a demonstration on a frozen Lake Clair.

● ● ●

American myth focuses on Ford working alone in a shed to build his Quadricycle. Americans like stories about "lone wolf" inventors who work (like Ford) in a shed or (like Steve Jobs) in a garage. But one of Henry Ford's greatest talents was an instinct for talent in others and his natural ability to build a team of really good people. The vehicles he developed after 1896 and 1898 were all the efforts of a company of talented people.

The Ford Motor Company's first car was the Model A—of 1903–1904, not to be confused with the Model A series of 1927–1931. It was a practical vehicle, available in two- and four-seat versions, looking significantly less like a carriage (horseless or otherwise) and more like an automobile. Most notably, it had a steering wheel rather than the tiller on Ford's 1896 and 1898 vehicles. Its 8-horsepower motor pushed the car to 28 mph, and its transmission offered two forward speeds and two in reverse as well. It was not cheap, at $800 to $900, and it was followed later in 1904 by a higher-end 24-horsepower Model B two-row, four-passenger touring car. The placement of the big engine, under a hood at the front of the vehicle, was a large step forward toward the look of a modern automobile. The price, however, was a steep $2,000 (equivalent to a $53,000 car today). A Model C was also offered, with a slightly more powerful engine than the Model A and a price of $850.

All of these were important vehicles, but all were inherently limited by their hefty price tags. A four-cylinder Model N, released in 1907, produced 15 horsepower and was priced at $500 to $600, a good enough value to make it the best-selling car in the country, which translated into just 7,000 units by 1908, the last year of production.

Ford believed he was going in the right direction—toward an affordable, high-value product. But he was impatient. Seven thousand cars counted as a success, but Ford dreamed much bigger. His disruptive vision was to manufacture a "motorcar for the great multitude." That is the assignment he gave to a select working group of his top employees. The result, introduced on October 1, 1908, was the Model T.

Easy to operate, maintain, and handle on rough roads—which were the nation had in 1908—the new model had a redesigned four-cylinder, 20 horsepower engine that could easily achieve 45 mph. It had many new mechanical features and could run on gasoline, kerosene, or ethanol. It was water-cooled with water pumps, and it had an improved and highly reliable ignition system. Most of all, it was built to be sturdy and reliable. Even at an initial price of $850, it was a runaway success. Ford knew that he could easily sell all the Model Ts he could make, but he was determined to make all that could be sold. He invested in a bigger factory, which was ready by 1910, in Highland Park, north of Detroit.

But Ford realized that a big factory was not enough. He needed to find many more ways to both increase production and lower costs. Ford introduced a version of the still-evolving assembly-line method of manufacture. But the real breakthrough came after one of his employees, William "Pa" Klann, took a tour of the Swift & Company slaughterhouse in Chicago. What he saw was something the meatpacker's managers called a "disassembly line." Animal carcasses were suspended from an overhead conveyor that ran past a succession of workers, each of whom was responsible for removing one specified portion of the carcass as the suspended animal moved by. This specialization—numerous workers removing an assigned piece over and over instead of a single skilled butcher laboring over one whole carcass at a time—greatly increased efficiency.

Pa Klann brought the idea back to Ford's Peter E. Martin, who, while skeptical, encouraged Klann to present the idea. Ford, who had recently toured an automated order-handling facility at the mail-order headquarters of Sears, Roebuck, was instantly excited by the possibility. Over a period of the next six years, through trial and error, a moving assembly line evolved within the new Highland Park plant.

In 1908, Ford produced 10,607 Model Ts that sold for $850. By 1916, when the assembly line had been perfected, the Highland Park plant turned out 730,041 cars at a retail price of $360, well within the reach of most American workers, including those who made the Model T. It was a sturdy, reliable, and generic product of mass production in one of its earliest incarnations. It changed not only America but civilization itself, fostering a consumer-driven society. The assembly-line-built Model T leveled economic classes by endowing them all with unprecedented mobility. The profusion of cars—by 1927, the final year of production, 15 million Model Ts had been manufactured—began the greater unification of the nation by stimulating a demand for an increasingly complex and far-reaching network of roads. The suburbanization of the country commenced. Equally profound was the impact of the Ford-perfected assembly line on the nature of work itself. The relation of labor to management was forever changed.

In some ways, it was not changed for the better. Ford workers grew restive over the demands of the assembly line, which forced them to keep pace with the machinery. The workday was repetitive and relentless. Turnover became a major problem, forcing the company to hire 53,000 people a year to keep 14,000 jobs staffed. Ford responded to the growing crisis with perhaps the most disruptive move any capitalist can make. In a single stroke, he doubled the wages of each assembly-line worker, paying an unheard-of $5 per day in 1914. The work was still miserable, but the pay could not be beat. As production rose, the price of the Model T dropped to a low of $269, and by 1922 one out of every two cars in the United States was a Model T.

Ford, wealthy as any plutocrat, was also a populist and an earnest antiwar activist who, in 1915, before U.S. entry into World War I, funded a "Peace Ship," in which he led a citizen pacifist mission to Europe.

On the other hand, after the war, Ford also funded publication of a weekly anti-Semitic national newspaper, *The Dearborn Independent*; reprinted the confabulated *Protocols of the Elders of Zion*, which purported to expose a secret plot for world domination by Jews; and published a collection of his own anti-Semitic articles in a volume titled *The International Jew*. for which he accepted in 1938 the Grand Cross of the German Eagle from the government of Nazi Germany. Hitler greatly approved of *The International Jew*, and, in a twist of tragic irony, the killing machine that was the Nazi death camps of World War II, in which millions of Jews were murdered and cremated with stunning efficiency, was inspired in part by Ford's moving assembly line.

DISRUPTION:
BRINGING WIRELESS
COMMUNICATION
TO PLANET EARTH,
THEREBY ANNIHILATING
SPACE AND TIME

GUGLIELMO MARCONI
(1874–1937)

In the 1973 revision of a 1962 essay titled "Hazards of Prophecy: The Failure of Imagination," the late British science fiction writer Arthur C. Clarke (1917–2008) proposed the third of his so-called Three Laws: "Any sufficiently advanced technology is indistinguishable from magic." This, it seemed, precisely described the advent of radio at the threshold of the twentieth century.

I n 1844, the American painter and inventor Samuel F. B. Morse (1791–1872) used his telegraph to send the message "What hath God wrought?" over forty-four miles of wires strung between Baltimore and Washington, D.C. On March 10, 1876, Alexander Graham Bell (1847–1922), laboring over a device to electrically transmit voice—not just the clicks of a telegraph—spoke the sentence "Mr. Watson, come here, I want to see you." It summoned, from an adjoining room, his assistant Thomas Watson, who heard the call through the receiver linked by wire to Bell's transmitter. These events were sufficiently magical to rapidly spawn civilization-altering technologies, the telegraph and the telephone, which, in the matter of communication, went a long way toward annihilating time and space—provided, of course, wires could be strung (or buried, or submerged) between place *A* and place *B*. The real magic? That would be communicating between place *A* and place *B* without wires—in fact, without any visible, humanly tangible connection between them. What hath God wrought, indeed.

In March 1897, the Irish-Italian inventor Guglielmo Marconi wirelessly transmitted Morse code across England's Salisbury Plain—site of Stonehenge—between stations set up 6 kilometers (3.7 miles) apart. On May 13 of the same year, he sent the world's first wireless message over open sea, from Flat Holm Island across the Bristol Channel to Lavernock Point, Penarth, Wales—again 6 kilometers. Later in the day, the location of the transmitter was moved ten kilometers farther, to 16 kilometers (9.9 miles). By the early 1900s, Marconi was transmitting to ships far out at sea and from station to station between Europe and North America.

It was magic, but it wasn't the whole story of one of the first great disruptive technologies to unfold in the twentieth century, an era in which disruptive technology exploded.

* * *

Born in Bologna, Italy, on April 25, 1874, Guglielmo Giovanni Maria Marconi was the second son of an aristocratic landowner, Giuseppe Marconi, and his Irish wife, Annie Jameson, daughter of Andrew and granddaughter of John Jameson, who had made the family wealthy by founding Jameson & Sons, distiller of Irish whiskey. Annie took her two sons to Bedford, England, in 1876, and the boys lived with her there until 1880, when they returned to Bologna. As a child, Guglielmo had an interest in science, especially physics and electrical phenomena in particular. He was befriended at eighteen by Augusto Righi (1850–1920), an eminent physicist on the faculty of the University of Bologna. Righi was a pioneer in the physics of electromagnetism and, following the work of the German scientist Heinrich Hertz (1857–1894), who proved the existence of electromagnetic waves, became the first person to generate microwaves. Righi invited the young Marconi to sit in on his university lectures and, even more important, to make use of his laboratory and the university library. The education was informal, but it was at the right hand of a master, and Marconi went on to Florence, where he enrolled at the Istituto Cavallero. Marconi, however, was less interested in gaining a full education in science than in quickly applying what he was learning. In 1894, when he was twenty, he set up his own laboratory in a room of his father's estate at Pontecchio. He was determined to develop *wireless telegraphy.*

For many, true magic requires making something out of nothing. Marconi did no such thing. When he started his work, the concept of wireless telegraphy already existed, and several scientists and inventors were working on it. The British physicist James Clerk Maxwell (1831–1879) had already provided theoretical and mathematical proof of the propagation of electromagnetic waves in free space; and various experimenters and inventors, including Thomas Edison, noted instances of electrical transmission without wires. In 1875, Edison stumbled across something he dubbed the "etheric effect" while working on a multiplexing telegraph capable of sending and receiving multiple messages over the same wire simultaneously. He noticed that a rapidly vibrating spark gap generated in one place produced a spark in a nearby relay, even if the relay was moved several feet away. No wires connected the spark gap and relay. In 1893, the prolific polymath innovator Nikola Tesla (1856–1943) demonstrated the rudiments of a wireless system that (he mistakenly believed) used the earth as a conductor. On August 14, 1894, the British scientists Oliver Lodge (1851–1940) and Alexander Muirhead (1848–1920) sent a wireless signal from Oxford University's Clarendon Laboratory to the nearby lecture hall of the Oxford Museum of Natural History. In November of that same year, the Indian mathematician and physicist Jagadish Chandra Bose (1858–1937) used microwave transmission to ignite gunpowder in a public demonstration at Kolkata's Town Hall. In 1895, the Russian physicist Alexander Stepanovich Popov (1859–1906) demonstrated a radio receiver, which he proposed to use as a lightning detector. Such work was innovative but not disruptive, because none of it was carried to full application and commercialization.

One year before Popov, in 1894, Marconi built his own lightning detector, which he called a "storm alarm," using a primitive coherer—essentially, two electrodes on either end of a glass tube with metal filings between them. When an electromagnetic signal was detected, such as the waves produced by lightning, the filings would come together, or *cohere*, allowing current to flow between the electrodes. If the coherer was attached to a battery and an electric bell (or other electrical device), the coming together of the metal filings closed the circuit, and the bell rang.

By the end of the year, Marconi modified his storm alarm into a primitive radio. In a demonstration for his mother, he wired a telegraph key to a circuit with a battery and an induction coil, pressed the key, and the bell wired to his coherer rang. Mrs. Marconi summoned Mr. Marconi, who was sufficiently impressed to finance his son's further research, and by 1895 Marconi had created a complete radio transmitting and receiving system, which included a spark-producing transmitter, an antenna (in the form of a metal sheet), a coherer-based receiver (more sophisticated than his first version), a telegraph key for sending Morse code, and a telegraph register (which printed out the Morse dots and dashes on a moving roll of paper tape).

All the components of Marconi's 1895 system were existing technology, which the young man assembled and, as needed, modified. In this sense, his "invention" was hardly original—except in another, more important sense, which was simply this: *nobody before him had brought together these components in this way.* Marconi himself acted as a "coherer," gathering the pieces, putting them together, and disrupting civilization by sending messages across great distances without paper or wires.

● ● ●

Marconi took his system to England in 1896, where he met with William Preece, engineer-in-chief of the post office, and performed a demonstration that helped him secure a British patent—the world's first for a complete system of wireless telegraphy. The Salisbury Plain and Bristol Channel demonstrations came in 1897, and in July he formed the Wireless Telegraph & Signal Company Limited (renamed three years later, in 1900, Marconi's Wireless Telegraph Company Limited). Later in 1897, he demonstrated his system to the Italian Government at La Spezia, home of the Italian naval fleet, sending a signal some twelve miles. Like most successful disruptors, Marconi moved along quickly with the momentum that developed behind him. In 1899, he set up wireless communication between France and England across the English Channel and then rapidly built permanent radio stations at The Needles on the Isle of Wight, at Bournemouth, and later at the Haven Hotel, Poole, Dorset.

On the threshold year of the twentieth century, 1900, Marconi took out his single most important patent, No. 7777, for "tuned or syntonic telegraphy." In December of the next year, he staged a spectacular demonstration to prove that his wireless waves would follow the curvature of the earth—and, therefore, that the range of radio signals was not limited by the horizon. (This is true of Marconi's AM radio signals; FM, developed later, does not follow the curvature of the earth.) He sent the first transatlantic wireless signals between Cornwall and Newfoundland, a distance of 2,100 miles.

Marconi continually worked to improve his system—and to further commercialize it. In 1904, his company established a commercial service to transmit nightly news summaries to ships that subscribed to the service. On October 17, 1907, the first commercial transatlantic wireless service was established between stations in Clifden, Ireland, and Glace Bay, Nova Scotia. The tragedies of the

Titanic, victim of an iceberg in 1912, and the *Lusitania,* torpedoed by a German U-boat during World War I in 1915, were spectacular proof that wireless communication could save lives. Both ships transmitted distress signals; indeed, the *Titanic's* radio operators were employees of Marconi International Marine Communication Company and not of the White Star Line, which owned the vessel. At the court of inquiry convened to investigate the loss of the *Titanic,* Britain's postmaster general went on record: "Those who have been saved, have been saved through one man, Mr. Marconi . . . and his marvelous invention." Thus, in its infancy, radio ascended from an exciting innovation to one that appeared to have become instantly indispensable.

• • •

The Italian Army commissioned Marconi a lieutenant in 1914 and subsequently promoted him to captain. The year after Italy entered World War I, in 1916, he was transferred to the navy, with the rank of commander, responsible for wireless communication. The government made him a member of the Italian mission to the United States in 1917, and in 1919 he was appointed Italian plenipotentiary delegate to the Paris Peace Conference, which resulted in the Treaty of Versailles and the Covenant of the League of Nations.

While he was working for the military, Marconi resumed his early experiments with Righi's short waves, which led, in 1923, to the development of the so-called beam system for long-distance communication between ships and from ship to shore. The system was also usable as an aid to navigation. Soon, "Marconi stations" equipped for long-distance shortwave communication were established worldwide and integrated into what the British government called the Imperial Wireless Chain. The first strategic system for international radio telegraphy, it networked the entire British Empire.

Beginning in 1931, Marconi researched the characteristics of even shorter waves—microwaves—the use of which was demonstrated in 1932 with the world's first microwave radiotelephone link, set up between Vatican City and the pope's summer residence at Castel Gandolfo. In 1935, Marconi demonstrated the use of a microwave radio beacon to aid ship navigation, thus bringing into being radio navigation, which revolutionized travel by sea and by air. The same year, he extended the application of microwaves to a set of concepts that, through the work of other researchers, soon became radar.

• • •

Born to wealth, Marconi became far wealthier, and the fruits of his work brought him many honorary degrees and national and international honors, crowned in 1909 by the Nobel Prize for Physics, which he shared with Karl Braun (1850–1918) for contributions to radio communication. An enthusiastic Fascist, he joined the Fascist Party in 1923 and, in 1930, accepted Benito Mussolini's appointment as president of the Royal Academy of Italy, which included membership on the Fascist Grand Council. The inventor's death on July 20, 1937, after suffering a series of massive heart attacks, took him from the world before Mussolini plunged the nation into the ruin of World War II. It was a war in which radio and radar technology were critical not only in tactics and strategy, but in moving the hearts and minds of warring peoples through the use of radio as a mass broadcast medium. It was the one use of his invention that Marconi had failed to foresee.

DISRUPTION:
BY MAKING FROZEN
FOOD GOOD FOOD,
BIRDSEYE CREATED
THE FROZEN FOOD
INDUSTRY AND GAVE
THE WORLD A NEW WAY
TO EAT

CLARENCE BIRDSEYE

(1886–1956)

Clarence Birdseye was a lot of things in his career. He grew up poor but not impoverished in Brooklyn and New Jersey, number six of nine children. He was always looking for ways to make money, and at the age of ten he heard about an English lord seeking wild game for his Long Island estate. The boy trapped a dozen muskrats, shipped them to the lord, and made a nine-dollar profit on the venture.

He was, it seems, not just a born entrepreneur, but a born naturalist. After graduating from Montclair High School in New Jersey, he enrolled in Amherst College, alma mater of both his father and older brother, where he majored in biology. To pay his tuition, he went trapping—always looking for animals within easy reach. He rounded up baby frogs, which he sold in bulk to the Bronx Zoo for use as reptile food. When an Amherst genetics professor was willing to pay for relatively rare black rats, to be used in a study, young Birdseye knew that a local butcher shop had a rat problem, and he offered to trap the pests. He killed all but the black ones.

But the money Birdseye made as a part-time trapper could not pay the bills past his sophomore year. So Birdseye dropped out and took a job as a taxidermist for the U.S. Department of Agriculture. This led to a position as an assistant naturalist with the department, stationed in New Mexico and Arizona. (Mostly, he shot surplus coyotes.) He moved on to Montana, where, during 1910–1911, he assisted the entomologist Orsdel King, who was attempting to isolate the vectors that spread Rocky Mountain spotted fever. Birdseye's task was to trap any and all small varmints, so that Orsdel could comb them for ticks to use in his research.

In 1912, Birdseye left the USDA to freelance for a New York furrier in search of pelts. For the next three years, he trekked by dogsled throughout Labrador, Newfoundland, trapping beavers for their pelts. His interest, however, was soon drawn to the Inuit Indians' methods of "quick freezing" the fish they caught. In the Arctic climate, this was not an especially complex procedure. Inuit fishermen just laid their catch on the ice, where the brisk wind froze the fish in an instant. Birdseye noticed that when the quick-frozen fish were cooked and eaten, they were as tender and flaky as fresh-caught. The fish frozen down south, in a process that took hours, were just awful by contrast: soggy, mealy, and tasteless.

Curious to see if the virtues of quick-freezing extended to foodstuffs other than fish, Birdseye stored cabbage heads, caribou meat, and geese outside his cabin. He took each item, laid it out on ice, and let the wind and air temperature do its work. These foods also held their taste and texture. Birdseye's two years at Amherst had taught him enough about cellular biology to lead him to conclude that the liquid within the cells of slow-frozen tissue froze in a way that formed large ice crystals, which tore up the cell walls, rendering frozen food mushy and unpalatable. Quick-freezing created much smaller crystals, which did not expand with such explosive effect. Since the cell walls were preserved intact, the tissue retained more of its texture and more of its flavor. For this reason, quick-frozen food tasted more like fresh food than conventionally frozen food did or ever could.

The person who could deliver quick-frozen food to market, Birdseye concluded, might well make a fortune. But quick-freezing food on the ice of Labrador and shipping it south was hardly practical. This is when Birdseye turned from the professions of taxidermist, hunter, trapper, and naturalist to full-on inventor.

● ● ●

Understand: Clarence Birdseye did not invent frozen food. People had been freezing food for centuries. But, excepting unique situations like the Inuit fishermen in Labrador, freezing food resulted in uniformly disappointing results. Frozen food was not just commercially unappealing to consumers; it was, in some cases, against the law. When thrifty jailers in New York State tried to feed their prisoners on reheated frozen food, the legislature banned it from the prison system, calling it inhumane. The food was not dangerous. It just was not worth eating.

Birdseye set about duplicating the results Inuit fishermen achieved in nature. To invent this, he understood, would be to invent an entire new industry. Like many disruptive innovators, Birdseye didn't invent anything new. He was going to figure out how to take something that already existed, apply it in a new and heretofore unthought-of fashion, and make it profitable.

In 1922, Birdseye began a series of fish-freezing experiments at the Clothel Refrigeration Company in New York. He concluded that he could quick-freeze fish fillets using air chilled to −45°F. Acting on this conclusion, he gathered backers for his own company, Birdseye Seafood Inc., and set to work inventing quick-freeze machinery. The biologist turned mechanical inventor. More astoundingly, his very first devices worked! Technologically, they were successful. The problem was that he could not entice retail consumers to buy frozen fish fillets, and the two-year-old Birdseye Seafood Inc. filed for bankruptcy.

In this commercial failure, Birdseye had something in common with Thomas Edison, whose very first invention was an automatic vote-tabulating machine Edison intended to sell the device to the House of Representatives and any other legislative body that had a need for rapidly registering and counting votes. The machine worked, and Edison presented it to the congressmen, only to be told that the very last thing they wanted was a quick way to register and count votes. In close votes, party whips used the time it took to poll members to threaten and cajole the necessary yeas and nays. From that point forward, Edison resolved that he would not invest time and effort in an invention without first determining that there was a market for it.

Birdseye, however, remained convinced that palatable frozen food *would* find a market. Even with his company in bankruptcy, he pressed on with perfecting his quick-freeze machinery. In 1924, the very year his company closed its doors, he invented a process of packaging fish fillets and other ready-to-cook food products in cartons—and *then* quick-freezing the contents by pressing the packed food between a pair of refrigerated surfaces. *Pressurized* quick-freezing not only made the freezing process more efficient from a manufacturing point of view, it was also better at preserving the cellular structure during freezing because it produced very small ice crystals.

Now Birdseye knew he had the basis of an industry. His only tasks were to persuade financiers and a skeptical shopping public, which, except for a handful of Inuit in Labrador, had only ever tasted terrible frozen food. Fortunately for Birdseye, he was living in the Roaring Twenties, an era in which a lot of big money was looking for big investments. He was able to quickly assemble a group of wealthy New York businessmen, who incorporated the General Seafood Corp. By the time it began operations in 1925, the indefatigable Birdseye had added yet another invention, which replaced the refrigerated plates with a pair of continuously moving stainless-steel belts, which were kept at the requisite sub-freezing temperature by a flow of cold brine. The belts moved the packaged fish through the factory even as they were carrying out the quick-freezing process.

Finally, the frozen food industry was born. Birdseye kept improving and extending the technology he had created, always looking to increase the speed of the freezing process, since the faster the food could be frozen, the smaller the ice crystals were and the better the food tasted. Yet it continued to be an uphill struggle, as consumers were won over very slowly. By 1927, he had patented machinery to freeze poultry, meat, vegetables, and fruit. He was making decent money, but had hardly disrupted the food industry. At last, in 1929, amid disappointing sales, Birdseye sold his company's assets and his own patents to the Goldman Sachs brokerage firm and the Postum Company. His price was $22 million—a spectacular sum. Moreover, his timing could not have been better. In October 1929, the bottom fell out of the stock market and the Great Depression commenced.

The hard times made Postum's management all the more anxious to build a market for what the company called "frosted foods." The company reorganized under the name General Foods Corporation and hired Birdseye to serve as president of its "Birds Eye Frosted Foods" division. Management backed a major launch campaign, which accomplished what Clarence Birdseye alone had been unable to do. It created a market for everything from frozen peas to fish to meats of all kinds.

From his position as president of Birds Eye, the inventor kept inventing. In 1934, he contracted with the American Radiator Corporation to develop and manufacture low-temperature cooling equipment for retail display of Birds Eye foods. The result revolutionized the way an entire class of groceries was marketed, merchandised, and retailed. In 1945, he leased a fleet of the first fully insulated railroad cars, which were capable of transporting frozen food products nationwide. This created the refrigerated shipping industry.

A true disruption is never just one thing, one effect. Whole systems are often changed. One disruption creates more disruptions. Everything Birdseye did for the technology of frozen foods created not only a market for the product: it expanded the availability from seasonal to year-round. This increased demand, which spawned large-scale agribusiness and stimulated innovation in agriculture.

As for Clarence Birdseye, he never stopped inventing. He experimented with methods of dehydrating foods, tinkered with reflecting lightbulbs, and even developed a recoilless harpoon for whale hunters. As he advised a college commencement audience shortly before he died in 1956, the secret of success was to "go around asking a lot of damn fool questions and taking chances." He was describing the very kernel of disruptive thinking.

DISRUPTION:
FRAMING THE THEORY
OF MODERN COMPUTING
WITH BOTH HIS
"TURING MACHINE" AND
WORK ON ARTIFICIAL
INTELLIGENCE

ALAN TURING (1912–1954)

Alan Mathison Turing lived four lives: He was a mathematician who framed the theory of modern computing, articulating and formalizing the concepts of both the algorithm and computation. He was an unlikely hero of World War II, who played a leading role on the British cryptology team that broke the infamous German "Enigma" cipher. After the war, he formulated the so-called Turing test to evaluate a machine's ability to exhibit intelligent behavior equivalent to or at least indistinguishable from that of a human being. And he was a gay man, which led to tragedy in a time and place in which open homosexuality was not only socially unacceptable but criminal.

··

Turing was born on June 23, 1912, in London, the son of a civil servant in the Indian service. Enrolled at the age of six in St. Michael's Day School, he attracted early recognition as a highly talented student. His natural affinity for science and mathematics was somewhat misplaced at his next school, Hazelhurst Preparatory School and Sherborne School, where instruction was oriented more toward the liberal arts. However, it was here that he met Christopher Morcom, with whom he formed a deep friendship that may be considered Turing's first love and that certainly was his first experience of tragedy. Morcom succumbed to complications of bovine tuberculosis in February 1930. Whatever else the boy had meant to Turing, he was an enduring intellectual inspiration, who introduced him to astronomy and other areas of science. After his death, perhaps as a way of coping with his intense sorrow, Turing turned to his studies with redoubled effort and gained admission in 1931 to King's College, Cambridge, from which he graduated in 1934 with first-class honors in mathematics.

Two years after earning his undergraduate degree, Turing published "On Computable Numbers, with an Application to the *Entscheidungsproblem*." The *Entscheidungsproblem*—the "Decision Problem"—was posed by the German mathematician David Hilbert in 1928. It asked: Is there an algorithm that, when fed any statement in the language of first-order arithmetic, determines in a finite number of steps whether or not the statement is provable using the usual rules of first-order logic? In 1931, the mathematician Kurt Gödel presented a formal mathematical proof that no such algorithm exists; Turing reached the same answer not through formal math, but by using a hypothetical computer, what he called a "universal computing machine," and what others, after him, have called a "Turing machine." As conceived by Turing, this device would be capable of performing any mathematical computation that could be represented by an algorithm. The point of Turing's paper was not that his imagined computer could not answer the *Entscheidungsproblem* in the affirmative, but that it could perform any calculation capable of being represented by an algorithm. This made it truly a universal computer.

As Turing conceptualized it in the 1936 paper, his "universal computing machine" was a mathematical abstraction of an entity capable of reading from, writing on, and moving forward and backward an indefinite tape, thereby providing a model for computer-like procedures. The behavior of a Turing machine is specified by listing an alphabet (that is, a collection of symbols read and written), a set of internal states, and a mapping of an alphabet and internal states, all of which determine what the symbol written and the tape motion will be, and also what internal state will follow when the machine is in a given internal state and reads a given symbol. Later, in a 1948 essay, "Intelligent Machinery," Turing provided a less abstract physical visualization of such a machine. It consisted of:

an unlimited memory capacity obtained in the form of an infinite tape marked out into squares, on each of which a symbol could be printed. At any moment there is one symbol in the machine; it is called the scanned symbol. The machine can alter the scanned symbol, and its behavior is in part determined by that symbol, but the symbols on the tape elsewhere do not affect the behavior of the machine. However, the tape can be moved back and forth through the machine, this being one of the elementary operations of the machine.

The physical components of the machine, as Turing imagined it in 1948, correspond to the major components of any modern digital computer:

- A *tape* divided into cells, each containing a symbol from some finite alphabet

- A *head* capable of reading written symbols on the tape

- A *transport and feedback system* linked to the head that moves the tape back and forth under or across the head, or that moves the head itself over the tape

- A *state register*, which stores the state of the machine

- A *table of instructions*, which, given the current *state* of the machine and the symbol that is currently under the *head*, tells the machine what to do—either erase or write a symbol; move the *tape* (or *head*) backward or forward; assume the same state or a new one.

From 1936 to 1938, Turing studied at Princeton University under the American mathematician Alonzo Church, who also addressed the *Entscheidungsproblem*, but did so mathematically. Princeton awarded Turing a PhD in 1938. His dissertation, "Systems of Logic Based on Ordinals," further developed the theoretical science behind computing by introducing the concept of relative computing, which carried computer theory beyond problems that could not be solved by Turing machines. While he was at Princeton, Turing also took the fateful step of studying the practical application of theoretical mathematics to cryptology, in the process actually constructing most of an electromechanical binary multiplier, a device capable of multiplying binary (base 2) numbers, the arithmetical basis of digital computing.

• • •

Turing returned to England and King's College in 1938. At the outbreak of World War II in September 1939, he volunteered his services at the headquarters of the Government Code and Cipher School at Bletchley Park, Buckinghamshire. Turing was made part of the elite team of "bright boys" (as they were dubbed) who were assigned to break the hitherto unbreakable German Enigma ciphers.

Enigma was the name of an electromechanical cipher encryption and decryption machine used by the German military, the *Abwehr* (German secret service), and the SS, as well as the German state railway system, during World War II. The original design had been patented in 1919 by a Dutch inventor, and it was modified and refined by a German engineer, Arthur Scherbius, in 1923. The German Army and Navy bought all rights to the machine from Scherbius in 1929.

At the time of World War II, Enigma was by far the most complex encryption-decryption device in the world. The basic Enigma machine—there were even more sophisticated variants—resembled a typewriter, but in addition to a keyboard and type keys, it also had an electrical plug board, a light board, and a set of three rotors. The rotors could be set independently to create a library of 16,900 ($26 \times 25 \times 26$) substitution alphabets, so that, provided the message was not longer than 16,900 characters, there would be no repeated use of a substitution alphabet within any given message. Since repetition is the key by which codes are traditionally broken, it seemed that the Enigma ciphers were inherently unbreakable. Moreover, the Enigma machine added additional complications. The sequence of alphabets used was different if the rotors were started in position ABC, as opposed, say, to ACB; there was a rotating ring on each rotor that could be set in a different position. Additionally, the starting position of each rotor itself was variable. The military version of the Enigma added yet another device, a *Stecker*, or electric plugboard, by which some key assignments (depending on the model) could be changed. Thus, even the most basic threewheel Enigma with six plug connections generated 3,283,883,513,796,974,198,700,882,069,882,752,878, 379,955,261,095,623,685,444,055,315,226,006,433,616,627,409,666,933,182, 371,154,802,769,920,000,000,000 coding positions—a staggering number.

Of course, complex encryption is useless if it cannot be readily decrypted by the intended recipient. The genius of the Enigma machine was that its complex combination key could be communicated by supplying just a few values: what rotors to use, the rotor order, the ring positions (within the rotors), the starting position, and the plugboard settings. German confidence in the security of Enigma was virtually unlimited.

Facing what seemed daunting odds, Turing and his Bletchley Park colleagues took some comfort in the fact that no matter how complex a coding system may be, the underlying alphabet is simple, consisting of very few letters. Moreover, although the Enigma gave the impression of bewildering randomness, it was grounded in one absolute principle: no letter could stand for itself. This immediately provided a basic key for codebreakers. Finally, another Achilles' heel was the absence of numbers. Engima ciphers were alphabetical, not alphanumeric. Numbers, therefore, had to be spelled out. This provided yet another key. And finally, the Germans had not counted on a final weakness of machine-generated code: the possibility that it could be broken by another machine.

The British codebreakers had one additional advantage. As early as 1932, well before the war began, Polish cryptologists were able to read some Enigma traffic. On the eve of the war, in mid-1939, the Poles passed much of their knowledge to the French and the British. This was the foundation on which Turing and the others were able to build during 1939 and the spring of 1940. Drawing on his experience at Princeton, Turing supervised the design and construction of a radically new codebreaking machine called the Bombe—after the Polish-built Bomba, an earlier, now outmoded decryption machine, which was named after a type of Polish ice cream. Turing's ever-evolving Bombes were early electro-mechanical computers, which allowed the Bletchley Park cryptanalysts to decode some 39,000 intercepted messages each month by 1942. Later in the war, this monthly volume rose to an astounding 84,000 messages.

Thanks to Turing's work, a great many German military and diplomatic radio messages were routinely decoded. The decrypts were part of "Ultra," the name the Allies applied to all intelligence derived from any important cryptanalytic sources, but especially to the Enigma decrypts. Although the Enigma decrypts came too late to be of help during the Battle of Britain in the skies over London and other British cities from July to October 1940, they were of great value in almost every encounter after this period. Prime Minister Winston Churchill later declared that "It was thanks to Ultra that we won the war." In particular, he believed that the Enigma intelligence was most valuable in tracking U-boats, which preyed upon Allied convoys and continually threatened to strangle the British lifeline from America. At the end of the war, Turing was made an officer of the Order of the British Empire (OBE) in recognition of what he had achieved.

• • •

After the war, in 1945, Turing joined the National Physical Laboratory (NPL) and began to design an electronic computer. His design for the Automatic

Computing Engine (ACE) was a nearly complete plan for an electronic stored-program general-purpose digital computer. But the machine, which his colleagues considered too complex, was never built. Discouraged, Turing left NPL and became deputy director of the Computing Machine Laboratory in Manchester. He designed the programming system for the Mark I, the world's first commercially available electronic digital computer.

Fully immersed in computer science after the war, Turing published "Computing Machinery and Intelligence" while he was on the faculty of the University of Manchester in 1950. In the paper, Turing considered the question "Can machines think?" Finding that "thinking" is a concept almost impossible to meaningfully define, he tried a less ambiguous question, asking if there are "imaginable digital computers" that could excel in the "Imitation Game."

In this parlor game with three players, player A is a man, player B is a woman, and player C, the interrogator, may be of either sex. Player C cannot see players A or B and can communicate with them only through written notes. By asking questions of A and B, C tries to determine which is the man and which is the woman. Player A is assigned to trick the interrogator into making the wrong decision, while player B attempts to assist the interrogator in making the right one. In the end, Turing concludes that it is impossible to argue definitively against the proposition that machines can think.

The "Imitation Game"-based Turing test and the conclusion Turing reached are fundamental to the philosophy, science, and technology of artificial intelligence (AI), which continues to assume a greater and greater role in many aspects of life today.

● ● ●

In 1951, Turing was accorded the high honor of election as a fellow of the Royal Society. But in March 1952 he was arrested and tried on charges of homosexuality—then a crime under British law—and sentenced to a year of hormone therapy in lieu of prison. In the depths of the Cold War, the British government also judged him to be a significant security risk, his homosexuality making him vulnerable to blackmail by Communist agents. He was immediately barred from continuing consulting work for GCHQ (Government Communications Headquarters, the British equivalent of the U.S. National Security Agency [NSA]), but he retained his academic position at the University of Manchester as the institution's first reader in the theory of computing.

Turing grew increasingly depressed, his condition aggravated by the synthetic estrogen he was forced to take, which made him impotent and caused enlargement of his breasts (gynecomastia). At Manchester, he embarked on research not merely into artificial intelligence but artificial life, using the Mark I computer to model chemical mechanisms by which genes could control the development of anatomical structure in plants and animals. But on June 7, 1954, he was found dead in his bed, the victim of cyanide poisoning. In his home, police investigators found a homemade device for silver-plating teaspoons, which included a cyanide reservoir. The cause of death was declared suicide, although Turing's mother insisted that his ingestion of the chemical was accidental. He was incorrigibly sloppy and careless, she said.

On September 10, 2009, in response to a petition, British Prime Minister Gordon Brown issued an official apology for the government's treatment of Alan Turing, and on December 24, 2013, Queen Elizabeth II signed a pardon, which was officially announced in August 2014.

TIM BERNERS-LEE

(1955–)

Tim Berners-Lee was born at the threshold of the digital age, four years after the introduction of the Ferranti Mark 1, popularly known as the Manchester Electronic Computer, which had been introduced by the British electrical engineering firm of Ferranti International in February 1951. It was the world's first commercially available electronic computer, and Berners-Lee's parents, Mary Lee Woods and Conway Berners-Lee, were members of the team that created it—4,050 vacuum tubes and all. It might be fair to say that Tim, one of the four Berners-Lee children, had computing in his blood, except that his first lessons in electronics came from tinkering with something a child of the 1950s could really get his hands on: his model railroad.

Whatever sparked the youngster's imagination, his intellect was recognized early. After his primary education, he earned a place in London's prestigious Emanuel School, which he attended from 1969 to 1973, when it was a "direct-grant grammar school," a highly selective secondary school financed directly by a British government deeply worried about the post–World War II "brain drain"—the outflow of high-performing Britishers to the United States and other places that promised more lucrative employment than the UK. Berners-Lee went on from Emanuel to Queen's College, Oxford, earning in 1976 a first-class B.A. in physics. After Oxford, he took a job at the Plessey telecommunications firm and moved on two years later to D. G. Nash, where he plunged into the creation of typesetting software for digital printers.

The 1970s were a pioneering era in software, and Berners-Lee approached his work in a pioneer spirit, moving on from the corporate world to a more intensively research-oriented environment. He left Nash in June 1980 and, until December of that year, worked as an independent contractor at CERN, the European Organization for Nuclear Research. As Berners-Lee had entered the advanced technology of electronics by modeling the nineteenth-century technology of railroading, so he approached the cutting edge at CERN by proposing a research project rooted in an idea that had appeared some thirty-five years earlier in the pages of *The Atlantic* magazine.

The article was called "As We May Think." Its author was Dr. Vannevar Bush, rather obscure today, but famous in 1945 as the director of the U.S. Office of Scientific Research and Development. He was a master of the aspect of World War II that Winston Churchill dubbed "the wizard war," warfare waged and won through the most disruptive of high technologies.

When Vannevar Bush had something to say, the world took note. His article declared that "The summation of human experience is being expanded at a prodigious rate, and the means we use for threading through the consequent maze to the momentarily important item is the same as was used in the days of square-rigged ships." Bush went on to write of the unprecedented explosion of knowledge, pointing out that "we can enormously extend the record" of human learning, "yet even in its present bulk we can hardly consult it."

Bush worried: "There may be millions of fine thoughts . . . but if the scholar can get at only one a week by diligent search, his syntheses are not likely to keep up with the current scene." He pointed out that when "data of any sort are placed in storage, they are filed alphabetically or numerically, and information is found (when it is) by tracing it down from subclass to subclass. It can be in only one place, unless duplicates are used; one has to have rules as to which path will locate it, and the rules are cumbersome. Having found one item, moreover, one has to emerge from the system and re-enter on a new path."

The problem?

"The human mind does not work that way. It operates by association. With one item in its grasp, it snaps instantly to the next that is suggested by the association of thoughts, in accordance with some intricate web of trails carried by the cells of the brain."

What if we could create a data storage-and-retrieval system that harmonized with the processes of the *human mind*?

Bush imagined "a future device for individual use . . . a sort of mechanized private file and library." *Memex*, he wanted to call it. It would consist of a desk with "slanting translucent screens, on which [microfilm-stored] material can be projected for convenient reading." He imagined on this desk "a keyboard . . . and sets of buttons and levers. Otherwise it looks like an ordinary desk." It would be capable of storing information that users could instantly access and apply whenever needed. Most important of all, one piece of information would be associated with others, connected via "a mesh of associative trails running through them, ready to be dropped into the memex and there amplified." Thus, the lawyer would have "at his touch the associated opinions and decisions of his whole experience, and of the experience of friends and authorities." As for the physician, "puzzled by a patient's reactions, [he] strikes the trail established in studying an earlier similar case, and runs rapidly through analogous case histories, with side references to the classics for the pertinent anatomy and histology."

In 1963, the American philosopher and information technologist Ted Nelson coined a word for what Vannevar Bush had imagined: *hypertext*, a model for linking content to associated content. At intervals during the Cold War, other thinkers pondered concepts of associated data linking, of "memex" and "hypertext," but none of them created a civilization-disrupting breakthrough.

The progress from concept to disruptive breakthrough had to await the availability of a technological infrastructure capable of implementing the idea. At CERN, Berners-Lee was in the epicenter of late twentieth-century applied physics. He had access to various computer systems, and he decided to apply, at long last, the concept of hypertext. He got as far as building a prototype system he called ENQUIRE—and then he left CERN to make some money in industry, at Image Computer Systems, Ltd, in Bournemouth, Dorset. Here he worked on the technology of computer networking, still in its infancy during the early 1980s. After four years, with this valuable hands-on networking experience under his belt, he returned to CERN, this time as a full-fledged research fellow.

● ● ●

In 1989, CERN was the largest Internet node in Europe. This was not saying a great deal, since the Internet was still very much in its infancy, but Berners-Lee understood that it was poised for explosive growth. He decided that he now had an opportunity to extend the hypertext concept to the Internet, thereby potentially giving each user deep access to what he believed would become the greatest repository and generator of information, knowledge, and experience civilization had ever known.

Too often, we tend to use the terms *Internet* and *World Wide Web* interchangeably. But they are not synonyms. Berners-Lee played no role in the "invention" of the Internet, which had its genesis in a 1969 project funded by the U.S. Department of Defense's Advanced Research Projects Agency (ARPA). The DoD was looking to build a rapid and robust computer network across which civilian contractors and military personnel could collaborate on defense-related research. The result, ARPANET, was the first digital network that implemented a common addressing system and protocol called TCP/IP—Transmission Control Protocol/Internet Protocol—which laid down uniform standards for end-to-end data transmission across big networks, including precisely how data should be addressed, transmitted, routed, and received. While ARPANET was being built, the National Science Foundation (NSF) created a similar and parallel network called NSFNet. In 1981, NSFNet was largely combined with ARPANET and, at length, NSF took over much of the ARPANET TCP/IP technology, establishing a more widely distributed "network of networks" capable of handling much more traffic. NSF called this super network the "internet."

The creation of unique addresses for each device connected to the Internet was an important breakthrough, analogous to rational mailing addresses for houses and businesses in the non-digital physical world. Unique addresses ensured that data from computer *A* intended to be transmitted to computer *B* would reach computer *B* rather than *C*, *D*, or *E*. What could be wrong with that?

Plenty, as Berners-Lee saw it. For, while addresses facilitated communication between one computer and another, they did not facilitate meaningful communication between and among the human beings who were using the computers. Berners-Lee decided to use hypertext to liberate addresses from individual computers and thereby facilitate the connection between human computer users and the data they wanted to access. He saw, for example, that John Q. Computer User had no interest in accessing the computer at IP address 216.58.216.164. These numbers were, in fact, meaningless to John Q., whose only interest was in accessing some bit of *data* that happened to reside at 216.58.216.164. It was no different from John Q.'s absence of interest in communicating with 1234 Elm Street versus his passionate desire for meaningful communication with the young lady who happened to reside at 1234 Elm Street.

Berners-Lee published online a document called "Answers for Young People," in which he explained how he invented the World Wide Web. It began not with a rush of inspiration but a flush of frustration. While he was working at CERN in the 1980s, he "found it frustrating that there was different information on different computers, but you had to log on to different computers to get at it. Also, sometimes you had to learn a different program on each computer. So, finding out how things worked was really difficult. Often it was just easier to go and ask people when they were having coffee."

In short, for Tim Berners-Lee, digital networks and the Internet were inadequately meeting his needs. They were, in fact, even failing to be at least as good as the most basic form of network: two people sharing information over coffee. At the same time, he realized that people connected with CERN were often not physically present at its Geneva headquarters—and so were unavailable for a face-to face talk. This led him to write some programs to convert data produced on one kind of computer using one kind of operating system to another, different computer using a different OS. The trouble was that, at the time, CERN researchers were not just using "Unix, Mac, and PC: there were all kinds of big mainframe computers and medium-sized computers running all sorts of software." Berners-Lee wanted to find a way not only to work with many incompatible computer and software systems spread out over a wide geographical area, but to make working with them easy, routine, and transparent.

"Can't we convert every information system so that it looks like part of some imaginary information system which everyone can read?" he asked. "And that became the WWW"—the World Wide Web.

The Internet is a physical network-of-networks, a material infrastructure, whereas the WWW is a virtual "information space." The WWW is accessed via the Internet, but instead of consisting of numerical addresses, it is a system of what Berners-Lee called Uniform Resource Locators (URLs), which can be keyed to and accessed via *hypertext* links. In short, it is the kind of linked information access Vannevar Bush imagined as memex. Hypertext is a way of linking keywords in one text or dataset to related information in another text or dataset, thereby enabling a computer user to depart from a linear narrative and, with a mouse click or two or more, drill down into subjects related to that narrative. Hypertext enables, enhances, and facilitates information sharing over the World Wide Web, which runs on the Internet.

The URL, as Berners-Lee devised it, is the address not of a machine but of a set of data. Today, computers (and other devices connected to the Internet) are actually identified by two numbers, a "media access control" (MAC) address and an "Internet protocol" (IP) address. The first is a kind of digital serial number hard-coded into network devices. The second is a number assigned to devices by networks that use the Internet protocol for communication. Unless you are an IT manager, engineer, or technician, you don't usually have to know either of these numbers because they won't help you find what you are looking for—which is not a particular device, but a particular set of data. It is true that when you want to access a certain set of data, you must communicate with the computer on which it happens to reside, but all you need to know is the URL, the address of the *dataset*—not the device—you wish to access.

In fact—and this is also thanks to Berners-Lee—you don't even absolutely need to know the URL. As Berners-Lee explained in his "Answers for Young People," when you click on a hypertext in the document that is displayed before you on your computer, tablet, or smartphone screen, you are not seeing everything there is to know about the link. "Behind the underlined or colored bit of text which you click on is an invisible thing like http://www.w3.org/." It is the URL, the name of the web page to which the link goes. Thanks to hypertext, however, all you see is the *link*—the word or phrase that has *human* meaning. When you click on that link, the computer takes you to the right URL.

The hypertext transfer protocol (HTTP) Berners-Lee developed allows a URL to be attached to a word or phrase that is relevant and meaningful to a human computer user. Let's say you go to the website of your county government. You need to renew your car's license plate. You see a colored phrase, "tag renewal." You recognize that as key to the data you need, and you click on it. Immediately, you are taken to the data or document you need. It may be on the same website you have open at the time, or it may be on a different site. Doesn't matter. The hypertext link will take you wherever you need to go. As for the physical location of the data, it may be in a server in the local county building, or it may be on the servers of a cloud service headquartered in a city or a nation halfway around the world. No matter. You don't need to know any of this to access the data you seek.

While you, the user, blissfully click away on words and phrases you easily understand, your computer, as Berners-Lee explains, "can't communicate with the webserver until it knows its computer number"—the unique Internet Protocol Address, or IP address, assigned by a network using TCP/IP for communication. When you click on a hyperlink, your computer must discover the IP Address before it can access the appropriate webserver and take you to the webpage with the data you want to access. To do this, your computer—creates a data packet that begins with the number of the computer—the IP Address—the packet is going to. Next comes the IP Address of the computer sending it. This is followed by what the data packet is about, and then the material your computer is sending to the other computer. Connected to the modern Internet are computers designated as Domain Name Service (DNS) servers. When you click a hyperlink, one of these servers retrieves the IP Address associated with that hypertext. Since the packet you sent by clicking on the link contains the IP Address of your device, the server sends the required IP Address information back to your computer, which is now enabled to access the desired webserver and webpage.

All of this is highly technical, and yet the end result—the effect—seems like magic. Indeed, the hypertext concept calls to mind the magic carpet of the *Arabian Nights* tales. Click the mouse, and you will fly to wherever you wish to go. Berners-Lee understood that the "magic" is built on technology—a well-designed digital infrastructure—but also on a human element in the form of coordination and cooperation. Berners-Lee is a modest man, who tells anyone who asks that inventing the World Wide Web was "easy." Getting everyone to use the same protocols, he says, was the hard part.

• • •

Tim Berners-Lee wrote his ENQUIRE proposal in March 1989. This led to the creation of the World Wide Web, for which he also designed and built the first web browser and the protocol (HTTP) to enable the exchange, or transfer, of hypertext across the World Wide Web. In fact, Berners-Lee built the world's first website, at CERN, which went online on August 6, 1991, at http://info.cern. ch/hypertext/WWW/TheProject.html. Three years later, he founded the World Wide Web Consortium (W3C) at the Massachusetts Institute of Technology, consisting of a number of companies that worked together to create ongoing www standards.

Perhaps no invention in the history of civilization has done so much so fast to further the sharing and creation of knowledge as the World Wide Web. Indeed, perhaps none has come closer to overcoming two of the most basic dimensions of our physical universe, space and time. No wonder that Berners-Lee has received so many awards and honors: knighthood (OBE and KBE) in 2004 and, in 2007, appointment to the Order of Merit (OM), a distinction restricted to just twenty-four living members. Some believe that the greatest honor of all was his inclusion, in 2012, on a new version of Sir Peter Blake's artwork for the Beatles' *Sgt. Pepper's Lonely Hearts Club Band* album cover.

KEVIN MITNICK

(1963–)

The early 1980s saw the rapid rise of the personal computer, which transformed computing from something government and big business did with monster mainframes in large locked and air-conditioned rooms, to something anyone could do at home. With this transformation, wide-area networking and the Internet emerged—as did the "profession" of the computer "hacker."

The first hacker group to be portrayed as a serious threat to network security called itself the "414s," after their Milwaukee, Wisconsin, area code. Members were indicted in 1983 for attacking some sixty mainframe computer networks, including those belonging to Los Alamos National Laboratory and the Memorial Sloan-Kettering Cancer Center. The idea that "kids" could penetrate serious government and institutional networks in places as far-flung as New Mexico and New York was at once upsetting and intriguing. Hackers began to achieve mythic status in pop culture, as evidenced in the 1983 John Badham blockbuster, *WarGames,* about a teenage hacker, played by a young Matthew Broderick, who uses his PC and an old-school acoustic modem to connect with a military supercomputer named WOPR, which he believes has given him free access to a new thermonuclear war simulation game. In fact, he nearly starts World War III.

By the mid-1980s, hacking escalated from a pop-culture phenomenon to a genuine law enforcement concern. Yet the public largely persisted in thinking of it as a form of social expression rather than a criminal enterprise. Call it cyber graffiti. It was in this social climate that Kevin Mitnick attained the stature of a digital Billy the Kid. He was not the world's first hacker, but he was the first to make a global name for himself and to demonstrate to a digitally challenged public that their cyber world was far from secure.

● ● ●

Kevin David Mitnick was born in Van Nuys, California, on August 6, 1963, and grew up in nearby Los Angeles, where, in high school, he was an avid amateur radio enthusiast. Now, "ham radio"—*that* had been good clean fun since at least the 1930s, but Mitnick did not confine himself to that hobby. When he was thirteen, he used a combination of in-person con-man tactics (called "social engineering") and document recovery ("Dumpster diving") to ride free on the LA bus system. It worked like this: Young Mitnick persuaded a bus driver to tell him where he could buy his own ticket punch, which he needed (he explained vaguely) for a "school project." He then raided a Dumpster outside a bus garage and found a cache of transfers, the paper slips that, if properly punched, allowed riders to change buses without paying a new fare. These two low-tech methods—social engineering and Dumpster diving—became cornerstones for hacking high-tech digital systems.

Mitnick proved himself a natural. Three years after ripping off the Los Angeles transit system, sixteen-year-old Mitnick breached the computer system of Digital Equipment Corporation (DEC), a giant of the computer industry from the 1950s through most of the 1990s, and copied advanced DEC operating system software. He had gotten into the system not through an act of genius, but because he had persuaded a friend to give him the phone number that allowed his PC modem to access "the Ark," the computer server DEC used to develop its OS software. He got away with this crime for nine years before he was tracked down, arrested, tried, convicted, and sent to prison for a year followed by three years of supervised release. Before that post-incarceration probation period had even ended, Mitnick broke into voicemail computers belonging to Pacific Bell—and then went on the lam, breaching dozens of computer networks while he was a fugitive, using cloned cell phones to disguise his location and copying software from national cellular companies and computer services firms. In the course of these operations, he stole computer passwords, breached and even altered computer networks, and purloined private emails.

In what was already being called the "hacker community," Kevin Mitnick earned the status of an unstoppable crime phantom, a digital John Dillinger without the gunplay. A concerted effort by federal agencies ran him to ground in 1995. Arrested and charged, he was confined to prison for four and a half years before he finally copped a plea. Facing monumental prison time on a thick catalog of offenses, he pleaded guilty to wire fraud, computer fraud, and intercepting a wire communication. His sentence was five years and change, but that included the pre-trial four and a half years he had already served. This left eight months, and prosecutors decided that it would not be easy time. The plea and the sentence had not created the public outrage over computer crime that authorities had hoped to provoke. This may have prompted prosecutors to convince the sentencing judge that Mitnick was unpredictable in the danger he actually posed. They argued that he knew how to start a thermonuclear war by whistling the launch code for NORAD missiles into a prison payphone. Such was the state of public naivete and sheer ignorance of the digital universe into which they found themselves thrust that the judge did not question what he was told. Mitnick therefore spent the next eight months in solitary confinement, not as a punishment for what was, after all, a nonviolent offense, but for fear that he might gain access to a phone, whistle up Armageddon, and extinguish life on the planet.

In the meantime, in the outside world, FREE KEVIN bumper stickers became a common sight on American streets. When he was finally released on January 21, 2000, he was subject to supervised release, which consisted of a three-year period in which he was barred from using any mode of communication technology other than a landline telephone. Mitnick's attorneys fought the decision and gained their client access to the Internet, which, by this time, had come to be considered very nearly a human right. Although he was barred for seven years from profiting from films or books based on his criminal activity, he was allowed to hold an amateur radio license, and he went on to become one of a new digital breed of security service providers known as "white-hat hackers." His consulting business, KnowBe4, still offers security awareness training and simulated phishing (email fraud) testing.

From the get-go, Mitnick's services were widely sought by organizations ranging from Fortune 500 companies to the FBI. While he can be counted among the pioneers of cybersecurity, the truly disruptive innovation for which he should be credited or blamed is having been a highly publicized virtuoso of crime in a new dimension—not the familiar kinetic space of the "real world," but the brave new digital "space" of a civilization networked by computers. His exploits offered the world a dramatic demonstration of the physical and financial consequences of a few keystrokes executed by a stranger, far away, invisible and unknown. The universe of the Internet, touted as a wonder of human intellectual evolution, perhaps an electronic force that would finally unite the peoples of the world as never before imagined or even possible, was revealed to have a dark side in which the volume, ease, and consequences of crime were multiplied exponentially.

5

ENTERPRISE

DISRUPTION:
MAKING THE
"PERSONAL
COMPUTER"
PERVASIVELY
PERSONAL

STEVE JOBS
(1955–2011)

Brilliantly conceived by Lee Clow, the creative director of the Chiat/Day advertising firm, and directed by Ridley (*Blade Runner*) Scott, the television ad that launched Apple's Macintosh computer was broadcast exactly once, on January 22, 1984, to a *Super Bowl XVIII* audience of 77.62 million viewers.

I t went like this: A woman athlete in bright orange running shorts and white tank top—which bears the outline image of a Mac—holds a long-handled sledgehammer. She sprints through a dismal gray hall, slicing through some vague yet unmistakably sinister bureaucracy where gray people stare zombie-like at an overwhelming screen from which a gigantic gray Orwellian Big Brother drones a barely intelligible message about "our Unification of Thoughts."

On the heels of the woman, shiny-helmeted, black-clad Thought Police are in hot pursuit as she races toward the giant screen. Suddenly, she winds up for an

Olympic-class hammer throw and, propelled by unstoppable momentum, hurls her hammer at the image on the screen. We see Big Brother shatter into shards amid a burst of brilliant white light and smoke.

The voiceover announcer intones: "On January 24th, Apple Computer will introduce Macintosh. And you'll see why 1984 won't be like *1984.*"

What in the world . . . ?

The merchandise being advertised was Apple's new computer. But all we saw of it was a glimpse of a line drawing on a running woman's tank top. The truth that was really being advertised was not a new computer, but the total disruption of so-called personal computing by a product hatched in the imagination of Apple's Steve Jobs.

● ● ●

Steve Jobs was notoriously private. Yet his life story has been told and retold in print and on screen, so that it now has the universal familiarity of myth. Like many mythic figures, Jobs was a foundling. Born in San Francisco on February 24, 1955, he was the child of Abdulfattah Jandali, a Syrian working on a PhD at the University of Wisconsin, and Joanne Schieble, a student there. Since Jandali's orthodox Muslim family forbade the marriage, Schieble decided before the birth that she would put the child up for adoption. After her initial choice of parents, wealthy and well-educated, suddenly bowed out, the adoption agency placed the boy with Paul and Clara Jobs, a blue-collar couple. Schieble refused to sign the adoption papers until the prospective parents promised to provide the child with a college education.

Steven Paul Jobs's early childhood unfolded in a modest ranch house in the San Francisco suburb of Mountain View. Paul Jobs, a skilled mechanic and carpenter, instilled in his adopted son a love of building things. The neighborhood was populated by the families of engineers working in the nascent industries of Silicon Valley, and Steve turned from woodworking and fixing cars to electronics. He became friendly not so much with the other neighborhood kids as with their engineer fathers. A loner among his age group, he was also restless in the classroom, bored, and instinctively rebellious against authority. His schoolwork improved when the family moved to Los Altos, populated by even more engineers and offering better public schools.

At thirteen, Jobs called Bill Hewlett, cofounder of Hewlett-Packard (HP), to ask him for some electronic parts for a project he was building. Hewlett gave him the parts—along with a summer job on the Hewlett-Packard assembly line. Through one of his few young friends, Bill Fernandez, Jobs met Steve Wozniak, an electronics hobbyist who was several years older. At the time, Jobs was just entering high school and was also getting turned on to marijuana, literature, and creative writing. He graduated in 1972 and enrolled in Reed College in Portland, Oregon. Aware that his education was a severe financial burden on his parents, Jobs dropped out as a full-time student but continued auditing classes, including a calligraphy course taught by the famed typographer Robert Palladino. Jobs later credited Palladino's class with awakening his lifelong obsession with beautiful design—something quite alien to the electronics industry at the time, which tended to build everything to suit the décor of a TV repair shop rather than a stylish home. "If I had never dropped in on that single calligraphy course in college," he remarked in a 2005 commencement address at Stanford University, "the Mac would have never had multiple typefaces or proportionally spaced fonts."

When he moved back to the Bay Area, Jobs reconnected with Wozniak, who gave him a new version of the video game Pong, which he had built on a circuit board. Jobs showed the board to the video game maker Atari, in Los Gatos, and let the person he spoke with believe that he, not Wozniak, had made the board. It got him a job as a technician. He saved enough cash to travel to India in 1974 in search of spiritual enlightenment. After seven months on the subcontinent, Jobs returned to California, experimented with LSD, and became a Zen Buddhist. He also returned to Atari, and was asked to design a new board for the arcade game Breakout. He split the job 50/50 with Wozniak—but cheated him, claiming that Atari had paid him $700 instead of $5,000.

In the meantime, Wozniak had been working on another project, a so-called blue box, a device that proto-hackers, known as "phone phreaks" or "phreakers," used to generate dialing tones that allowed them to make all the free long-distance calls they wanted. Wozniak and Jobs began marketing the illegal blue boxes, which led them in 1975 to involvement in the local Homebrew Computer Club hobbyist group. This led to Wozniak's creating what became the Apple I personal computer. With a third high-tech enthusiast, Ronald Wayne, they formed, on April 1, 1976, Apple Computer. The name was inspired by Jobs's visit to an Oregon commune, which had an apple orchard, and the company was based in the garage of Jobs's home. Apple was formally incorporated on January 3, 1977, without Wayne, who had sold his interest back to Jobs and Wozniak for $800.

Based on the success of the Apple I—which was nothing more than a motherboard, with no keyboard, storage, or monitor—Jobs and Wozniak obtained $250,000 from an investor, and Wozniak designed the Apple II, which was introduced on April 16, 1977. In some ways, it was similar to the other early hobbyist machines of the era, such as the Commodore PET and Tandy's very popular TRS-80, but it featured two breakthroughs that instantly set it apart: color graphics and open architecture, the latter allowing it to use a wide variety of software. Jobs also saw to it that it was beautifully designed, and Software Arts, creators of VisiCalc, the first popular spreadsheet program, chose the Apple II as its platform. This catapulted the machine far ahead of its competition.

With the introduction of the Apple III in 1980, Jobs became determined to compete with IBM and IBM's software supplier, Microsoft. By all appearances, this was a longer shot than pitting David against Goliath. But Jobs had a vision for dramatically differentiating Apple from IBM.

Jobs knew that IBM was about to introduce its "personal computer," the PC. He also knew that IBM walked onto the field as the company whose name was virtually synonymous with the word *computer*. The firm's massive mainframes were used by every major business, institution, and government agency. Its ownership of the computer market was symbolized by a mantra commonly heard among executives: "Nobody ever got fired for buying IBM." Yet Jobs saw in IBM's marketplace incumbency not a strength but a weakness. Personal computing was all about the cutting edge. IBM, however, was all about holding on to what it already had. Jobs knew that IBM had hired Microsoft to create the operating system software, called DOS (for Disk Operating System), for their PC. This told him that IBM was thinking of its product not as a truly innovative desktop computer but something more like a desktop computer terminal, emulating those connected to an IBM mainframe. Jobs understood something else. As with the mainframes, IBM's PC would present to the user a steep learning curve. Since it used Microsoft's DOS, the IBM PC would be a text-based machine dependent on a text-based operating system. This meant that computer users who bought IBM were obliged to learn the language of the computer (MS-DOS) to communicate with it. It was, therefore, not a machine built to serve people, but one that demanded that people serve it. While you might never get fired for buying IBM, you might be sentenced to serve that IBM machine for the rest of your life.

Jobs upped the ante on how the Apple II had differentiated itself from the competition with its color graphics and greater hardware and software flexibility. Now, he replaced the text-based operating system with a Graphical User Interface—a GUI, pronounced *gooey*—which used icons and a clickable mouse rather than arbitrary and obscure keyboard commands to communicate between user and machine. Instead of the user learning the machine's language, the *machine* communicated in a visual language that *human* users already understood.

• • •

Steve Jobs saw the technological breakthrough of the GUI as a breakthrough in civilization. The Super Bowl *1984* commercial declared that IBM was not just an Apple competitor: it was the enemy of a free humanity. He imagined and portrayed the IBM PC as a machine for those already committed to a lock-stepping life sentence in a corporate "cube farm." The truth he wanted to reveal was that the IBM personal computer was not really "personal" at all. Like a mere terminal, it was a machine primarily intended to connect to an IBM mainframe. The PC was meant to get *many* people serving *one* really big machine.

The Macintosh did spectacularly well in the marketplace—at first. But its high price, compared to the IBM PC, and initially limited range of software slowed follow-up sales and led, in 1985, to a power struggle between Jobs and John Sculley, whom Jobs had hired as CEO two years earlier. Jobs lost round one of the fight and was ousted from his own company. He turned around and founded NeXT, which he hoped would take much farther what had been started with the Mac. In fact, however, NeXT struggled.

But, without Jobs, Apple approached total collapse as Microsoft, with its own new GUI operating system, Windows, gained the ground it had earlier lost to Apple. In 1996, Apple's new CEO, Gil Amelio, bought NeXT and brought Steve Jobs back to the company. Jobs set about leading further innovations to the Mac—but he took the company beyond innovation and deeper into disruption.

Jobs had already changed the relation between user and computer. He also changed the way computers looked by making the design of the machines truly beautiful. The Macs led the way from desktop computers to laptop computers, which made the machines more portable and therefore more personal. In his second tenure at Apple, Jobs continued changing how people viewed and used technology. The year 1998 saw the introduction of the iMac, teardrop-shaped and candy-colored PCs that announced a sharp pivot from the machines' standardized beige and boxy look. In 2001, Jobs brought out the iPod, the digital music player that in 2002 spawned the iTunes Music Store, creating the business of (legal) downloaded and streamed music. The iPod was a handheld computer that resembled nothing that had come before it. The iTunes store it created brought massive change to the music industry at every level. Sales of CDs imploded as music lovers downloaded only the songs they wanted when they wanted them.

The iPod also paved the way for the iPhone, introduced in 2007. Arguably, this device is the single most disruptive invention brought into being under Jobs's leadership of Apple. This was not the original "smartphone" but it was the first to find success in the marketplace. A small, versatile, handheld computer, the iPhone served as a portal to the Internet and World Wide Web; allowed communication via text and email; and hosted an emerging array of "social web" applications, such as Facebook, Twitter, Instagram, and others. It spawned an industry dedicated to creating "apps," which performed a variety of computing, search, and commerce functions. It also did everything the iPod did—and more, providing a platform not only for music but video as well. It was a still and a video camera and an audio recorder. And, yes, it was also a cell phone. In short, the iPhone, through all its iterations, became a universal computing machine that fits in the pocket.

• • •

Jobs led Apple to even more innovations, including the iPad, a kind of scaled-up iPhone (without the phone), which may be seen as an evolutionary hybrid between the laptop computer and iPhone. It was introduced in 2010, the year before Steve Jobs succumbed, at the very premature age of fifty-six, to complications resulting from pancreatic cancer. The final revolutionary innovation that he personally led was Siri, a speech-recognition system that transformed the iPhone into a true personal digital assistant. With this, the *graphical* user interface morphed into a *vocal* human-computer interface that was little different from the human-human interface based on speech. Computers were no longer personal. They were intimate, heralds of an emerging world of advanced artificial intelligence and robotics. In 1950, Alan Turing, the father of computer science, published a paper that set out to answer the question "Can computers think?" By the year of his death, Steve Jobs had delivered a resounding *Sure looks like it.*

DISRUPTION:

TRANSFORMING ALL
PARADIGMS OF GLOBAL
COMMERCE WITH AN
ONLINE "EVERYTHING
STORE"

JEFF BEZOS

(1964–)

Founding Amazon, the online "everything store," which disrupted commerce even more radically than Aaron Montgomery Ward did with his massive mail-order catalog in 1872 or Richard Warren Sears with his far more massive catalog in 1894, was a product of what Jeff Bezos called his personal "regret minimization framework." The digital transformation of commercial civilization started in 1994 with a company Bezos planned to call Cadabra until he did a double take when his lawyer misheard the name as Cadaver. That set him on a fast search for a new label, and he didn't feel he had much time to find one. He was in the throes of anxious regret, believing he had missed his chance to get a jump on market competition because he had been unwilling to risk entry into the Internet business boom of the early 1990s. Driven by regret, he had already left a lucrative Wall Street job as vice president of the hedge-fund firm D. E. Shaw & Co. so that he could sink everything into the new company with, it turned out, a name that sounded like a synonym for corpse.

eaving the safety of Shaw had been part of a uniquely entrepreneurial move, compounded of chance, impulse, insight, and preparation. *Cadabra*, the name, misfired because at least one person heard it wrong. But nobody wants a Cadaver on their hands. *Amazon* wasn't Bezos's next first choice, either. He bought the URL Relentless.com, only to back away when more than one friend said it sounded "sinister." So, he resorted to research—very little research, because there was so little time. But it turned out to be just enough. He tore through the dictionary, limiting himself to the *A*'s, because he wanted to be at or near the top of any list. He chose *Amazon* because it was "exotic and different." *As* a rationale, it showed an instinctive understanding of Internet marketing, which required above all else the quality of being different and exotic to attract a click. But there was also substance to the "Amazon" method. It was the biggest river on the planet, and Bezos intended to build the biggest store, one that offered everything, one that invited exploration of the unknown.

But before he got to everything, he needed to start somewhere. Reasoning that there was always a high demand for literature, he decided to start by selling books. The universe of this product was huge, much larger than could be contained in any store built of bricks and mortar; the price point per unit was relatively low; and the merchandise was easily shipped. His first world headquarters was the garage attached to his house in Bellevue, Washington.

● ● ●

He was born Jeffrey Preston Jorgensen in 1964, in Albuquerque, New Mexico. His mother, Jacklyn Gise, and his father, Theodore John Jorgensen, divorced when Jeffrey was less than a year old. Jacklyn had married young, at seventeen, and remarried when her son was four. Her father, Lawrence Preston Gise, was the regional director of the U.S. Atomic Energy Commission (AEC) in Albuquerque and had earlier worked for DARPA (Defense Advanced Research Projects Agency), the Department of Defense agency that had commissioned the creation of ARPANET, direct precursor of the Internet. Her second husband was Miguel "Mike" Bezos, who had immigrated to the United States on his own at age fifteen. When he adopted Jeff, the kid's name became Bezos, and the family moved to Houston, where Mike went to work as an engineer for Exxon, and Jeff entered public school, where he quickly showed great aptitude for science and technology. By the time he was ready for high school, the Bezos family had moved to Miami and high schooler Jeff enrolled in a pre-college Student Science Training Program at the University of Florida.

After graduating from high school first in his class and valedictorian as well as a National Merit Scholar, Jeff Bezos enrolled in Princeton University, from which he graduated Phi Beta Kappa in 1986 with bachelor degrees in electrical engineering and computer science. His first job was on Wall Street with FITEL (First International Telecom), building a digital network for global trade. After a stint with Bankers Trust, he joined D. E. Shaw, specializing in Internet hedge-fund investment opportunities.

• • •

As a digital geek who also had high-end hedge-fund chops, Bezos combined and confounded the stereotypes associated with technocrats and plutocrats. He presented the persona of a loose, impulsive, charismatic experimentalist entrepreneur, yet possessed the drive implied by the earlier name of his company: he was *relentless*. An August 15, 2015, *New York Times* article portrayed Amazon as a company of "Big Ideas in a Bruising Workplace," describing the environment as "soulless" and "dystopian," a "workplace where no fun is had and no laughter heard." Bezos strenuously denied the characterization.

But there was undeniably a disruptively contradictory quality about his company. In contrast to the great majority of start-ups, especially in the digital space, Bezos presented a business plan that promised no profit for at least four to five years. This made for a great deal of controversy, but when Amazon emerged as one of the survivors of the early twenty-first-century "dot-com bubble," when legions of start-up dot-coms became instant dot-bombs, the plan began to make sense. While the Amazon business model was all about speed and frictionless agility, the business plan was drawn up for the long term and not for day traders. By 2011, Amazon had 30,000 full-time employees in the United States. By the close of 2016, it employed over 300,000 people worldwide.

The company made its name as the preeminent digital bookstore, the success of which put most big brick-and-mortar chains out of business by the second decade of the twenty-first century, save Barnes and Noble. But Amazon evolved beyond books, becoming the "everything store" Bezos had originally envisioned. Bezos did much to bridge the gap between cyberspace and physical space, creating innovative systems for the rapid and accurate fulfilment of orders—with some merchandise even offering same-day delivery. Bezos also launched an experimental program in the use of drones to air-deliver merchandise.

As Amazon expanded its retail offerings, it invested in other digital companies and began acquiring or spinning off what is today more than forty full-fledged subsidiaries, among them Zappos (online clothing and shoes), Shopbop (fashion), Diapers.com (diapers and other infant-related consumables), Amazon Robotics (formerly Kiva Systems, maker of mobile robotic fulfillment systems), Audible (audio books), Goodreads (social catalog site for books), and IMDb (the movie database). In 2005, Amazon acquired CreateSpace, originally an online distributor of on-demand DVDs, which Amazon in 2009 expanded into a comprehensive provider of self-publishing services for authors, publishers, film studios, and music labels. Thus, the company that started out as a digital bookstore also became a digital publisher. As for films, Amazon Studios, established late in 2010, began producing television programming and feature films, often selecting scripts through crowdsourcing.

Today the world's biggest Internet retailer as measured by revenue and market capitalization, Amazon has made Jeff Bezos the richest person in the world, with a net worth of $121.3 billion as of early 2018. He has used the wealth generated by Amazon to launch new and highly diverse enterprises, including Blue Origin, a company dedicated to human spaceflight, and the acquisition of the *Washington Post*. His Bezos Expeditions entity is a vehicle for his personal investments, which include the likes of Airbnb, Google, TeachStreet (a search engine to find teachers), and Uber. He has also founded and funded several philanthropic enterprises, mostly educational and medical or related to generally liberal political causes.

Most profoundly, though, Bezos has used digital technology to tear down most of the walls separating business sectors. Amazon both sells and publishes books, along with just about everything else. It streams entertainment of all sorts, and it creates entertainment. It is a formidable storefront, warehouse operation, and distribution empire, all in one. And it is a source of funding for the research and development of technologies of all kinds, including those dedicated to manned space flight. Vertical monopolies are not new. Famously, early in the twentieth century, John D. Rockefeller created in Standard Oil a company that controlled the means of exploring and drilling for and extracting, refining, delivering, distributing, and retailing petroleum products. Jeff Bezos started Amazon as an online bookstore, but he never intended to stop there. Today, it is best described as an online business, which makes it sufficiently agile to do whatever can be done over the global World Wide Web.

DISRUPTION:
TRANSFORMING
FUTURISTIC
DAYDREAMS INTO
LARGE-SCALE
ENTREPRENEURIAL
ENTERPRISES

ELON MUSK
(1971–)

As a child, Elon Musk often gazed far away while his parents were speaking to him. It happened so often, they thought he was hearing-impaired, and physicians were sufficiently in agreement to perform an adenoidectomy. The result? Elon Musk still gazed into the distance, even when people were talking to him. The correct diagnosis was not adenoid trouble, but daydreaming, and, as his mother told a Musk biographer, "He goes into his brain, and then you just see he is in another world . . . designing a new rocket or something."

In imaginative capacity, character, attitude, mindset, and ambition, Musk is the twenty-first-century icon and avatar of the disruptive thinker. While not all he daydreams about has come to realization, let alone commercialization, Musk has already transformed banking and payments with PayPal, has cracked the code on creating commercially viable electric cars, and has gone a long way toward commercializing space travel in the private sector.

• • •

Elon Reeve Musk was born on June 28, 1971, in Pretoria, Transvaal, South Africa. His South African father, Errol, was an electromechanical engineer, pilot, and sailor. His Canadian mother, Maye Haldeman Musk, worked as a model and dietitian. Elon is the eldest of their three children.

Musk's parents divorced in 1980, and he lived mostly with his father in suburban Pretoria but is now estranged from him. He grew up a loner, who read extensively and taught himself programming, selling his first video game—he called it Blastar—to a computer magazine for $500. He admits to being bullied and beaten at school, severely enough—he was hurled down a flight of stairs—to have been hospitalized. Educated in private elementary schools and at Waterkloof House Preparatory School, Musk graduated from a public high school in Pretoria and left South Africa for Canada in 1989, just before he turned eighteen, having become a Canadian citizen through his mother. He enrolled at Queen's University in Kingston, Ontario, when he was seventeen and, after his sophomore year, in 1992, transferred to the University of Pennsylvania, from which he graduated in May 1997 with a Bachelor of Science degree in physics and a Bachelor of Science degree in economics from the university's Wharton School of Business. By this point in his life, the daydreaming, reclusive child and victim of bullying had become significantly more socialized—and entrepreneurial. With another Penn student, he rented an entire ten-bedroom frat house and turned it into an ad hoc (unlicensed) nightclub.

When he was twenty-four in 1995, Musk moved to Palo Alto, California, to begin a PhD program in applied physics and materials science at Stanford—only to quit after two days, having decided to become an Internet entrepreneur instead. To this ambition he soon added projects in renewable energy and the exploration of space.

• • •

Having wasted no time in leaving Stanford, Musk wasted no time in plunging into his first company. With his brother, Kimbal, and some angel investor cash, he started a web software company called Zip2. It was an Internet-based city guide designed specifically for the newspaper industry, and the Musks launched it only after having secured contracts from the *New York Times* and *Chicago Tribune*. In 1999, his own company's board rejected his bid to serve as CEO and sold Zip2 to Compaq, at the time a leading maker of PCs, for $341 million in cash and stock. Musk netted $22 million and was free to go on to bigger things. In March 1999, one month after the Zip2 sale closed, he cofounded X.com, an online financial services and email payment company, which merged in 2000 with Confinity and its PayPal online money-transfer service. The following year, the merged company became PayPal.

The rapid growth of PayPal into the ubiquitous online money-transfer company carried a profound lesson for Musk. Growth was due to viral marketing, with customers recruited when they received money via the service. Musk instantly recognized the power of viral marketing, even as he understood that viral marketing would work only if the underlying product was compelling. This encouraged him to develop his own most compelling passions into businesses. Once again, however, his desire to maintain control as CEO was thwarted. While the board removed him as PayPal CEO late in 2000, he remained on the board, and when the company was acquired by eBay in 2002 for $1.5 billion in stock, Musk received a payout of $165 million as PayPal's largest shareholder.

His early Internet ventures made Musk a wealthy man—but he daydreamed like a much wealthier man. In 2001, Musk laid out Mars Oasis, a plan to land an experimental greenhouse on Mars, grow food crops, prove the viability of Mars for eventual colonization, and generally reignite the greatly dimmed public interest in space exploration. With Adeo Ressi, the Penn classmate with whom he ran the impromptu "nightclub," and an aerospace equipment buyer named Jim Cantrell, Musk flew to Russia in hopes of buying surplus Dnepr ICBMs to refurbish as vehicles capable of lifting payloads into space. His ambition was to privatize and commercialize space travel, space commerce, and space exploration. His overtures in Russia were rebuffed, and the trio returned to the States empty-handed. Musk tried again the following year, with an aerospace insider, Mike Griffin, and this time received an offer—which Musk summarily rejected as too expensive. He decided then and there to create a company that would build its own spacecraft.

What happened next revealed Musk's genius for transforming an apparently wild daydream—what kid doesn't want to build his own rocket ship?—into a plausible business proposition. He looked at aerospace from a disruptively new business perspective, calculating that the materials that go into building a rocket account for no more than 3 percent of what a rocket costs. He reasoned that, if he applied what he knew from software development—chiefly modular design—and vertically integrated all aspects of space travel, his proposed company could build and launch a rocket ten times cheaper than NASA, could—while realizing a spectacular 70 percent gross margin. Having turned his daydream into a value proposition, he restored the dream-vision aspect to it by setting as the long-range goal of the company that he now called SpaceX the creation of a "true spacefaring civilization."

In May 2002, Musk sank $100 million of his own money into SpaceX and assumed leadership as both CEO and CTO (chief technology officer). The company has so far built a line of rocket engines, a family of nine Falcon launch vehicles, and the SpaceX Dragon, a reusable multipurpose spacecraft. In September 2008, the Falcon 1 became the first privately funded liquid-fueled vehicle to put a satellite into earth orbit. That same year, SpaceX won a $1.6 billion NASA Commercial Resupply Services program contract for a dozen flights of the Falcon 9 rocket and Dragon to service the International Space Station (ISS) after the Space Shuttle was retired, as scheduled, in 2011. On May 25, 2012, the SpaceX Dragon docked with the ISS, making SpaceX the first private-sector firm to launch and dock a vehicle to the ISS. The company had another first on December 22, 2015, when it successfully re-landed on the launch pad the first stage of its Falcon rocket, demonstrating history's first reusable launch vehicle. By the end of 2017, SpaceX had landed and recovered the first stage on sixteen missions, and in February 2018 the company successfully test-launched the Falcon Heavy, a partially reusable superheavy-lift launch vehicle that is currently the most powerful rocket in the world.

• • •

With SpaceX, Musk has looked to the future, setting a goal of establishing an 80,000-resident Mars colony by 2040. He has pointed out that, in an atmosphere without oxygen, transportation on Mars would be powered by electricity—electric cars, trains, and aircraft. Not coincidentally, of course, Musk is chairman of an electric car company, Tesla, Inc. It had been incorporated in 2003 by Martin Eberhard and Marc Tarpenning, and Musk became a major investor in February 2004, joining the board of directors as chairman. He took a hands-on role in the development of some of the company's vehicles and, following the 2008 global economic meltdown, took over management as CEO and "product architect."

Although Toyota debuted its hybrid gas-electric Prius in 1995 and marketed its first production model in 1997, all-electric cars had been considered a dead technology, killed by a combination of Big Oil and the auto industry. The demise of electric vehicles was even chronicled in a successful 2006 documentary titled *Who Killed the Electric Car?* It was the Tesla that brought the electric car back to life and made it exciting, and it was Elon Musk who was the Lazarus of this technology. In contrast to the first generation of electric vehicles, which offered mediocre performance and very limited range, the Tesla Roadster was a sexy sports car with a more-than-supercar 0-to-60 acceleration of 1.9 seconds, a supercar price of between $200,000 and $250,000, and a range in excess of 300 miles on a single charge. Just under 2,450 of the vehicles were sold, but they paved the way for the models that followed, each with greater horsepower and longer range. Musk has plans to build a compact Tesla, which would sell for a mainstream price of below $30,000, and he also intends to sell electric powertrains to automakers who want to produce their own electric vehicles. Currently, the company sells powertrain systems to Daimler (Mercedes) and Toyota (RAV4 EV). Musk has been called the Henry Ford of the modern electric car.

• • •

Tesla started out as a niche vehicle for the very wealthy and is gradually evolving into a vehicle that most drivers can afford. A key aspect of Musk's disruptive process is to broadly commercialize niche technology, to democratize radical innovation. In 2006, brothers Peter and Lyndon Rive founded SolarCity on the suggestion of Elon Musk, their cousin. In 2016, Musk merged SolarCity with Tesla as its subsidiary to market commercial solar panels and to provide other alternative energy services and products.

In 2013, Musk took alternative power beyond cars and solar panels when he unveiled his plan for the Hyperloop, a high-speed transportation system in which passenger pods driven by a linear induction motor—a maglev (magnetic levitation) system—run at 700 miles per hour in sealed, partially evacuated tubes. His initial proposal is for a Hyperloop between Greater Los Angeles and the San Francisco Bay Area. In connection with the project, Musk announced in 2015 a SpaceX-sponsored design competition for the Hyperloop passenger-carrying "pods." In 2017, SpaceX built a Hyperloop test track and began work on a test tunnel.

• • •

There is a limit to Musk's techno-utopian vision. He founded OpenAI in 2015 as a not-for-profit artificial intelligence (AI) research company, specifically with the mandate to develop AI in ways that ensure it will be both beneficial and safe for the future of humanity. Musk believes that the evolution of AI is both inevitable and important, but that it might result in super-intelligent systems that could be used by governments to "oppress their citizenry." He believes that by promoting open-source development of AI now, the concentration of proprietary corporate power can be curbed, if not entirely avoided. As part of his AI initiative, Musk founded Neuralink in 2016. The startup is focused on creating brain-implantable devices to enable human beings not merely to use digital technology but to merge with it, thereby ensuring human control over AI. Mind-computer interfaces, Musk believes, will allow "our brains to keep up in the intelligence race. The machines can't outsmart us if we have everything the machines have plus everything we have."

OpenAI and Neuralink again suggest comparisons with Henry Ford. Ford's development of the moving assembly line brought the benefits of technology to untold millions, but it also changed the nature of work forever, chaining workers to the tyranny of an automated assembly line. Ford understood this, and he responded by increasing the pay of his line workers to an unheard-of $5 a day. It was sufficient, he calculated, to enable any of them to afford to purchase one of the cars they were building. In this way, Ford believed the laborers in his plants would be less alienated from their relentlessly automated work. Musk now proposes the equivalent of internalizing automation by the human implantation of AI. In the end, this may turn out to be his single most disruptive innovation.

6
EDUCATION

GUTENBERG LAUNCHED
A PRINTING REVOLUTION
WITH MECHANICAL
MOVABLE TYPE, THE
FIRST TECHNOLOGY OF
MASS MEDIA, WHICH
DECENTRALIZED
CONTROL OF KNOWLEDGE
AND ENABLED AN
INTELLECTUAL AWAKENING
THROUGHOUT EUROPE
AND THE WORLD

JOHANNES GUTENBERG
(c. 1400–1468)

Invention is not synonymous with disruption. Gutenberg did not invent print-ing. Woodblock printing—printing of words and images carved onto a block of wood—is known to have been used as far back as the Han Dynasty of China, which puts its origin before CE 220. But Gutenberg was also not the first to intro-duce movable-type printing, the invention with which he is most widely credited. The earliest known movable-type system also came from China, using porcelain type, about 1040, during the Song Dynasty. Two centuries later, in Korea, a system using movable metal type was introduced, and the *Jikji*, a volume of Zen Buddhist teachings, is the first known book printed using movable type.

ndeed, printing in which each page of text was carved from a wood block did not appear in Europe until the early fourteenth century, when it was used to print patterns on cloth. About a hundred years later, block printing was used for books. It was regarded as a cheap—and not altogether desirable—alternative to hand-copied manuscripts.

Johannes Gutenberg was born in Mainz, Germany, during this early period of European woodblock printing, the youngest son of a prosperous family. His father, Friele Gensfleisch zur Laden, was an engraver for the ecclesiastic mint, a hereditary position. Young Gutenberg—he adopted his surname from the house his father and his paternal ancestors inhabited, zu Gutenberg—learned the goldsmithing trade, which included engraving, from his father. Although his family was not royalty, they were patrician and, as such, it is likely that Johannes Gutenberg was well educated at a grammar school and continued his studies at the University of Erfurt. Preparation for the printer's trade required a high degree of literacy, including a thorough knowledge of Latin and some Greek. Beyond this highly credible speculation regarding his education, almost nothing is known about Gutenberg's early life. What is known is that in 1411 a popular uprising in Mainz drove out of the city more than a hundred patrician families, including Gutenberg's.

For the next fifteen years, there is no sign of either the Gensfleisches or the Gutenbergs. Then, in 1434, Johannes sent a letter from Strasbourg, saying that he was living there as a goldsmith. In or about 1439, Gutenberg became involved in an apparently unsavory enterprise in which he polished and peddled metal mirrors, claiming that they could be used to capture holy light from religious relics. The following year, 1440, writing again from Strasbourg, Gutenberg claimed to have perfected what he called "*Aventur und Kunst*" (Enterprise and Art)—that is, the secret of printing. Whether this "secret" was a movable type system or some variation on traditional block printing is unknown, and four years passed before the historical record concerning Gutenberg resumes. The year 1448 finds him back in Mainz, where he borrowed money from his brother-in-law and may have used it to advance his experiments with movable type. In any case, by 1450 the new movable-type press was in operation.

Working from Hof Humbrecht, a building owned by a relative, Gutenberg was enjoying a lucrative business printing a variety of books. We know that he invented some method of rather quickly producing movable type intended for use on a wooden printing press with an oil-based ink. It was a system in which every component was intended to speed the near-mass production of books. This said, nothing of Gutenberg's press or other paraphernalia survives or was ever illustrated. The details of Gutenberg's technique for making the movable type are unknown. What is abundantly clear from specimens of Gutenberg's work, especially his famed Bible of 1455, is that the typeface he created reproduced the characters standard in manuscripts of the period. Gutenberg produced two different forms of each letter. In one, the letter was separated. In the other, the letter was linked, so that it could be closely joined to the adjacent type, thereby avoiding gaps in the printed page.

Historians of printing technology speculate that the individual pieces of type were created by engraving their letter into hard steel and then punching it into a softer metal to build a mold in which multiple copies of each character could be cast. The cast type was arranged into a wooden tray called (in modern English) a galley. When all the type was set into the galley, the raised letters were inked with leather-covered ink balls, and a sheet of paper or parchment was placed on top of the galley. The inked galley, with the paper on top of it, was then slid under a pad and into the press. The screw-threaded press plate was lowered down onto the sandwiched pad, paper, and galley, the resulting pressure creating the impression that became the printed page. We know that Gutenberg prepared a special ink for this process—a sticky, very black ink, which, unlike traditional water-based woodblock ink, used a combination of linseed oil, resin, and soot.

Gutenberg was already enjoying a brisk business when he took on as partner a wealthy burgher named Johann Fust. Gutenberg borrowed 8,000 guilders from him to finance a series of books, and then another 8,000 to finance the creation of the 42-line Bible of 1455. This, the so-called Gutenberg Bible, is considered the first book of true merit printed in Europe with movable type. In Gutenberg's own time, it was recognized for what it is universally considered today—not only *his* masterpiece of printing, but one of the most beautiful printed books ever produced. It is monumental. Printed in two volumes, it consists of a total of 1,282 pages and was the work of Gutenberg directing a staff of twenty skilled printers. The 1455 Bible employed a font of 290 different cast letters and symbols. This 1455 edition consisted of 180 copies—150 on paper and 30 on vellum parchment. The price for the paper version was 30 florins each—a lordly sum, representing perhaps three years' wages for a skilled worker, such as a clerk.

Alas for Johannes Gutenberg, the Bible turned out to be the high-water mark of his career. He fell into a bitter financial dispute with his partner, Fust, who sued him in the archbishop's court for misusing the funds he had loaned him. When the decision went against Gutenberg, he forfeited control over the printing establishment to Fust, and he relinquished to him half of the printed Bibles. Bankrupt, Gutenberg subsequently opened another print shop and continued as a printer in Mainz, but he never succeeded in replicating his earlier success. He struggled until 1465, when the Archbishop Adolph von Nassau conferred upon him the title of Hofmann (court gentleman) in recognition of his movable-type printing system. The honor carried with it a generous stipend, which saw Gutenberg through his final few years. He died in 1468.

● ● ●

While Gutenberg himself died in some degree of obscurity—living chiefly on his stipend—the printing system he created spread very rapidly. Unlike the much earlier Chinese and Korean inventions, Gutenberg's press was a truly transformative technology. Thanks to the mass production of books, knowledge and news spread rapidly throughout Europe. The new technology propelled the Renaissance with redoubled force and consequence. Printing spawned the Reformation, the Age of Enlightenment, and the Scientific Revolution. No longer was written knowledge confined to a small circle of individuals and institutions wealthy enough to own manuscripts. The *written* word had become the *printed* word, and what people thought and read could no longer be controlled exclusively by governments, churches, and individual rulers. Like the Internet of today, movable-type printing presses, which quickly appeared in all the major cities of Europe, became a kind of political, cultural, religious, and scientific network—a nervous system, if you will, of a civilization now capable of continually challenging and renewing itself.

As for the basic technology of movable type and the Gutenberg press, it remained remarkably unchanged until the nineteenth century, when steam and electric power exponentially increased the speed, volume, and reach of the printed word. Still, the basics of cast movable type remained the principal technology underlying the production of all books until the early 1960s, with the perfection and spread of photographically based offset printing. Today, the digital revolution has finally disrupted printing on paper—but it has yet to replace it and does not seem likely to do so.

MARGARET MEAD

(1901–1978)

Published in 1928, Margaret Mead's first book, *Coming of Age in Samoa: A Psychological Study of Primitive Youth for Western Civilization*, was a blockbuster. Not only was it the most widely read book in anthropology of the twentieth century, it made its twenty-seven-year-old author the world's most famous anthropologist. It explored in detail the sexual life of teenagers in Samoan society, and it reached the conclusion that social and cultural norms have greater influence on sexuality and sexual behavior than nature does, thereby coming down on the side of nurture in the enduring nature-versus-nurture debate. Furthermore, the book asserted that "developed" Western societies have much to learn from "primitive" societies such as the one in Samoa. Mead's study disrupted Western notions of sexual norms, gender roles, adolescence, and morality.

M ead's first book is often identified as one of the intellectual foundations on which the "sexual revolution" of the 1960s is based, but perhaps the even more disruptive aspect of Mead's debut publication, as well as the rest of her long and highly influential career, is best expressed in the foreword her Columbia University mentor, the pioneering anthropologist Franz Boas, wrote:

> Courtesy, modesty, good manners, conformity to definite ethical standards are universal, but what constitutes courtesy, modesty, good manners, and definite ethical standards is not universal. It is instructive to know that standards differ in the most unexpected ways.

Any thoughtful and candid reader of Margaret Mead could not come away from this or her subsequent work without feeling that concepts of normality and morality are relative to culture and not absolute. Coming after Albert Einstein showed in his Special Theory of Relativity (1905) that the nature of physical reality is relative to the observer's frame of reference, Mead's study was the second blow to absolutism Western civilization had absorbed in the twentieth century.

● ● ●

Margaret Mead was born in Philadelphia and raised in suburban Doylestown. She was the daughter of Edward Sherwood Mead, professor of finance at the Wharton School of the University of Pennsylvania, and Emily (née Fogg) Mead, a sociologist well known for her work among Italian immigrants. An early influence in her life was the varied Christian religious affiliations of the members of her family. This absence of unanimity among her relatives prompted her to search on her own for a denomination that seemed most aligned with her view of Christianity. She chose the Episcopal Church, and while her own later views on sexual mores would certainly fall well outside of expected Episcopal morality, she remained committed to the Church and even played a role in writing the 1979 revision of the Episcopal *Book of Common Prayer.*

Mead was educated at the Buckingham Friends School, a Quaker institution in Lahaska, Pennsylvania, and received her bachelor's degree from Barnard College in 1923. She next enrolled in Columbia University, where she studied with Boas and another pioneering anthropologist, Ruth Fulton Benedict. She earned a master's degree in 1924 and set out the following year to do anthropological fieldwork in Samoa, which became the basis of her PhD dissertation and her first book. After she returned to New York in 1926, Mead took a position as assistant curator in the American Museum of Natural History and was awarded a PhD from Columbia University three years later.

Her private life was emotionally rich and included sexual relationships with the anthropological linguist Edward Sapir and with Ruth Benedict. Sapir had been one of Boas's students and was a close friend of Benedict, but his ideas on marriage and the "appropriate" social role of women were resolutely conventional and drove Mead away. Mead was married three times: from 1923 to 1928 to theology student Luther Cressman, who turned from the study of religion to anthropology; from 1928 to 1935 to New Zealand-born anthropologist Reo Fortune; and from 1936 to 1950 to the British anthropologist Gregory Bateson. This last union produced a daughter, Mary Catherine Bateson, who herself became an eminent anthropologist.

Mead's sexual, bisexual, and serial marital history (unusual at the time) is consistent with the open-minded orientation she brought to her anthropological fieldwork. The birth of her daughter occasioned a professional relationship with Dr. Benjamin Spock, whom she chose as the girl's pediatrician. Mead became an important influence on Spock's ideas of "permissive" child-rearing, which found their way into his own social and cultural blockbuster, *Baby and Child Care*, first published in 1946. While Mead's marriage to Bateson ended with his leaving her, she remained devoted to him and kept his photograph on her bedside table. Nevertheless, from 1955 until her death in 1978, Mead lived with the anthropologist Rhoda Métraux, with whom she had both a romantic and professional, collaborative relationship.

• • •

Although none of her published work following *Coming of Age in Samoa* had the same cultural impact as that first book, Mead's 1935 *Sex and Temperament in Three Primitive Societies* exerted an influence on feminism even greater than that of the 1928 book, largely because it identified the people of the Chambri Lake region of the Sepik basin of Papua New Guinea as female-dominated. Mead's point was that this social organization was, within the Chambri frame of reference, perfectly normal and certainly not in any way dysfunctional. Some subsequent anthropologists have challenged Mead's observations, contradicting her claim that the society she observed was ever dominated by women.

Mead went on to write ten more major books and was editor or coauthor of eight others. Her influence over the academic field of anthropology has been powerful, despite many challenges not only to her conclusions but also to the accuracy of her recorded observations. Somewhat underappreciated today was her highly engaging, provocative, and always entertaining media presence, which continued late into her life. During the tumultuous years of the sexual revolution and the rise of the 1960s counterculture movement, she was a frequent guest on popular television talk shows and was often commissioned to write articles for mass-circulation magazines. She brought to these popular forums the same message that she had brought to her students and to the readers of her academic anthropological texts.

The citation that accompanied the Presidential Medal of Freedom President Jimmy Carter posthumously presented to Mead on January 19, 1979, characterizes her popular achievement aptly: "To a public of millions, she brought the central insight of cultural anthropology: that varying cultural patterns express an underlying human unity."

DISRUPTION:
CREATING A REVOLUTION
IN AMERICAN
CHILD-REARING BY
ENCOURAGING PRACTICES
THAT SOME CONDEMNED
AS "PERMISSIVE" BUT
HE CALLED "COMMON
SENSE"

BENJAMIN SPOCK

(1903–1998)

The title of the 1946 work that made Dr. Benjamin Spock famous hints at its disruptive impact: *The Common Sense Book of Baby and Child Care*. Just compare that to the child-rearing guides that had come before: Luther Emmett Holt's 1894 *The Care and Feeding of Children: A Catechism for the Use of Mothers and Nurses* and John B. Watson's 1928 *Psychological Care of Infant and Child*. From *Catechism* and *Psychological* to *Common Sense* is a breakthrough journey. In contrast to previous child-rearing manuals, which assumed that parents knew nothing and were therefore in dire need of strict prescriptions, Spock began with two disarming sentences: "Trust yourself. You know more than you think you do." Within six months after the first copy rolled off the press, half a million had been sold. By the time of its author's death in 1998, 50 million had been distributed worldwide in 39 languages.

O ver the years, some—and not a few—have been appalled by the success of the man everyone knew as "Dr. Spock." His advice—which boiled down to doing what comes naturally, to loving your child and showing that love whenever and wherever you can, to letting both parents and children be themselves—was condemned as launching and fostering an era of "permissive parenting." When the first edition came out in 1946, everything from delinquency to anarchy was predicted. Others—a growing majority—came to see the era of Spock as liberation for both children and their parents.

• • •

Benjamin Spock's approach to child-rearing was not an arbitrary formulation. A physician, he began his pediatric practice in 1933 and quickly concluded that the prevailing approaches to pediatric care made the grave mistake of devoting little or no attention to the emotional needs of the child. Some widely accepted notions seemed downright cruel to Spock. As a young pediatrician, he saw that the medical profession gave him only two choices: either fall back on accepted practice, no matter how flawed, or challenge it. He chose the latter and mounted the challenge by investigating what was behind the questions parents continually asked him. They concerned such issues as toilet training and breastfeeding and infant and child sleep problems—basic stuff that should not have been controversial but was.

Spock's first step was to seek training in psychoanalysis—and, in fact, he became the first American pediatrician to acquire a formal background in the discipline. He became an apostle of Freudian insights into the early causes of so many adult problems. Yet instead of merely coercing parents into acting in accordance with Freud's theories, Spock worked to translate psychoanalytic insights into specific child-rearing recommendations and then to merely suggest that parents try them out and report back to him on the outcome. He continually sought feedback and refused to issue rigid, inflexible instructions. Instead, he counseled, recommending courses of action and monitoring the results they produced. He understood that he had something in common with the parents of his patients, namely dissatisfaction with prevailing methods of child-rearing. His solution was to work together with them to find better ways. The only constant he adhered to was encouraging parents to show their children affection.

Benjamin Spock was born on May 2, 1903, in New Haven, Connecticut. He was the first child in what grew into a large New England family. His father, a Yale graduate, was a lawyer for the New Haven Railroad, his mother, a homemaker. Both were descended from very early settlers in the area, and both were strict—"puritanical," as Spock described them. He was sent to private preparatory schools and then to Yale, which he graduated from in 1925 with a major in English literature, a background that was good preparation for an author. A standout member of a standout Yale rowing crew, he sailed with the crew to Paris to represent the United States in the 1924 Olympic Games.

In 1925, Spock enrolled in medical school at Yale. But, partially in defiance of his father, he transferred in 1927 to the College of Physicians and Surgeons of Columbia University in New York City, graduating first in his class two years later. His wife, Jane Davenport Cheney, was a civil-liberties advocate and liberal political activist. Even before beginning his medical studies, he made the decision to specialize in the care and treatment of children, feeling that they had "their whole lives ahead of them." He regarded pediatrics at the time as too narrowly focused on the physical aspects of child development, and so he supplemented it with his pediatric training in psychoanalysis.

From 1933 to 1944, Spock practiced pediatric medicine and taught pediatrics at Cornell Medical College. He also worked as a consultant in pediatric psychiatry for the New York City Department of Health. His reputation and influence within the profession grew rapidly, and as early as 1938 he had been approached by the publishing house Doubleday to write a manual on childcare. At that point in his career, he did not feel that he was sufficiently prepared to do so; but in 1943, while he was on a summer vacation, he began to write the book that would make him world famous. In 1944, with World War II raging, he joined the U.S. Navy as a medical officer, serving until 1947. In his spare time, he continued to write his book, which was published to spectacular success in 1946. The timing was perfect, since that was the first year of the postwar baby boom generation.

• • •

The book, which was continually updated and revised between 1957 and 2012, outsold, in the United States, every book on every subject that had come before it, except for the works of William Shakespeare and the Holy Bible. (In 1976, cumulative sales of *Baby and Child Care* actually did surpass Shakespeare.)

As the 1950s gave way to the 1960s, Spock's once-revolutionary "common sense," "flexible," and "permissive" approach to child-rearing came to seem increasingly mainstream, going with the flow of a generation that cherished free expression. The young people of the 1960s were, in fact, a generation raised by parents that his book had influenced. At this juncture, looking around him at children who embodied values he himself had nurtured, Spock, influenced by his wife, became a political activist. To him, activism seemed a natural extension of his concern for children's health. In 1962 he became cochairman of the National Committee for a Sane Nuclear Policy (SANE), an organization dedicated to halting nuclear bomb testing in the earth's atmosphere. Growing up in a radioactive environment, Spock reasoned, was not healthy and, therefore, was of urgent concern to a pediatrician. In 1963, he actively campaigned for Medicare, which was part of President Lyndon B. Johnson's "Great Society" portfolio of social-welfare programs. His advocacy of what many fellow physicians condemned as "socialized medicine" brought an angry reaction from the American Medical Association, which condemned Spock as a lightweight popularizer rather than a dedicated academic researcher. Undaunted, Spock plunged even deeper into the era of protest, becoming a fierce antiwar activist in opposition to the escalating Vietnam conflict. Why labor, he asked, to preserve the health and well-being of children only to send them into an unjust, ill-advised, and ultimately fruitless war? Spock found himself marching and protesting alongside young people who had not even been born when he had embarked on his quietly revolutionary medical career.

While those who supported the war joined Spock's medical critics in condemning his books on *Baby and Child Care* for having produced a spoiled generation of grungy hippies and drifting dropouts unwilling to fight for their country, Spock persisted in his protests—even as he pointed out that the antiwar movement had also spread among Third World youth, whose parents had never read his books.

• • •

Yet some of what Benjamin Spock saw in the late 1960s disturbed him. When he revised his book in 1968, he added material advising parents not to be afraid to set limits to their children's behavior, pointing out that "common sense" argued against limitless permissiveness. The advice was clearly out of step with his target audience, and, for the first time ever, *Baby and Child Care* showed a sharp—50 percent—decline in sales. Spock attributed this not to his advice about setting limits, but to the unpopularity of his antiwar activism. Indeed, on May 20, 1968, he was brought to trial, with other high-visibility protesters, on charges of conspiracy because he had actively counseled young men to resist the draft. Although he was convicted, the verdict was set aside on appeal over a procedural issue. The verdict and its reversal provoked some long-time users of *Baby and Child Care* to return their copies of the book in protest. More, however, found the prosecution of the aging baby doctor absurd.

In the 1970s, Spock published *Decent and Indecent: Our Personal and Political Behavior* and *A Teenager's Guide to Life and Love*, both of which were more traditional in their approach to sexual behavior and general morality. After running for president on the People's Party ticket in 1972, he returned to *Baby and Child Care*, revising the book in 1976 in response to feminist objections that he had perpetuated gender-role stereotypes of fathers and mothers. Conceding the validity of their objections, Spock revised what he himself considered "sexist" material and advocated a more equitable sharing of parental responsibility.

Spock's health began to decline in the 1980s, and he withdrew from public life. He lived to ninety-four, dying on March 15, 1998. His books continue to enjoy substantial sales, and mainstream child-rearing, which had been highly prescriptive and restrictive before the advent of Spock, has never returned to the earlier rigid models that reflected a more absolutist view of society.

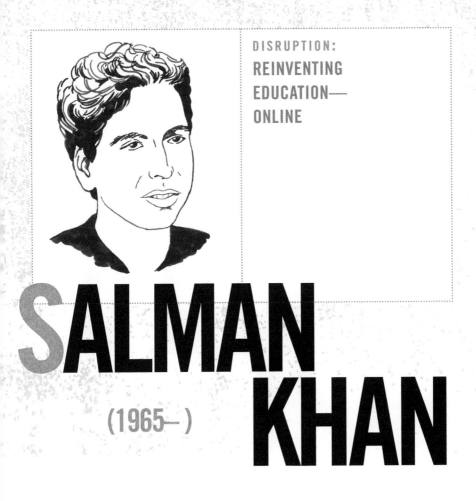

SALMAN KHAN

(1965–)

Salman Amin Khan has a mission: to deliver "a free world-class education for anyone anywhere." The operative words here are *free* and *world-class*. In 2017, combined U.S. spending—federal, state, and local—on education was $1.1 trillion. It may be too much, it may be too little, but, either way, anything expressed in a trillion or more is the opposite of *free*. For this expenditure, the United States produces students ranking 24th in science, 39th in mathematics, and 24th in reading out of students in 72 nations, based on the performance of fifteen-year-old Americans who took the 2015 Program for International Student Assessment. This level of performance is not, perhaps, the opposite of *world-class*, but it is certainly far from it.

As the rapper Big Sean sang in 2015, "One Man Can Change the World," and that is what Khan set out to do. Russian physicist and Facebook, Twitter, and Groupon venture capitalist Yuri Milner called him "the world's first superstar teacher."

• • •

Salman Khan was born in the New Orleans suburb of Metairie on October 11, 1976, to a mother and father who immigrated to the United States from, respectively, West Bengal and Bangladesh. Sal was educated in the local Metairie public schools, and he recalls that Grace King High School was a mixed bag, with "a few classmates . . . fresh out of jail and others . . . bound for top universities." He excelled in his studies, serving as valedictorian of the Class of 1994. He went on to accrue degrees in electrical engineering and computer science from the Massachusetts Institute of Technology (MIT) and an MBA from Harvard Business School.

Khan interned at Palo Alto Research Center, Inc. (PARC), the legendary Xerox research and development company, and from 2003 through 2009 he was a hedge-fund analyst at Connective Capital Management. But his real love was teaching—*his* way.

In a 2014 interview for *Forbes*, writer Peter High asked Khan about "the famous story of your cousin, Nadia, who needed some help with her math class in seventh grade as the genesis of the idea that has become Khan Academy." Khan responded by explaining that he had grown up "with plenty of smart people," who could beat him at chess and "solve brain teasers before I could, but then they would struggle in algebra. These were incredibly smart people who simply did not have the foundation in math that I had."

He saw this in his cousin Nadia. Although she had received As and Bs in every math class she took, her math instruction had left very basic gaps in her knowledge. It was not her fault: it was an inherent flaw in standard American classroom education. Even if everything was covered, there was no guarantee that every student would understand every principle, leaving many students without fundamental building blocks for their understanding of math.

Khan saw this flaw as "a real opportunity." With his background in software, he gave free rein to what he called his "romantic notions of . . . writing software that could help people learn." He created a software tool designed to give students like Nadia productive "practice problems." Khan "didn't trust them when they said how long it took them or whatever else," so he integrated into the practice-problem program a database that revealed where each user's gaps were. Armed with this information, derived from his students' own efforts to solve the problems, Khan found that he "could intervene appropriately" and "give them as much practice as they needed" *where* they needed it.

Nadia and the handful of others Khan tutored were hooked—but so was he. Convinced that he had a tool that not only helped his *students* but helped *him* to be a better teacher because it directed him to each student's gaps, he decided that he needed to scale up his process. "The software was appropriate for tens of people," he told Peter High, "but video together with analytics connecting the software to the videos would be necessary to take it to the next level." Accordingly, he began doing YouTube videos "to complement the software idea, and they took on a life of their own and it reinforced that there was a need that was not being met effectively."

Khan's disruptive insight was combining high technology with no technology. Software practice programs plus YouTube videos were the high-tech. Khan himself was the no-tech. He was the teacher. Students moved at their own pace. His database software identified the gaps, and Khan concentrated on these, either with live video or a recorded video designed to address the gap he identified. Since he recorded all of his presentations as he gave them, he soon accumulated a large and growing collection of videos available on various subjects. Students always had the option of seeking out extra help on their gap issues and areas by replaying the relevant portions of the videos as often as they needed to.

Khan's takeaway was that "many people . . . are very good students, but they think of themselves as bad students." Why? He concluded that traditional classroom teaching was "missing . . . [a] way to understand where their gaps are and a way to address those gaps. The problem is by the time you are in algebra class and if you are a little shaky on decimals, there has not been a good way to address that traditionally. The class is going to move on." In the Khan approach, each student sets the pace and can repeat and repeat material that initially escapes understanding.

Conventional education is mostly a one-way broadcast: *I teach, you learn.* Khan's approach was two-way. He sought feedback so that he could learn how to teach each student based on the performance of that student. He discovered that this approach did not merely transfer subject-matter knowledge to his students; it also transformed their intellectual assessment of themselves: "Some of the strongest testimonials that I got back in the early days were from students who indicated that they thought they were simply bad at a given subject, and they were on the verge of giving up hope when they found our videos." They did not merely discover calculus or algebra: they discovered that they were capable of learning calculus or algebra—and then they discovered they were capable of learning anything. Khan told High about a member of the Khan Academy team who had failed calculus repeatedly and dropped out of college because of it. When he later started a successful IT career, he found that he had to go back and learn calculus. This time, however, he used Khan Academy. Subsequently, he joined the Academy "team and now is one of our top engineers," Khan told High. "He didn't realize he had all these gaps in his formative mathematics and that was what was keeping him [from] passing calculus."

Khan discovered that the American educational system was separating students into *smart* and *not smart* or *motivated* and *not motivated*. He disrupted this dysfunctional approach by addressing the gaps in a student's mastery of a given subject. It wasn't about *smart/not smart* or *motivated/not motivated*, but "how strong your foundation is, and how confident you are. One's perception of themselves has a much bigger role than has been acknowledged to determine who succeeds and who does not."

• • •

Khan kept teaching online and recording videos in the process of discovering the process. In 2009, the popularity of his online teaching material prompted him to give up his financial-analyst job to devote himself full time to developing his YouTube channel, which he called Khan Academy. He formed a 501(c)(3) nonprofit organization, which was chiefly funded by donations from philanthropic organizations, such as the Carlos Slim Foundation, and from corporate sponsors, including Google and AT&T. The latter funded the creation of mobile versions of the content, to make it fully accessible through smartphone apps. This, Khan understood, was especially important since smartphones are, for many young people, especially from lower-income families, their main digital screen and portal into the Internet.

Khan found himself doing well by doing good, making an annual salary between $350,000 and $556,000. The video courses are free to students. In 2012, Khan took a step toward integrating the Academy's approach into the conventional classroom with a feature called Coach, which connects teachers with students through videos and monitor tools. By 2017, Khan Academy YouTube videos had piled up more than 1.2 billion views.

Criticism of the Khan approach has been mainly focused on Khan's lack of formal training in teaching and pedagogy, but these critics have yet to demonstrate that the absence of such credentials has had a negative effect on results. Indeed, *Research on the Use of Khan Academy in Schools*, a 2014 study funded by the Bill and Melinda Gates Foundation and developed by the SRI International research non-profit showed that 85 percent of teachers who used

Khan Academy materials believed they had a positive impact on their students' learning. Khan himself is modest in his assessment, telling Eric Westervelt on an NPR *Here & Now* radio broadcast (January 5, 2016) that he believes his programs are "valuable, but I'd never say they somehow constitute a complete education." Of course, the only "complete education" is life itself.

7
SOCIETY

TOUSSAINT LOUVERTURE

(1743–1803)

He was called the Black Napoleon for his tactical and strategic brilliance in leading a slave rebellion and shaping it into a fight for national independence. Little is known of the early life of François-Dominique Toussaint (his full birth name), except that he was certainly born on May 20, 1743, on a plantation called Bréda, at Haut de Cap, in Saint-Domingue (modern Haiti), at the time a French colony. Most sources agree that he was the oldest son of Gaou Guinon, the King of Allada, which was located in what is today the West African country of Benin. Gaou Guinon had been captured in war, sold into slavery, and sent to Saint-Domingue. Toussaint's mother, the captive king's second wife, was named Pauline, and their son was born into slavery. It is also possible that Toussaint was born elsewhere in the colony and brought to Bréda as late as 1772, when he was 29, perhaps under an overseer named Bayon de Libertat.

The French colonies at this time were governed by the *Code Noir* (Black Code), a set of laws that sanctioned harsh treatment of "human property." Yet Toussaint was treated with kindness and even educated by his godfather, Pierre Baptiste, known to history as the "savant slave." He taught his godson to read and write. Local Jesuit missionaries may also have contributed to Toussaint's early education, and it is said that Bayon de Libertat, the Bréda plantation overseer, was so impressed with the boy's quick wit that he gave him the run of his personal library. Whatever combination of people and circumstances contributed to his education, by the age of twenty Toussaint was widely read and was fluent in both French and Creole, with a fair command of scholarly Latin to boot. He became well known for his medical knowledge, which drew on African herbal folk medicine traditions in addition to European medicine as it was practiced in the local hospitals run by the Jesuits.

For many years, it was believed that Toussaint remained a slave until the start of the revolt. But a marriage certificate from 1777 shows that he had been freed the year before, when he was 33. Some authorities believe that he secured his emancipation through the intervention of Bayon de Libertat, but that he remained on the Bréda plantation as the manager of his former owner's household slaves and served as the owner's coachman. In any event, he lived in comfort on the plantation for years, marrying Suzanne Simone Baptiste (c. 1743–1816) in 1782. She may have been his cousin, or the daughter of Pierre Baptiste. The union produced two sons, Isaac and Saint-Jean. Toussaint was a shrewd manager, who carefully husbanded his money, invested in property, and grew prosperous. He was sufficiently wealthy to own slaves himself, setting them to work on a coffee plantation that he acquired.

Thus, when Toussaint made the decision to join the slave rebellion that began on the "Night of Fire," August 22, 1791, he did so less out of desperation born of a sense of personal oppression, and more because of some higher calling or purpose. As the name given to August 22 implies, the revolt began when slaves put the torch to plantation houses and fields in and around Haut de Cap. They also killed every white person they encountered. Those participating in the revolt prevailed on Toussaint to join them. He decided to do just that, but—and this was another sign that he did not act on impulse—first saw to it that his wife and sons were safely evacuated from the French half of the island of Hispaniola and lodged in the Spanish-controlled eastern half, called Santo Domingo. In addition, he also put Bayon de Libertat and his wife aboard a ship bound for the United States.

Well-read and thoroughly aware of events beyond his island home, Toussaint drew inspiration from the ideology of liberty, equality, and fraternity that were driving the French Revolution of the same period. But the initial revolt was soon suppressed, except for sporadic fighting between the slaves, free blacks, and planters. In the aftermath, some of the free blacks sided with the slaves and others with the white planters. Toussaint remained on the side of the insurgents, joining forces led by Georges Biassou, serving both as a doctor to the troops and as commander of a small unit. He was instrumental in creating strategy and in negotiating with the Spanish, who were eager to support any rebellion against French power on Hispaniola. Some authorities identify Toussaint as Biassou's military secretary.

Toussaint combined skillful negotiation with strategic restraint. In December 1791, he led negotiations between the insurgents and the French governor, Philibert François Rouxel de Blanchelande. At this point, the rebellion had been largely suppressed, but a core of insurgents still held white prisoners. Toussaint offered their release in exchange for a legal ban on flogging slaves and an agreed-on extra rest day each week. Blanchelande rejected the demand, whereupon Biassou ordered the massacre of the prisoners. Toussaint intervened, however, negotiated terms for their release, and escorted them to Le Cap, where he hoped his demonstration of goodwill would earn an audience with the colonial assembly. It did not.

Convinced that the French attitude toward the slaves would remain unyielding, Toussaint began to mold the uprising into a full-scale bid for independence. He concurred with Biassou's decision to make a formal alliance with Spain against France, and he assumed a major role in the negotiations. He also took charge of a line of outposts, the Cordon de l'Ouest, which defended the rebel-held territory against counterattack by the French. His ability to maintain order and discipline among fighters who until recently had been illiterate fugitive slaves was greatly admired. Toussaint worked hard to create a genuine army, capable of fighting with European discipline on the one hand, but also using guerrilla tactics when necessary. Even the French came to admire him.

• • •

Toward the end of 1792 or the beginning of 1793, Toussaint took *Louverture* (*opening*) as a surname, identifying himself as a leader who opens the way. It was a fitting sobriquet. Although a self-taught military tactician and strategist, Louverture had an uncanny way of finding or creating openings in the enemy's position. Politically, Louverture began to speak more and more in the idealistic rhetoric of the French Revolution. His bargaining position progressed from his earlier efforts to improve the conditions of slavery to a demand for the abolition of slavery— a major step toward creating an independent black republic.

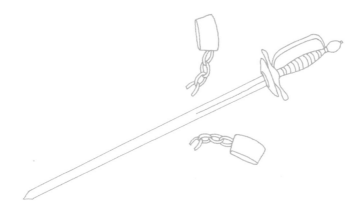

"Brothers and friends," he addressed the black residents of Saint-Domingue on August 29, 1793, "I am Toussaint Louverture; perhaps my name has made itself known to you. I have undertaken vengeance. I want Liberty and Equality to reign in Saint-Domingue. I am working to make that happen. Unite yourselves to us, brothers, and fight with us for the same cause." The French colonial commissioner, Léger-Félicité Sonthonax, responded by proclaiming the emancipation of the slaves. Clearly, it was a move to win over the blacks, but Louverture reminded his fellow leaders that Sonthonax did not actually have the authority to issue such a proclamation. This was sufficient to prevent the blacks from leaving the Spanish alliance—until the French National Convention (the French revolutionary ruling body) ordered the emancipation on February 4, 1794.

Now Louverture, who had maintained an "opening" with the leading French general, made his move. Sensing that some other rebel leaders were growing jealous of him, and, more important, that the Spanish had begun expressing their displeasure at the power he had acquired over a large portion of the island, Louverture embraced the French in May 1794, rallying his troops to General Étienne Maynaud de Bizefranc de Lavaux.

Allying his forces with those of France against Spain, Louverture emerged during 1794 to 1802 as the dominant political and military leader in the colony. He promoted himself to general-in-chief of the army, and led not just the formerly insurgent blacks, but the French colonial forces as well, in pushing the British off the island and then in capturing the half of Hispaniola controlled by the Spanish.

It was unheard of. A *black* commander had united former black slaves with white French soldiers in conducting a successful campaign against the troops of two major European powers, Britain and Spain. In 1798, Louverture negotiated treaties with Britain and with the United States—not as Toussaint Louverture, rebel leader, but on behalf of the French Republic. What is more, he parlayed his military and diplomatic successes on behalf of that Republic into his own political takeover of the colonial government. By 1801, Saint-Domingue was still officially a French colony, but Louverture was governing it as an independent state. Boldly, he drew up a constitution, enshrining in it the abolition of slavery and appointing himself governor for "the rest of his glorious life."

• • •

Louverture never claimed to be an enemy of France. On the contrary, he called himself what he believed himself to be: a free French citizen, who was loyal to Napoleon Bonaparte. He even wrote to him, but never received a reply.

The fact was that Napoleon had had enough of Toussaint Louverture. He sent his brother-in-law, General Charles Emmanuel Leclerc, to meet with Louverture, offer peace, and recover control of the colony through diplomacy. At the same time, he would keep secret Napoleon's order to deport all black officers. The sagacious Louverture was suspicious of Napoleon and persistently refused Leclerc permission to land. He attempted to unite the blacks in defending against the landing of the army, but a sizable number of his officers were convinced that Leclerc had honorable and peaceful intentions. They trusted Napoleon's promise of diplomacy. At length, a fierce fight between the French and those blacks still loyal to Louverture broke out. The fighting grew in intensity, prompting Leclerc to resume his plea for peaceful talks. The talks commenced, only to break down quickly. Fighting resumed, and on May 6, 1802, Louverture personally ventured into Cap-Français to negotiate with Leclerc. The French general agreed to a cease-fire and an amnesty for Louverture and his top lieutenant. This accomplished, Toussaint Louverture retired to his plantations.

General Leclerc was taking no chances, however. He ordered one of his generals, Jean Baptiste Brunet, to arrest Louverture and his aides. Brunet effected this arrest by sending Louverture a letter in which he professed himself a friend, who wanted to take him to Paris, where he could negotiate personally with Napoleon Bonaparte. In fact, Brunet had set a trap. The black leader was arrested and, with his entourage, deported to France on charges of fomenting an uprising. "In overthrowing me," Toussaint Louverture declared with quiet humility, "you have cut down in Saint-Domingue only the trunk of the tree of liberty; it will spring up again from the roots, for they are numerous and they are deep." His ship landed in France on July 2, 1802. On August 25, Toussaint Louverture was clapped into a cell at Fort-de-Joux in the Jura Mountains. The following year, in April, he died, of pneumonia probably complicated by exhaustion, malnutrition, and tuberculosis.

Toussaint Louverture's prophecy concerning the tree of liberty neverthe-less proved true, as his follower Jean-Jacques Dessalines revived the rebellion, defeating the French on January 1, 1804, after nearly twelve and a half years of war. Absent Toussaint's moderating influence, Dessalines led a massacre of the remaining white population on the island. Between three and five thousand French residents were killed.

DOROTHEA DIX

(1802–1887)

Dorothea Lynde Dix revolutionized the treatment of a grossly abused segment of society, and also introduced a new standard of hygiene and humanity to nineteenth-century American medicine. The odds were heavily against her in both endeavors, and there was nothing in her early life to suggest that she would make any impact on the world. Indeed, there was much that portended a brief life as an invalid. Yet she proved herself a force of nature, so fierce in her determination that friends and enemies alike called her "Dragon Dix."

Born in Hampden, Maine, Dorothea Dix soon moved with her family to Worcester, Massachusetts. Both of her parents traced their lineage to the founding of the Massachusetts Bay Colony in the seventeenth century. Dorothea's father, Joseph Dix, was an itinerant Methodist minister. Like his wife, Mary Bigelow, he was an alcoholic. Where Mary was feckless and negligent, Joseph was violently abusive. When she turned twelve, Dorothea decided that she could take her hellish home life no more. She fled to Boston and the house of her grandmother, Dorothea Lynde, for whom she was named, and her grandfather, Dr. Elijah Dix, a physician.

Young Dorothea's grandparents had the means and the generosity to take the girl in. While still living with them, the nineteen-year-old started a school, which attracted the children of wealthy Bostonians. Dix took to teaching with a passion—but instructing the well-to-do left her wanting to do more. In her spare time, she took in neglected and impoverished students, whom she taught in an improvised schoolroom set up in a barn on her grandmother's property.

Young Dorothea Dix worked to exhaustion. Her health was frail, and she suffered from increasingly severe and frequent spells of profound depression, which exacerbated a growing list of physical ailments. She soon retreated from active teaching to the privacy of her room. There she began writing religious books and children's stories, which occupied much of her time between 1824 and 1830. Among her works was one best seller, *Conversations on Common Things*, first published in 1824 and appearing in a *sixtieth* edition in 1869. She also turned out a dictionary of flowers titled *The Garland of Flora* in 1829. Her breakthrough publication, *Prisons and Prison Discipline*, would not come until 1845.

During her long spell of ill health, Dix supplemented her writing income with a position as governess for the family of the country's most celebrated Unitarian preacher: William Ellery Channing. She traveled with the Channing family on a tour of St. Croix in the Caribbean, where she had her first glimpse of slavery. The experience created a deep impression, and she became a committed abolitionist.

Dix's stint as a governess seemed to restore her health, and in 1831 she opened a girls' school in Boston. Five years later, however, in 1836, she was swept by another wave of despair, depression, and illness. This being the Victorian age, when most physicians believed the sovereign cure for just about any ailment was travel, Dix's physicians recommended a European tour. If the doctors envisioned a span of relaxation for her, however, they were very much mistaken. On the trip, she met a group of social reformers. Elizabeth Fry, Samuel Tuke, and William Rathbone were advocates for the rights of the "feebleminded" and the "insane." They espoused the radical position that those afflicted with mental illness should be granted rights equal to those of any other person. Rathbone invited Dorothea to stay as a guest at Greenbank, his family's ancestral seat in Liverpool. As Quakers, the Rathbones were all ardent social activists, and Greenbank was always alive with visiting reformers, most of whom held to the socialist doctrine that government had a duty to ensure the economic and social welfare of its citizens. Of special interest to the Rathbones was an issue referred to before the mid-nineteenth century as "lunacy reform." It is through the Rathbone family and their circle that Dix was made aware of the horrific conditions in asylums in England. She was privy to the studies the Rathbone circle made of English and Scottish asylums, even before they were published and debated in the House of Commons.

• • •

After her return to the United States in 1840, Dorothea Dix volunteered to teach a Sunday school class at the East Cambridge, Massachusetts, jail. In this squalid prison, she found her calling. Appalled by the primitive, brutal treatment of prisoners—especially those suffering from mental illness—Dix set out on a mission of reform. It began with her own one-woman fact-finding investigation into how the indigent mentally ill were treated throughout Massachusetts. She found that most towns simply contracted with local people willing to provide the service, requiring neither credentials nor evidence of competence. The result was predictable: underfunded care and mistreatment of the persons entrusted to the contractors' custody. Fraud and corruption were rampant. Dix wrote a report to the Massachusetts legislature, which was widely published. She described how "Insane Persons [were] confined . . . in cages, stalls, pens! Chained, naked, beaten with rods, and lashed into obedience."

To Dix's immense satisfaction, her "Memorial to the Legislature of Massachusetts," a comprehensive report on the treatment of the mentally ill in that state, moved passage of a bill to expand the state mental hospital in Worcester. The report also made Dix a national celebrity. She used her notoriety in 1844 to launch an investigation into similar conditions in New Jersey. She took it upon herself to visit every almshouse and jail in the state—New Jersey having no state hospital for the indigent mentally ill at the time.

Dix was meticulous in compiling facts; but, even more, she was a keen and coolly empathetic observer. She wrote of human beings, not of mere statistics. Her description of an inmate confined to a cot in the basement of one New Jersey county almshouse is typical: a "feeble and depressed old man, a pauper, helpless, lonely, and yet conscious of surrounding circumstances, and not now wholly oblivious of the past." She asked: "This feeble old man, who was he?" The passage, typical of many in her reports, would have been affecting in itself, but Dix had taken time to answer her own question *before* she published the example. She knew that the old "pauper" had been a distinguished New Jersey jurist, now fallen on hard times in his old age. She knew that many of the state's legislators knew this man, and she was not above shaming them into action. In March 1845, the New Jersey legislature appropriated funding to build the state's very first public facility to house and treat the indigent mentally ill.

Between 1844 and 1852, Dix toured more states, including New Hampshire, Rhode Island, Louisiana, Illinois, North Carolina, and Pennsylvania. In 1853, her efforts led to the building of the first public mental hospital in Pennsylvania. Her efforts often moved legislators to build new facilities or to expand and modernize existing institutions. In fourteen states, she helped pass reform legislation to provide what she described as "moral treatment" for the mentally ill, defining this as treatment that promoted three values—modesty, chastity, and delicacy. Among the most basic reforms Dix advocated were the separation of mentally ill persons from the general prison population and the humane incarceration of the mentally ill, without ropes, chains, or the other prevalent and primitive methods of restraint and control.

Her work at the county and state levels was innovative, but in her appeal to the federal government she was downright disruptive. In the 1850s, there was strong opposition to federal appropriation for anything resembling "welfare" programs. These were considered the province of private philanthropy, religiously funded charities, and local and state initiatives. Dix promoted a Bill for the Benefit of the Indigent Insane, which got around the issue of cash appropriation by using something the federal government had in abundance: public lands. The bill set aside 12,225,000 acres for sale, the proceeds of which were to be distributed to the states for the benefit of the mentally ill—with some portion also benefitting the blind and deaf. Congress responded with passage in both houses, but President Franklin Pierce refused to sign the legislation, arguing that he did not want to set a precedent for federal financing of social welfare projects. Congress lacked the votes to override his veto.

Staggered by this blow, Dix did what she had done as a young woman when illness and depression assailed her: she traveled to Europe. This time, she made no pretense of a pleasure tour, but instead undertook to investigate conditions in mental hospitals and institutions in Scotland, the Channel Islands, and throughout the Continent. The Methodist Dix even gained an audience with Pope Pius IX, who, at her urging, visited the asylums in and around Rome and was duly shocked at conditions in them. He publicly endorsed her work.

● ● ●

Despite President Pierce's shortsightedness where federal involvement with welfare expenditures was concerned, Dorothea Dix had successfully involved local and state government in the struggle to bring humanity to the treatment of the mentally ill. Her work also launched a dialogue about the proper role of government in promoting the welfare of its citizens, a dialogue that continues to this day, often in rancorous tones.

In 1861, with the outbreak of the American Civil War, Dix confronted a new problem. Most immediately, it was how to provide a decent level of medical care for the overwhelming number of wounded the war was producing every day. More generally, it was how to reconcile the values of civilized society with warfare.

In Europe, the Crimean War (1853–1856) had already revealed the appalling inability of the British military to care for those wounded in battle. In that theater of conflict, it was a woman, Florence Nightingale, who not only brought professional nursing into the war, but who cast a glaring light on the neglect and abuse of wounded and sick soldiers, effectively shaming the government into action. The Crimean War introduced a new class of weaponry into warfare, firearms and artillery produced on an industrial scale. The American Civil War (1861–1865) brought that industrialized warfare to a far more devastating level. The rifle-musket and the minié ball (precursor of the modern rifle round), dramatic improvements in the destructiveness of artillery and ammunition, the emergence of iron warships and their vastly more destructive firepower, all ratcheted up the ruin.

The technology of devastation outstripped the progress of medical science, which lagged far behind in its capacity to repair flesh torn and bones shattered by iron, lead, and high explosives. The Civil War produced a volume and severity of wounds that even the most experienced military surgeons had never imagined. Rapid amputation was virtually the only treatment available for wounds to extremities. Gut and head wounds were generally untreatable and therefore almost invariably fatal.

A minority of those wounded were taken to poorly equipped field hospitals. Most were treated at so-called dressing stations, which were far more rudimentary. If a soldier survived amputation, the odds were very high that, in an era before the germ theory of disease was fully understood, he would later succumb to infection. There was a great need for medical volunteers with the courage to stand up to such grueling sights. Already famous as a tireless crusader for the humane treatment of the mentally ill, Dix secured an appointment as Superintendent of Women Nurses for the Union Army. In this post, she created the basis of what would become the U.S. Army Nursing Corps.

In the days of high Victorian morality, because medical work brought them into intimate contact with any number of men, female nurses were typically regarded as little better than prostitutes. The army had long employed untrained male nurses. Convinced that women naturally made better nurses than men, Dix set about recruiting women of impeccable moral character, strength of mind, and sternness of will. Determined and deliberately overbearing, she ruled her nursing corps with an iron hand. Despite her own bouts of depression and ill health, she presented an unassailable exterior, and the men with whom she worked, from generals down to privates, took to calling her "Dragon Dix." Her demeanor made enemies of some and created resentment among others, but she not only eased unspeakable suffering and saved untold lives, she created a legacy that made the profession of female nursing both respectable and respected.

Indefatigable, Dix was everywhere in the war—in the front lines and the rear-echelon hospitals. She supervised all recruitment and training personally, and she did so with an absolute genius for combining high moral purpose with unglamorous, practical effectiveness. She was careful to discourage her nurses from romanticizing or sentimentalizing their work. She demanded both a strong attitude of compassion and a high level of basic sanitation. Both, she was convinced, were essential to ameliorating suffering and preventing death from post-traumatic infections.

Like Florence Nightingale in Europe and fellow Civil War nurse Clara Barton, Dix's example inspired a higher level of medical treatment for soldiers. It also influenced an ongoing movement to bring a degree of humanity to warfare, with the series of Geneva Conventions in the twentieth century drawing their inspiration from her work.

During and immediately after the Civil War, Dix established thirty-two hospitals in the United States and influenced the creation of others internationally. Her antebellum work to bring compassion to the treatment of the mentally ill extended to a campaign to improve the treatment of prisoners and the disabled, including the many permanently disabled by war wounds. After the war, she personally toured the South in the immediate aftermath of the war and reported comprehensively on the damage to the region's prisons, hospitals, and asylums.

Among the hospitals Dix founded was New Jersey's Trenton State Hospital, where she herself took up residence in 1881. By this time, she was ill and all but spent, a semi-invalid. The grateful state had established a suite in the hospital for her to use as long as she might live, and from this facility she spent the last six years of her life corresponding with politicians, administrators, and citizen activists in the United States, England, Japan, and elsewhere. She died on July 17, 1887.

DISRUPTION:
DEFINING THE RELATION
OF CAPITAL TO LABOR
AS IMMORAL, UNJUST,
AND DYSFUNCTIONAL,
THEREBY SETTING
THE STAGE FOR
THE COMMUNIST
REVOLUTIONS OF THE
TWENTIETH CENTURY

KARL MARX

(1818–1883)

At the funeral of Karl Marx, who died on March 14, 1883, poor and mostly forgotten, his friend and collaborator Friedrich Engels (1820–1895), coauthor with Marx of *The Communist Manifesto,* delivered a eulogy. It is a fair statement of what would prove to be the magnitude of this economist-philosopher's disruptive transformation of social thought. "Just as Darwin discovered the law of development of organic nature," Engels told mourners, "so Marx discovered the law of development of human history: the simple fact, hitherto concealed by an overgrowth of ideology, that mankind must first of all eat, drink, have shelter and clothing, before it can pursue politics, science, art, religion, etc.; that therefore the production of the immediate material means, and consequently the degree of economic development attained by a given people or during a given epoch, form the foundation upon which the state institutions, the legal conceptions, art, and even the ideas on religion, of the people concerned have been evolved, and in the light of which they must, therefore, be explained, instead of vice versa, as had hitherto been the case."

t is significant that Engels compared Marx to Charles Darwin, who explained biological evolution. Engels went even farther, effectively comparing Marx to Isaac Newton. Like Newton, Marx "discovered the special law of motion," a law "governing the present-day capitalist mode of production, and the bourgeois society that this mode of production has created." Engels was specifically referring to the concept of "surplus value," which Marx defined as the increase in the value of capital that results when workers add their labor to it. This "surplus value" is commonly called *profit*, and it is entirely appropriated by the capitalist when the products of labor are sold. In societies in which capitalists own the means of production, workers are exploited by being deprived of any share of the surplus value they create. Thus, the foundation of capitalist civilization is theft and therefore inherently corrupt.

Engels celebrated Marx as a scientist, but pointed out that "Science was for Marx a historically dynamic, revolutionary force" and "Marx was before all else a revolutionist." While he took "great joy" in his scientific discoveries, his "real mission . . . was to contribute . . . to the overthrow of capitalist society and of the state institutions which it had brought into being, to contribute to the liberation of the modern proletariat, which he was the first to make conscious of its own position and its needs, conscious of the conditions of its emancipation."

Marx founded the International Working Men's Association and laid the ideological foundation of communism, which argued for an end to nations and nationalities and the beginning of a global union based on the common value of labor. For this, Engels told his fellow mourners, Marx "was the best hated and most calumniated man of his time. Governments, both absolutist and republican, deported him from their territories. Bourgeois, whether conservative or ultra-democratic, vied with one another in heaping slanders upon him. All this he brushed aside as though it were a cobweb, ignoring it, answering only when extreme necessity compelled him. . . . His name will endure through the ages, and so also will his work."

* * *

Karl Heinrich Marx was born on May 5, 1818, into the kind of family he would later deride as *bourgeois* (comfortably middle class), in the German town of Trier. Although both his mother and father were descended from rabbis, his father, Heinrich (born Herschel) allowed himself to be baptized a Lutheran to avoid losing his position as a prominent attorney. At seventeen, Marx began to follow in his father's footsteps by enrolling in the Faculty of Law at the University of Bonn. He also took a step toward a bourgeois life by becoming engaged to Jenny von Westphalen, daughter of Baron von Westphalen, who was highly placed in Trier society. Ironically, perhaps, it was the baron who directed young Marx to the works of Claude Henri de Rouvroy, comte de Saint-Simon (1760–1825), a political philosopher who foresaw a social evolution toward true equality based on a universal, international union of working people. With the support of his father, Marx left both the University of Bonn and the study of law for the more prestigious and academically oriented University of Berlin. Here, he became a disciple of the philosophy of Georg Wilhelm Friedrich Hegel (1770–1831), especially his analytical method of thesis, antithesis, and synthesis and his concept of the master-slave dialectic. Marx joined the Young Hegelian movement, which articulated a radical criticism of Christianity and, by extension, opposition to the Prussian autocracy.

Marx's identification with the Young Hegelians prevented his pursuing an academic career, since the Prussian government approved all university appointments, so Marx turned instead to journalism, becoming the editor, in October 1842, of the *Rheinische Zeitung*, a liberal newspaper based in Cologne. Refusing to compromise his views, he wrote articles that blatantly offended the Prussian government. Predictably, the government soon closed down the paper. This sent Marx in flight to Paris, where, shortly after his arrival at the end of 1843, he gravitated toward various organizations of expatriate German workers and French socialists. For a brief period, he edited the *Deutsch-Französische Jahrbücher*, which combined the interests of French socialists and radical German Hegelians. It was a rarefied group, which naturally limited the journal's paid readership. The enterprise quickly folded.

In Paris, Marx became a communist and, in his *Economic and Philosophical Manuscripts* of 1844 (unpublished until the 1930s), he hammered out a humanist version of communism that was based on contrasting the alienated nature of labor under capitalism with the engaged state of labor as it would be under communism. Marx argued that communism would leave people free to develop their nature in cooperative production. In Paris, he met Engels, with whom he would develop a lifelong friendship and intellectual collaboration.

By the end of 1844, Marx's radicalism had become unpalatable even for Paris, and the French government expelled him. He moved, with Engels, to Brussels, which remained his home base for the next three years—though he frequently visited England with Engels, whose family owned cotton mills in Manchester. In Brussels, Marx also turned to the study of history in the light of economic theory and Hegelian philosophy. This led him to develop "materialism." As explained in *The German Ideology* (which Marx composed at this time but that was published posthumously), materialism viewed history as being created by "the material conditions determining . . . production." Marx focused on the history of various modes of production through the ages and thus predicted the inevitable collapse of the currently prevailing mode, industrial capitalism, which would be replaced by communism.

In Brussels, he also joined the Communist League, which consisted of German expatriate workers. The League was centered in London, and Marx and Engels quickly became the driving intellectuals of the organization. When members convened in London at the end of 1847, they commissioned Marx and Engels to write a declaration of their organization's position. This was *The Communist Manifesto*, published in 1848, the very year in which all Europe was swept by a tidal wave of revolution, in part driven by Marx's journalism and intellectual presence.

● ● ●

Revolution was the environment in which Marx thrived. He moved back to Paris and then returned to Germany, where he founded, again in Cologne, the *Neue Rheinische Zeitung*, which took a radical democratic line against the Prussian autocracy. Predictably, the new paper was soon suppressed and, to escape arrest, Marx fled to London in May 1849. This was the commencement of what he deemed a lifetime of exile.

From London, Marx predicted that the recently suppressed fires of revolution would soon rekindle, and he wanted to play a leading part in the conflagration. He rejoined the Communist League and wrote two long pamphlets on the 1848 revolution in France and its aftermath, *The Class Struggles in France* and *The 18th Brumaire of Louis Bonaparte*. All that was required to reignite wholesale revolution, he wrote, was some new crisis. While he waited for it, he and his family, which at the time included his wife, Jenny, and their four children, lived in poverty in London's Soho. Engels was Marx's chief source of income—which put both communists in an ideologically uncomfortable position. Engels worked ruthlessly to increase the revenue produced from the family business in Manchester. He was, in fact, a capitalist. Marx did manage to steadily supplement his income by writing weekly articles as a foreign correspondent for the *New York Daily Tribune*.

In the meantime, he labored on a study of political economy, largely in an effort to articulate the nature of the coming crisis. The deeper he delved, the more voluminous the work became. In 1857, he halted, having produced a manuscript of 800 pages, which he called the *Grundrisse* ("Outlines") of a projected study of the nature of capital, real property, wage labor, the state, foreign trade, and the world market. He laid the *Grundrisse* aside (it would not be published until 1941) and turned instead to writing *Theories of Surplus Value*, a three-volume tome reviewing the major authors of what was at the time called "political econ-omy" and is today more simply called economics. The two most extensive anal-yses in this book were devoted to the Scottish apostle of capitalist economic theory, Adam Smith (1723–1790), and David Ricardo (1772–1823), one of the founders of classical economics.

At last, in 1867, Marx returned to the material in *Grundrisse* and wrote vol-ume one of *Das Kapital* (*Capital*). This would prove to be his masterpiece, a com-prehensive and upending analysis of the capitalist process of production. It was a work of materialist history. The next two volumes, which with the first comprised the complete book, were essentially finished during the 1860s, but Marx would not let them go. He tirelessly, obsessively made revisions. Left unpublished at his death, it was Engels who did the final editing and saw to their publication.

In *Capital*, Marx fully developed his analysis of the relationship of labor to capital and his theory of surplus value, which explained the historical oppression of the proletariat (working classes) by the bourgeoisie (capitalists). At the same time, however, *Capital* predicted the inevitability of the collapse of industrial capitalism due to the inescapable decline in the rate of profit built on surplus value. *Capital* was Marx's exploration of social conflict as the playing-out on the world stage of Hegel's process of *thesis* versus *antithesis*. What Marx saw as the crisis of this conflict, a crisis that history itself made inevitable, was the *synthesis* that would bring an end to industrial capitalism.

• • •

Three things had slowed Marx in creating his *Capital*. The first was the sheer ambition of the project, which was nothing less than providing the historical explanation for the economic structure of a complex modern society. The second was his poverty, which forced him to take on many other writing projects to keep his family afloat. The third was that he was never content merely to study and write.

Marx devoted a large amount of time and effort to the First International Workingmen's Association—or, more simply, the First International—to whose General Council he was elected when it was founded in 1864. This organization, he believed, gave the proletariat its best chance to reignite a successful revolution. But it was threatened from within by its own anarchist wing, led by the Russian founder of collectivist anarchism, Mikhail Bakunin (1814–1876). Marx led the struggle against this wing and prevailed. In 1872, having ousted Bakunin, he went on to support moving the headquarters of the General Council from Lon-don to New York, believing that social and political change would come more readily in the New World than in the Old. Instead, the move precipitated the rapid decline of the International. Nevertheless, Marx was able to witness the Paris Commune of 1871, in which the citizens of Paris rose up against the government, which had suffered a humiliating defeat in the Franco-Prussian War (1870–1871). The "communards" held the capital for two months before the Commune was crushed in bloody battle. Marx's stirring pamphlet *The Civil War in France* briefly injected fresh life into the International, but the ray of hope proved fleeting.

• • •

Marx was plagued by declining health from the 1870s on. Sustained composition became burdensome and then simply impossible. He lacked the strength to combat some of his major followers, who now opposed revolution and instead proposed compromise in the form of the mild socialism some liberal European states permitted and even favored. Marx did not fade into irrelevance, but he did diminish as a presence. Others picked up the revolutionary cause in his name; but, in attempting to create a comprehensive system of governing philosophy under the banner of dialectical materialism—by its nature a dynamic ideology rather than a settled governing philosophy—they damaged the theoretical foundation Marx had laid. (And, in fact, *dialectical materialism* isn't Marx's term at all, but was coined in 1887 by Joseph Dietzgen.)

Without question, Marx's approach to history has been a powerful influence on how history is written, studied, and thought about to this day. Economic factors are now at the heart of modern academic history, political science, and sociology—thanks largely to Marx. But perhaps the most compelling gauge of the disruption created by this rebellious thinker's work is the fact that, until as recently as the end of the twentieth century, half of the world lived under governments claiming to be "Marxist."

USHERING IN THE AGE OF THE PROGRESSIVE JOURNALIST, WHO USED THE POWER OF THE PRESS TO PIT DEMOCRACY AGAINST THE SOCIAL INJUSTICES WROUGHT BY THE EXCESSES OF INDUSTRIALIZED CAPITALISM

JACOB A. RIIS
(1849–1914)

The closing quarter of the nineteenth century and the first decade of the twentieth in the United States are often called the "Gilded Age." It was a name Mark Twain and Charles Dudley Warner coined for the period in the title of their 1873 satirical novel, *The Gilded Age*. These years were a period of American economic expansion, explosive growth of the nation's cities, and great American optimism and opulence. Yet, as the historian Sean Cashman wrote, "Throughout the Gilded Age, the specters of poverty and oppression waited on the banquet of expansion and opportunity."

t was an era with an insatiable demand for labor, so long as that labor was dirt-cheap. As economic historian Clarence Long noted, the mean hourly wage of male factory workers, age sixteen and older, was 16 cents in 1890, with a low of 11 cents for cotton-mill workers and a high of 29 cents in the printing industry. Such wages ensured that unskilled and even semiskilled labor would always be the working poor, consigned to industrial shantytown slums and, in the largest cities, to tenements that were nothing more than miserable warehouses for human beings.

During the closing quarter of the nineteenth century, New York City spawned more tenements and tenement slums than anywhere else in the nation. It was New York that attracted a massive influx of immigrants looking to the United States for a better life than they could find in the Old World. On balance, many achieved their dream, but many also were consigned to the squalor of neighborhoods packed with badly overcrowded, ill-lit, and suffocatingly narrow apartment buildings. By 1900, some 2.3 million people—two-thirds of New York City's population—lived in such places.

Life in the tenement slums was both grim and dangerous. But as the demand for cheap labor increased, so did the immigration of Europe's poorest people, and the tenements were continuously occupied. The city's middle and upper classes avoided the Lower East Side of Manhattan, turning a blind eye to conditions there—until 1890, when a journalist named Jacob August Riis published *How the Other Half Lives*, an exquisitely detailed, eloquently reported exposé of life in the slums of New York.

The remarkable documentary narrative quoted extensively from the slum-dwellers themselves, thus giving them a voice hitherto seldom heard. It was accompanied by Riis's own stark photographs, which illuminated the darkest corners of tenement life using the harsh light of flash powder. The Victorian approach to social injustice, poverty, and suffering was often softened with romantic sentimentalism, whether the subject was the slums of London or those of New York. Riis purged the sentimental, presenting instead the naked truth with a hard-edged compassion born of painful objectivity.

* * *

Jacob Riis was himself an immigrant. He was born in Ribe, Denmark, one in a family of fifteen children of Niels Edward Riis, a schoolteacher who also wrote part time for the local newspaper, and Carolina Riis, a homemaker. The desperately poor conditions in Riis's Denmark can be gauged by the fact that only three of the Riis children, including Jacob, survived to witness the opening of the twentieth century.

Jacob's father saw his son as a talented writer and urged him to develop and pursue a literary career, but Jacob, seeing the poverty all about him, apprenticed himself to a carpenter instead. When the father of the girl he loved rejected him as a prospective son-in-law, the twenty-one-year-old Riis immigrated to the United States in 1870. For the next seven years, he scraped and scrambled to make it as a carpenter. For long stretches, he was close to starvation—even though he was actually a very good carpenter.

Frustrated, he finally wandered back toward the path his father had wanted for him. Riis found freelance work writing occasional news stories and was able to cobble together a small amount of cash along with a wad of promissory notes, which bought him a bankrupt weekly newspaper. He made a go of it before selling the enterprise at a handsome profit. He used the funds to return to Denmark, where the young woman, whose father had rejected him years earlier, now accepted his proposal of marriage. Riis brought his bride back to New York, where he briefly worked for a Brooklyn paper before joining the staff of the *New-York Tribune* in 1877.

He was assigned as a police reporter and given a desk in a dingy press office on Mulberry Street across from police headquarters. Savvy New Yorkers called Mulberry Street "Death's Thoroughfare." It was the heart of the Lower East Side immigrant slums and a beat with rarely a dull moment. Riis walked the streets of this district relentlessly, especially between the hours of two and four in the morning, determined, as he said, to catch the neighborhood "off its guard." He was, in effect, a voyeur with a social conscience, gliding noiselessly in the godless hours through places like Bandits' Roost, Bottle Alley, Bone Alley, Thieves' Alley, and Kerosene Row.

Riis prowled and reported his beat for years. As the 1880s approached their close, he recognized that the nation, now in the gathering throes of Progressivism, was ready to see what he saw. A new crop of social activists and politicians was bent on improving American civilization, including the lot of the immigrant, and Riis had good reason to believe that the stories around him could earn a place on something other than a police blotter. The message he wanted to deliver was that the Lower East Side "was not fit for Christian men and women, let alone innocent children, to live in, and therefore it had to go."

He took up the pencil and camera that had served him so well as a newspaper reporter, and he used them, all with his journalist's nose for a compelling story, to systematically document the district he had known intimately for more than a decade. He believed that what most broke his heart would break the hearts of his readers as well, and so he focused most sharply on the children of the neighborhood. The book he published in 1890, *How the Other Half Lives*, billed as a document of New York City tenement life, is mostly a book about the doomed children of the Gilded Age slums. He wrote:

> A little fellow who seemed clad in but a single rag was among the
> flotsam and jetsam stranded at Police Headquarters one day last
> summer. No one knew where he came from or where he belonged.
> The boy himself knew as little about it as anybody, and was the least

anxious to have light shed on the subject after he had spent a night in the matron's nursery. . . . . He sang "McGinty" all through, with Tenth Avenue variations, for the police, then settled down to the serious business of giving an account of himself. The examination went on after this fashion:

"Where do you go to church, my boy?"

"We don't have no clothes to go to church." And indeed his appearance, as he was, in the door of any New York church would have caused a sensation.

"Well, where do you go to school, then?"

"I don't go to school," with a snort of contempt.

"Where do you buy your bread?"

"We don't buy bread; we buy beer," said the boy, and it was eventually the saloon that led the police as a landmark to his "home." It was worthy of the boy. As he had said, his only bed was a heap of dirty straw on the floor, his daily diet a crust in the morning, nothing else.

How the Other Half Lives was a bestseller. No less a Progressive than Theodore Roosevelt hailed it as "an enlightenment and an inspiration." It not only exposed slum conditions in New York but also alerted the entire nation to such conditions elsewhere. No one who read the book and looked at its photographs could any longer claim ignorance of the misery of "the other half."

How the Other Half Lives inaugurated programs of slum clearance throughout urban America. It was almost as if a switch had been thrown. Before Riis's book, there had been no concerted efforts to clear the slums. Riis was but one of a small legion of Progressive writers who appealed to the conscience of the Gilded Age. Collectively, they were called the "muckrakers," a word adopted by Theodore Roosevelt from John Bunyan's seventeenth-century allegory, *The Pilgrim's Progress*, which portrayed a man armed with a "muck-rake" to sweep up the filth around him while he remained unaware of the celestial glory above his head. American muckraking was born from the marriage of the Progressive movement and the professionalization of journalism.

Following the muckraking trail that Riis had blazed was Upton Sinclair, whose 1906 novel *The Jungle* told the story of Jurgis Rudkus, a Lithuanian immigrant who worked in a Chicago meatpacking plant. Rudkus represented the plight of millions of immigrants, who were soft targets for exploitation by employers, policemen, and others with power. Sinclair described Rudkus's workplace in nauseating detail, including, among other things, the big meatpackers' use of tubercular beef and the grinding up of rats. Six months after the novel's publication, Congress passed the Pure Food and Drug Act and a Meat Inspection Act.

Other Riis-esque muckrakers included Ida Tarbell, who exposed the evils of industrial monopoly in her *History of the Standard Oil Company* (1904), and Lincoln Steffens, whose *Shame of the Cities* (1904) reported on the machinations of the nation's corrupt urban political machines. These and others issued unblinking reports on business corruption, political skullduggery, child labor, slum conditions, racial discrimination, prostitution, sweatshop labor, insurance fraud, and illegal stock manipulations. Together, they disrupted business-as-usual, creating real, documented, and measurable change in American society. They did not tear down American capitalism, but did their best to saddle it with a conscience.

DISRUPTION:
USING NONVIOLENT
RESISTANCE BASED
ON PUBLIC SELF-
SUFFERING TO DEPRIVE
OPPRESSIVE LEADERS
AND REGIMES OF ALL
POWER AND THEREBY
EFFECT PROFOUND
SOCIAL CHANGE

MOHANDAS GANDHI
(1869–1948)

"Generations to come will scarce believe that such a one as this ever in flesh and blood walked upon this earth," Albert Einstein wrote of Mohandas Gandhi. The reality-redefining physicist could barely comprehend and only wonder at how a human being would so willingly embrace self-suffering rather than inflict suffering on another, no matter how oppressive that other was. Even more wonderful, in Einstein's eyes, was Gandhi's avowed expectation—the fulfilled expectation—that self-suffering was the ultimate weapon against tyranny.

As Einstein's classic equation $E=mc^2$ was the most elegantly simple expression of nature ever devised, so Gandhi's method of creating social change was as simple in concept as it was difficult in execution. Through self-suffering, one human being can end some degree of injustice and oppression. It was an act of faith, but not merely of faith, for it was based on a logical understanding of motivation and political, social, and economic action. You cannot prevent another from causing you pain. If, however, you possess the courage to endure the pain that comes with refusing to yield to tyranny, you defeat the tyrant by rendering impotent the only weapon the tyrant possesses: coercion. It is a concept both simple and awesome to contemplate.

• • •

Mohandas Karamchand Gandhi was born on October 2, 1869, in the coastal town of Porbandar, now a part of Gujarat, which borders Pakistan to the northwest and the Indian state of Rajasthan to the north and northeast. He was the youngest child of Hindu parents. His father, like *his* father before him, served as a *diwan* of Porbandar state, a liaison between the prince of Porbandar and the British government's political agent (chief colonial administrative officer). Young Mohandas grew up greatly admiring his father's practical political wisdom, his talent for resolving conflict, and his personal courage as a social leader. In Karamchand Gandhi, he saw a selfless public servant. In his mother, Putlibai, Mohandas saw an example of religious devotion and spiritual willpower. She was a follower of Jainism, a Hindu sect committed to nonviolence and vegetarianism—since killing animals was an unacceptable act of violence against the sacredness of life.

Mohandas Gandhi attended primary school and high school, and in 1883 he was married to Kasturba (whom Gandhi affectionately called "Ba") in a traditional Hindu arranged marriage. The couple's early life together was often tumultuous, and Gandhi came to regret his vain efforts to compel Kasturba to conform to his will. He became persuaded that voluntary obedience was the only valid and viable form of compliance. The Gandhis would have five sons, of whom all but one lived to adulthood.

In 1887, Gandhi enrolled in Samaldas College in Bhavnagar, Gujarat, but left after a single term for England to study law. The decision resulted in Gandhi's excommunication from his caste, which forbade overseas travel. Craving acceptance by English society, young Gandhi began to dress and behave in emulation of an "English gentleman," even though his circle of English friends consisted of people who held unconventional, even radical ideas. Before long, he rejected his worship of all things English and reasserted his Indian identity. In 1891, he qualified as a barrister and returned to India—only to discover that his London training had not adequately prepared him for a career in Indian law. He accepted a job offer from an Indian firm in South Africa and, in April 1893, once again left his native land, this time with his young family.

Gandhi discovered that the small South African Indian community was intensively oppressed by the white majority, which regarded Indians as nothing more than a source of cheap manual labor. Heavily taxed, Indians were nevertheless denied the rights of citizens, including the right to vote. Racial discrimination was pervasive, and in May 1893, while traveling by train from Durban to Pretoria to prosecute a lawsuit for a Muslim client, Gandhi was forced out of the first-class compartment for which he held a ticket. When the guard (conductor) told him he had to go to a third-class van, Gandhi protested: "But I have a first-class ticket." The guard repeated his demand and threatened to "call a police constable to push you out."

It was at this point that Gandhi uttered words that changed his life.

"Yes," he replied, "you may. I refuse to get out voluntarily."

He had discovered nonviolent "passive resistance."

As a result of this incident—the police ejected him from the train, but he was not forced to "get out voluntarily"—Gandhi resolved to lead the Indian community in a campaign to transform the South African government and society. He met with local Indian community leaders and proposed forming an association to win rights. He organized laborers and sympathizers in passive resistance campaigns and founded the Natal Indian Congress to coordinate the movement. When, in the course of this work, a white mob nearly beat him to death, Gandhi responded by publicly forgiving his attackers. In 1903, he started a journal, *Indian Opinion*, and in 1904 he founded the Phoenix commune on three principles: that the good of the individual is contained in the good of all; that all work is equally valuable; and that only a life of labor is worth living. In 1907, he mounted a nonviolent campaign to overturn the newly passed Transvaal Asiatic Registration Act (TARA), a South African law requiring Indians living in the Transvaal to be fingerprinted and issued government registration certificates. He called the protest a "satyagraha campaign," using a Hindu word meaning "quest for truth." The campaign employed nonviolent civil disobedience to compel change: the entire South African Indian community refused to obey the registration law. The resisters were jailed, soon creating so great a burden on South African prisons that General Jan Smuts, the nation's premier, repealed the registration law in exchange for voluntary submission to registration. When Smuts subsequently reneged, Gandhi led public burnings of the voluntary registration certificates and encouraged illegal crossings of the Transvaal border.

Securing 1,100 acres outside of Johannesburg, Gandhi founded Tolstoy Farm, a communal center of resistance and self-sufficiency. On the morning of November 6, 1913, in protest of a tax imposed on Indians, he led a "Great March" of

2,200 men and women in a mass illegal border crossing. There were arrests and incarcerations, but the world was watching the movement Gandhi had begun and, under international pressure, Smuts repealed the tax and relaxed the immigration laws.

* * *

Having emerged as a remarkable leader of change in South Africa, Gandhi returned to India after twenty-one years. In May 1915 he founded the Satyagraha Ashram. Two years later, he embarked on his first Indian satyagraha campaign to liberate the indigo tenant farmers of Champaran (a district in northern Bihar) from oppression by their planter landlords. He was arrested and summoned to court to answer charges. He offered no defense but admitted his guilt, explaining that his obedience was to a higher law of conscience. The case was dropped, and Gandhi traveled throughout the district taking down stories of hardship from farmers. This moved the government to appoint a committee of inquiry in June 1917, and, in the end, the landlord planters were ordered to make restitution to their tenant farmers.

Gandhi conducted more satyagraha campaigns. While leading a textile-mill strike in 1918, he introduced the fast as a means of applying moral pressure on the mill owners to accept arbitration. The owners did not want to be responsible for the self-starvation of Gandhi, so they agreed to binding arbitration, which resulted in a substantial wage increase. Gandhi applied satyagraha to other campaigns, and soon the Indian peasants were awakened to the power of mass civil disobedience. This prompted the British government, early in 1919, to pass the Rowlatt Acts, which criminalized the possession of any antigovernment document with the "intention" to circulate it. The satyagraha Gandhi led against the law swept up all of India, and the country effectively ground to a halt in a general strike, protest, and boycott. Colonial officials arrested Gandhi. Against his will, violence erupted in response; however, the protests also managed to unite Muslims and Hindus for a common purpose.

Gandhi's satisfaction in this result was short-lived. On April 13, 1919, British general Reginald Dyer attacked a mass meeting of some ten thousand in Amritsar at the Jallianwala Bagh, a public space of seven acres enclosed by a wall through which there were just five exits. Two British armored cars, each with machine guns, opened fire on the protesters, killing more than a thousand Indians in ten minutes. At the next meeting of the Indian National Congress, Gandhi called for a new round of nonviolent resistance, including the revival of traditional Indian hand spinning and weaving as alternatives to importing British cloth. The boycott was economically devastating to the British textile industry.

Soon also, the British government broke its pledge to support the Ottoman sultan of Turkey against the republican revolution seeking to overthrow him. Indian Muslims saw any contribution to the sultan's overthrow as an attack on Islam. Gandhi rallied Indian Hindus to join in supporting the nation's Muslims and proposed what he called "non-cooperation" with the British government—a massive program of nonviolent civil disobedience that amounted to a large-scale boycott of British laws, institutions, mercantile concerns, and import merchandise. With this, Gandhi led India to turn its back on Britain—the first step toward *swaraj*, or home rule for India. The *swaraj* movement called for renunciation of all titles and honors conferred by the British government and a total boycott of law courts, educational institutions, councils, elections, imported merchandise (especially foreign cloth), and all functions of government. If Britain had no one to rule in India, it could not rule India. Gandhi promoted a program of Indian national education and Indian home industries, especially the spinning and weaving of homespun cloth.

As noncooperation swept the nation, Indians in 1921 bestowed on Gandhi the title of Mahatma—roughly, "Great Soul"—and he was widely worshipped as a quasi-messiah. The government responded with mass arrests, which only inflamed India. As violence broke out, Gandhi appealed to the Congress to suspend the campaign. He himself was arrested, tried, and sentenced to six years' imprisonment for sedition, but released in 1924 for an appendectomy. With the country still roiled by violence, he fasted for three weeks in a bid to restore nonviolence. He launched a new satyagraha in 1928, protesting a sharp increase in land taxes with an expanded anti-British boycott. Indian officials resigned en masse, so severely crippling the colonial government that officials released political prisoners, returned seized lands, and compensated individuals for other property loss. Gandhi believed the time was now ripe for the "Salt satyagraha."

After the British viceroy rejected his demands for self-government, Gandhi decided to attack the salt law, which taxed salt—a staple of rich and poor alike—and outlawed the manufacture of one's own salt as well as the purchase of untaxed domestic salt. On March 12, 1930, in a demonstration extensively covered by the international press, Gandhi led a 240-mile march to the sea, where he intended to break the law by "making salt"—gathering the natural sea salt that had crystallized under the sun on the beach. When Gandhi reached the ocean and picked up a fistful of salty mud on April 6, Indians began making and selling illegal salt everywhere. Although Gandhi and others were arrested, international pressure moved the viceroy to repeal the salt tax and other repressive measures.

● ● ●

Mahatma Gandhi was now one of the most famous men in the world. He went to London to attend the Round Table Conference of 1931 as the representative of the Indian National Congress. He visited the English textile workers, who were hard-pressed by the Indian boycott, yet who expressed enthusiastic solidarity with Gandhi's movement. No sooner did the world-famous Gandhi return to India, however, than he discovered that the government had arrested his movement's key leaders. When Gandhi protested to the viceroy, he himself was arrested and the Indian National Congress declared illegal. As the British endeavored to create division among the Hindus by making the segregation of the lower from the upper castes a matter of colonial law, Gandhi announced from prison a "fast unto death" beginning on September 20, 1932. The fast succeeded in uniting the Hindus against the segregation. This persuaded Gandhi, weak and near death, to break his fast.

The outbreak of World War II in September 1939 brought a new crisis. Britain took India into the war without even consulting Indian leaders. Gandhi launched a civil disobedience campaign against the curtailment of freedom in wartime; but when Japan joined World War II in December 1941, posing an immediate threat to India, the British proposed granting India dominion status, which would give the individual Indian states and provinces the authority to secede from the empire after the war. Gandhi saw this as an attempt to dismember India, and the Congress rejected it, passing instead a "Quit India" resolution on August 8, 1942, setting total and complete independence as its objective. Gandhi and other Congress leaders were jailed, and, absent his direct leadership, the independence movement became violent.

While both Gandhi and his wife, Kasturba, were in prison, Kasturba died from pneumonia on February 22, 1942. In deep despair, Gandhi suffered a decline in his own health, which alarmed his jailers, who released him in May. The end of World War II in September 1945 brought the Labour Party to power in Britain, and the liberalized government began to cooperate with Gandhi and the Congress to work out terms of independence. The British wanted to partition India into three provincial groups, one dominated by a Hindu majority, the other two by Muslim majorities. Gandhi was adamant against dismembering the nation. The dispute between the Hindus and the Muslims grew violent, even as Gandhi walked from house to house in Calcutta barefoot, to talk and to listen to both sides, desperate to reconcile them. At the very verge of independence, India was also on the brink of civil war. The Congress defied Gandhi by creating an independent Pakistan. While some celebrated independence on August 15, 1947, Gandhi embarked on a new "fast unto death" in a successful effort to restore peace between Calcutta's Hindus and Muslims.

Hindu extremists were horrified that, in the end, Gandhi served India and not the Hindus of India. He was denounced by the extremist fringe as a traitor. Various attempts were made on his life, including the detonation of a bomb at one of his regular prayer meetings. Gandhi, however, refused to allow the fear of death to deter him from working to unite Muslims and Hindus. At 5:10 in the afternoon on January 30, 1948, as he walked onto the lawn of Birla House, where he was living in New Delhi, to join about five hundred others in prayers, he was shot at point-blank range by Nathuram Vinayak Godse, a Hindu extremist. Although Mahatma Gandhi's Hindu supporters insisted that he died with "Hey Ram" (Oh God) on his lips, others present recalled only a sigh or perhaps the single syllable "Ah," which they interpreted as an expression of empathy for the state of humanity.

His end was tragic, but what Gandhi had achieved was real and momentous. Not only did his life of nonviolent resistance bring about the dismantling of the British Empire and signal a reversal of European imperialism generally, it inspired the many nonviolent leaders who followed him—most notably, in the United States, the Reverend Dr. Martin Luther King, Jr.

MARGARET SANGER

(1879–1966)

Disruptor is not a synonym for *hero*. Whatever disruptive innovations do *for* us, they almost always also do something *to* us. Many times, they challenge familiar concepts of morality, forcing us to weigh one set of rights and imperatives against another, and often—very often—make us uncomfortable.

I n an era of Progressive reform and the intense awakening of concern over women's rights, Margaret Sanger chose to advocate for a right unique to and basic for women, yet one that challenged long-held views of morality. Sanger opposed what she called "enforced motherhood" as "the most complete denial of a woman's right to life and liberty" and for that reason became an advocate of birth control. As her social philosophy developed, however, she came to see birth control as a way "to limit and discourage the over-fertility of the mentally and physically defective." As both creative destruction and destructive creation, social and moral disruption can be an ethically troubled process.

• • •

She was born Margaret Higgins in Corning, New York, on September 14, 1879, to a free-thinking Irish immigrant stonemason named Michael Hennessey Higgins and Anne Purcell Higgins, Michael's devoutly observant Roman Catholic Irish American wife. Her father's radicalism influenced Margaret more than her mother's piety. An even stronger influence was her having been born and raised one of eleven children, the bearing of whom, Margaret believed, contributed to her mother's early death.

Armed with her father's social iconoclasm and the cautionary tale she saw in her mother's life, Sanger was determined to avoid what she regarded as the twin traps of frequent pregnancy and poverty. Seeking an education, she attended Claverack College and Hudson River Institute. Seeking a profession outside the home, she enrolled at White Plains Hospital as a nurse probationer. Supporting herself as a practical nurse in the White Plains women's ward, she worked toward earning a registered nursing degree, but her marriage in 1902 to architect William Sanger put an end to her training. Moreover, despite recurring bouts of tuberculosis, Sanger bore three children and attempted to settle into a life as a homemaker and mother in comfortable suburban Westchester, New York.

The trouble was that the Sanger marriage proved to be anything but blissful. In an effort to save their union, the Sangers decided in 1911 to leave the suburbs and make a bold move into the milieu of radical political activism and "bohemian" moral revisionism sweeping Lower Manhattan's Greenwich Village. The Sangers opened their new urban home to a community of "liberals, anarchists, socialists and IWW's," as Sanger later wrote. She eagerly allowed herself to be radicalized, joining the Women's Committee of the New York Socialist Party and pitching in on strikes and demonstrations staged by the IWW (Industrial Workers of the World).

Her infatuation with the world of bohemian radicalism, like her move from Westchester to the city, might have begun as nothing more than an attempt to relieve boredom. Soon, however, it became far more sharply focused. Sanger found herself identifying deeply with the feminist movement, and this, combined with her education and experience in nursing, prompted her to accept in 1912 an invitation to write a column on female sexuality and "social hygiene" for the *New York Call*, a daily newspaper affiliated with the Socialist Party of America. The column was called "What Every Girl Should Know." It was so full of frank medical advice that an article devoted to venereal disease was branded as obscene, leading U.S. postal inspectors to ban delivery of that edition of the paper.

Soon, Sanger's interest in women's health and sex education narrowed to a topic that was bound to draw the attention of more than the postal authorities. She became increasingly interested in what was at the time called "family limitation." Her move to New York had prompted her to resume nursing, this time as a visiting nurse working among the poor immigrants living in Lower East Side tenements. In these sordidly overcrowded quarters, it was impossible to deny the dire consequences of frequent childbirth and the presence of more children than a family could support. Along with this reality came an elevated incidence of miscarriage and self-induced abortion, which often produced catastrophic results.

Sanger wanted to educate poor women in methods of contraception, but was legally blocked by the 1873 Comstock Act, which barred the "Trade in, and Circulation of, Obscene Literature and Articles of Immoral Use," including contraceptives, "abortifacients" (substances and devices to induce abortion), and "any information regarding" these and other items considered obscene. An abundance of state laws also introduced their own prohibitions. Conversation with the anarchist-feminist Emma Goldman persuaded Sanger that contraception was a means of empowerment being denied mainly to poor and working-class women. To Sanger and other like-minded activists, keeping women pregnant was an important way of keeping them out of the workforce and under the thumb of their husbands. By the same token, fear of unwanted pregnancy was a way by which men kept women "faithful."

Sanger believed that women had the inherent right to have control over their own bodies, including reproduction. She also believed that liberating women from the risk of unwanted pregnancy would bring about more fundamental social change. It was apparent to her that the older generation of feminists could accept only one method of "family limitation": sexual abstinence. Sanger believed that abstinence imposed an unacceptable level of self-denial on women and men. As for the Socialists, they regarded the fight for birth control as a distraction from other political objectives. Sanger saw an unmet social and psychological need that both society and the government opposed. She took it upon herself to create and carry out a campaign to challenge federal and local censorship of contraceptive information. She also challenged laws banning birth control and abortion. Sanger believed that if she could bring these to public consciousness, she would find the support she needed.

• • •

Margaret Sanger completed her personal transformation from suburban homemaker to radical activist by beginning publication in March 1914 of *The Woman Rebel*. A radical feminist monthly magazine, it called for militant action to assert the right of every woman to be "absolute mistress of her own body." She also challenged conventional, prevailing feminism, arguing that educational, economic, and political equality were meaningless if women were still subjected to unwanted pregnancies. The key to equality, the basis of human rights for women, she argued, was contraception.

Sanger did not espouse abortion in *The Woman Rebel*, only contraception, which was not itself illegal. What *was* illegal was disseminating information about contraception through the mail. Postal authorities seized five of the magazine's seven issues. Despite this, Sanger continued publishing and distributing. She also wrote and published a sixteen-page pamphlet titled *Family Limitation*, which included graphic instructions and information covering a variety of various contraceptive methods. This resulted in a federal indictment in August 1914 for violation of postal obscenity laws. Although she made bail, she evaded what she believed would be certain conviction and imprisonment, fleeing to England even as she ordered the distribution of *Family Limitation*. When federal authorities jailed her husband, William Sanger, for giving a copy of the pamphlet to an undercover agent, national interest in birth control exploded. As often happens when authorities seek to suppress knowledge, the clamor for that knowledge became irresistible.

While self-exiled in England, Sanger became involved in linking birth control to socioeconomic and medical issues of eugenics—attempts to "improve" the race. She also came under the influence of the work of Havelock Ellis, who believed that contraception would free women to enjoy sexual intercourse. Sanger, in effect, espoused the then-revolutionary idea that women—and men—had a right to sexual pleasure.

She put theory into practice in her own life. Separation from her husband ended her marriage, and she embarked on sexual relationships with a number of men, including Ellis and the novelist H. G. Wells. Sanger returned to New York in October 1915, now determined to face trial because she was convinced that she had public support. Tragically, that support was boosted by the sudden death, in November 1915, of her five-year-old daughter. A public outpouring of sympathy dissuaded the government from continuing to press its case against her. She embarked on a national tour, enduring frequent brushes with the law—and exploiting the publicity generated by each.

Her boldest act of defiance came on October 16, 1916, when she opened America's first birth control clinic, in Brooklyn. Predictably, the clinic was raided, and Sanger and her clinic staff were tried and convicted. She was jailed for thirty days, and her conviction was upheld on appeal—except that the appellate court did stipulate that physicians were lawfully permitted to prescribe birth control "when medically indicated." This gave Sanger a basis on which to establish a birth-control distribution system through clinics staffed with physicians.

In 1922, Sanger married wealthy oilman James Noah H. Slee, who provided considerable financial support for the birth-control movement she now led. Having founded the American Birth Control League, she lifted issues of birth control into the social mainstream. But she also engaged the support of the eugenics movement and began advocating birth control for those with genetically transmitted mental or physical defects. She even supported compulsory sterilization for the mentally incompetent. At the time, this was hardly a radical idea. In 1927, Oliver Wendell Holmes Jr. wrote the Supreme Court decision (*Buck v. Bell*) upholding a Virginia law that authorized the state to surgically sterilize "mental defectives" without their consent. But, after the already scientifically specious and morally repugnant theory of eugenics was enthusiastically seized upon by Nazi Germany during the 1930s and early 1940s, Sanger's position was almost universally condemned. She never advocated eugenics based on class, ethnicity, or race; nevertheless, her reputation in the human-rights community became tainted and controversial.

By the mid-twentieth century, Margaret Sanger's feminist crusade had morphed into a movement for birth control on more general human ecological grounds. A much-publicized "population explosion" was seen as threatening global welfare, especially in economically disadvantaged countries. In 1952, Sanger was instrumental in founding the International Planned Parenthood Federation (IPPF), winning widespread support from world leaders but disrupting domestic politics in some countries, including, to this day, the United States. She retreated from her earlier advocacy of eugenics and now insisted that the IPPF mission was to do no more than make birth control information and measures available on a global basis. She steadfastly refused to support controls mandated by governments. Sanger retired as president of the IPPF in 1959 and, increasingly frail, withdrew from activism. Her death, at the age of eighty-six on September 6, 1966, came after the introduction of oral contraception ("the Pill") and a year after the United States Supreme Court upheld the right of married couples to use birth control.

DISRUPTION:
MAKING CIVIL RIGHTS
THE PREEMINENT
SOCIAL ISSUE OF THE
1960S, CULMINATING
IN THE CIVIL RIGHTS
ACT OF 1964 AND THE
VOTING RIGHTS ACT
OF 1965

MARTIN LUTHER KING, JR.
(1929–1968)

The son of a prominent black pastor and religious leader in Atlanta, Georgia, Martin Luther King, Jr. was very much raised in the church, but it was by no means certain that he would follow his father's call to the ministry. Angry, chronically depressed, deeply resentful over conditions in the Jim Crow South, he survived a suicide leap out of a second-story window when he was just twelve years old, and the following year caused a ripple of scandal in his church when he denied in Sunday school the resurrection of Jesus Christ. He clearly had doubts about faith, compounded by a contentious relationship with his father, who regularly beat him, swearing to the boy that he "would make something of him even if he had to beat him to death."

Martin Luther King, Jr. had doubts, but he read the Bible avidly, even fiercely. He came to believe it offered what he later called "profound truths which one cannot escape." After graduating from Atlanta's Morehouse College with a BA in sociology in 1948, he almost grudgingly enrolled in Crozer Theological Seminary in Chester, Pennsylvania, earning a bachelor of divinity degree in 1951. Fearful that it would make a career in the ministry impossible, he broke off a serious romance with a young white woman in Atlanta and, in 1953, went on to marry Coretta Scott, an accomplished musician and civil liberties activist.

While studying at Crozer, King found himself drawn to Mohandas Gandhi's philosophy and methodology of nonviolent protest. He enrolled in Boston University as a doctoral student in systematic theology while serving as assistant minister in Boston's Twelfth Baptist Church, a storied African American house of worship established in 1840. The twenty-five-year-old King was called as pastor of the Dexter Avenue Baptist Church in Montgomery, Alabama, in 1954, and the following year received his PhD from Boston University.

King was presiding at Dexter Avenue when, on December 1, 1955, Rosa Parks, a local seamstress-tailor by trade and an NAACP activist by conviction, was arrested for violating Montgomery's Jim Crow laws: she refused to give up her seat to a white passenger on a public bus.

Her arrest was not an accident, but a strategic provocation. Montgomery's civil rights activist community had been planning a boycott of the city's buses to compel their integration. When E. D. Nixon, director of the local NAACP chapter, heard of Parks's arrest, he posted bond and enlisted her cooperation in initiating the action. Flyers were distributed urging a one-day boycott of the buses on the day that the Parks case was to be heard. Local black ministers, including King, agreed to spread the word in their Sunday sermons. King had predicted 60 percent cooperation with the boycott. When the buses were almost completely empty on Monday, he suddenly realized the power of strategic nonviolence. He and other activists quickly formed the Montgomery Improvement Association (MIA), of which King served as president. Under his leadership, the boycott was extended—until such time that the segregation policy was ended.

On the fourth day of the boycott, King and other MIA members met with representatives of the bus company and the city commissioners. The MIA presented a desegregation plan, which the bus company summarily rejected. City officials, moreover, informed King and the others that any city cab driver who charged less than the authorized 45-cent minimum fare would be prosecuted; black taxi services, in solidarity with the boycott, had begun charging black passengers a dime, the same as the bus fare. To avoid making the black businesspeople victims, King and the MIA drew up a "private taxi" plan, a precisely organized volunteer carpool, which transported boycotters to and from work.

Throughout the boycott, city commissioners and others repeatedly approached individual black community leaders in an effort to sabotage the boycott. When these efforts failed, some whites resorted to violence. King's home was fire-bombed on January 30, 1956, and Nixon's on February 1.

Both men and their families refused to yield.

City officials brought about the indictment, later in the month, of 89 black activists under a rarely used statute prohibiting boycotts. King was among those arrested. At the same time, the "private taxi" system was attacked through cancellation of liability insurance on church-owned station wagons. King responded by securing insurance through a black agent in Atlanta, who obtained underwriting from no less a firm than Lloyd's of London. At that point, the police resorted to arresting black drivers for trumped-up traffic offenses.

King led the boycotters through more than a year of harassment and physical danger. The Montgomery business community suffered as the black community stopped patronizing downtown stores. Moved by increasingly dire economic necessity, business owners formed a group called the Men of Montgomery to negotiate directly with the MIA. The negotiations soon stalled. In the meantime, however, representatives of the boycott sued the city and the bus company in federal court, securing a judgment that found segregation on buses unconstitutional. When the city appealed, the U.S. Supreme Court upheld the ruling of the lower court on November 13, 1956. The decision officially ended the Montgomery Bus Boycott on a note of high triumph—although King and other leaders refused to call off the boycott until December 21, 1956, when the court's mandate came into force.

King's leadership of the boycott, especially his eloquence in explaining and justifying it not only to black but also to white America, enlarged its scope far beyond Montgomery. Thanks in large part to King, the Montgomery boycott effectively launched the national civil rights movement. Determined to build upon the success of the action, King organized the Southern Christian Leadership Conference (SCLC), which would serve as a base of operations and a forum from which he could deliver his message nationally. As leader of the SCLC, King became a national figure, a much-sought-after lecturer, and, for most black and white Americans, the primary spokesman and face of the civil rights movement. In February 1959, he and other members of the SCLC traveled to India, where King discussed the philosophy of Gandhi with Indian prime minister Jawaharlal Nehru. This experience crystallized for King the nonviolent approach.

Early in 1960, Martin Luther King Jr. was named co-pastor of Atlanta's Ebenezer Baptist Church with his father. He continued to lead nonviolent protests, and in October 1960 was arrested with 33 others while protesting segregation at an Atlanta department store lunch counter. Although charges in this case were dropped, King was sentenced to a term at the state prison farm on fabricated traffic charges. Now that he was a national figure, the sentence provoked nationwide outrage. Despite public pressure, President Dwight D. Eisenhower declined to intercede in the controversy. But presidential candidate John F. Kennedy made a successful appeal on King's behalf. This act gained JFK much-needed support from the African American community, who overwhelmingly voted for him in November's general election. In turn, King's commitment to nonviolence earned him the ongoing gratitude and support of President Kennedy and his successor, Lyndon Johnson; though King was frequently frustrated by what he saw as both presidents' reluctance to move aggressively on civil rights.

In 1963, in Birmingham, Alabama, King led a campaign to end segregation in such facilities as lunch counters and in hiring. The protestors were, as usual, nonviolent; however, the police reaction was brutal. Images of the fire hoses, police batons, and police dogs used against demonstrators by order of the city's openly racist Commissioner of Public Safety "Bull" Connor were broadcast on the nightly news. King was jailed along with many other protestors. When some of Birmingham's black clergy joined with some local white clergy in denouncing King and the demonstrations, King addressed his widely published April 16, 1963, "Letter from Birmingham Jail" to them.

In this landmark document of the civil rights movement, King explained the very basis of nonviolent protest. He broke it down into "four basic steps":

> collection of the facts to determine whether injustices exist;
> negotiation; selfpurification; and direct action. We have
> gone through all these steps in Birmingham. There can be no
> gainsaying the fact that racial injustice engulfs this community.
> Birmingham is probably the most thoroughly segregated city in
> the United States. Its ugly record of brutality is widely known.
> Negroes have experienced grossly unjust treatment in the courts.
> There have been more unsolved bombings of Negro homes and
> churches in Birmingham than in any other city in the nation.
> These are the hard, brutal facts of the case. On the basis of these
> conditions, Negro leaders sought to negotiate with the city

fathers. But the latter consistently refused to engage in goodfaith negotiation.

King closed his letter to the critical clergy with the "hope that circumstances will soon make it possible for me to meet each of you, not as an integrationist or a civil rights leader but as a fellow clergyman and a Christian brother":

> Let us all hope that the dark clouds of racial prejudice will soon pass away and the deep fog of misunderstanding will be lifted from our feardrenched communities, and in some not too distant tomorrow the radiant stars of love and brotherhood will shine over our great nation with all their scintillating beauty.

The "Letter from Montgomery Jail" was a high point in King's leadership, but an even greater height followed. On August 28, 1963, King addressed more than 200,000 men, women, and children gathered on the National Mall, in front of the Lincoln Memorial, in Washington, D.C., and delivered "I Have a Dream," the single most important speech of the entire civil rights era and one of the great public utterances in American history. "I have a dream. . . ." The phrase was intoned over and over in the speech. "I have a dream that my four children will one day live in a nation where they will not be judged by the color of their skin but by the content of their character." It rang out like a great bell throughout America, and it rang in—against the formidable odds against it—passage of the Civil Rights Act of 1964.

• • •

In December 1964, King was awarded the Nobel Prize for Peace, in essence a global certification of what was at that moment his virtually unquestioned leadership of the civil rights movement.

But the moment dimmed. The next year, challenges from both white and black communities began to pile on. The brutality of the white response to the Selma, Alabama, SCLC demonstration in 1965 created outrage in the civil rights community. When a first march was literally beaten back on "Bloody Sunday," March 7, 1965, King led a second on March 9, but refused to provoke a direct confrontation with a phalanx of state troopers. After asking his followers to kneel in prayer before them, he declined to lead them on, but instead turned back with them.

In one important sense, the Selma demonstration was successful. It prompted passage of the Voting Rights Act later that year. But the rising generation of black activists questioned King's leadership and accused him of having become overly cautious by backing down on March 9. Some even suggested that he had avoided direct confrontation because of some prearrangement with white officials. The Selma controversy marked the ascendency of the militant civil rights wing, which steadily gained influence, posing increasingly serious challenge to the nonviolent approach. The summer of 1965 saw a massive race riot in the Watts neighborhood of Los Angeles, the costliest and bloodiest urban riot since the New York Draft Riot of July 1863 during the Civil War. Worse, the summer of 1965 was the first in a succession of "long hot summers," in which racial violence and urban rioting became increasingly commonplace in American cities.

Partially in response to the rise of urban militancy, King took his message up into the urban North. In 1966, he began a campaign against racial discrimination in Chicago, especially in the highly explosive area of housing. Although King hammered out an agreement among a coalition that included black and white activists as well as labor organizations, calling for an end to discrimination in housing, little practical progress was made against entrenched forms of urban discrimination that rivaled anything King had witnessed in the South. Yet again, the younger activists challenged King and his nonviolent methods.

At this point, with his civil rights leadership already being challenged, King—who had said in 1965, "I'm much more than a civil rights leader"—deliberately and daringly jumped into another controversial fray. Speaking at New York's Riverside Church on April 4, 1967, he proclaimed his opposition to the Vietnam War. This met with objections from two fronts. Some activists believed his stance, though overlapping with the anti-war sentiments of Gandhi, blurred and blunted the focus on civil rights. It also caused President Johnson, already mired in the increasingly unpopular war, to qualify his support for King. Although he would be portrayed later in popular history almost strictly as a nonviolent campaigner against racism, King's fierce and disruptive advocacy on a range of issues defied easy categorization.

Instead of retreating from controversy, however, King kept pushing. He worked to broaden the fight from civil rights for the black community to equal rights for all people, especially poor people, regardless of race. Over the objections of many black activists, King announced a Poor People's Campaign and March on Washington, which focused on economic rights for all Americans, regardless of race.

But first, he lent his support and presence to Memphis sanitation workers, a heavily black and chronically underpaid work force, who had been on strike ever since two of their members were crushed to death by a malfunctioning truck.

The night of April 3, 1968, King delivered what came to be known as his "I've Been to the Mountaintop" speech at a church. His flight into the city had been delayed by a bomb threat against his plane, and that incident gave the speech an elegiac, valedictory cast: "Well," he said, "I don't know what will happen now. We've got some difficult days ahead. But it doesn't matter with me now. Because I've been to the mountaintop.... And I've looked over. And I've seen the promised land." He paused, before continuing with ringing conviction. "I may not get there with you. But I want you to know tonight, that we, as a people, will get to the promised land. So, I'm happy, tonight. I'm not worried about anything. I'm not fearing any man. Mine eyes have seen the glory of the coming of the Lord."

The next evening, at 6:01 p.m., April 4, 1968, King was assassinated by James Earl Ray, a racist white small-time crook, as he stood on the balcony of Room 306 of the Lorraine Motel. He was cut down in the midst of some of the heaviest challenges he and his nonviolent movement had yet faced. But at the time of his death, he was nevertheless the one leader who had done the most to transform disparate racial protests into a unified national campaign. The movement he led not only forged a generation of leaders like John Lewis and Jesse Jackson, who drove substantive changes in law, policy, and government, but that spoke directly to the consciousness and conscience of both black and white America. As his model, Mohandas Gandhi, had universalized the Indian struggle for independence, Martin Luther King, Jr. had elevated the struggle for black civil rights into a timeless and universal campaign for justice and for humanity that remains today a powerful example of positive and constructive disruption.

BY ERASING THE "COLOR LINE" IN MAJOR LEAGUE BASEBALL, BRANCH RICKEY INITIATED A TRANSFORMATION IN AMERICAN SOCIAL JUSTICE

BRANCH RICKEY

(1881–1965)

Born in Stockdale, Ohio, Branch Rickey played catcher on the Ohio Wesleyan University baseball team and professional football for the Shelby Blues of the Ohio League, predecessor to the modern NFL. He befriended teammate Charles Follis, who had the distinction of being the first African American pro football player in the United States. Rickey saw that Follis's presence on the team was not always welcome, and he later praised him for his grace under the pressure of racial tension and prejudice. Also before graduating, Rickey played minor league baseball in 1903 and went on to coach baseball, basketball, and football when he worked as athletic director at Allegheny College, Pennsylvania. During 1905–1907, he played catcher in the American League (St. Louis Browns and New York Highlanders) before returning to college, this time the University of Michigan law school, from which he earned a JD, financing his education by coaching the Michigan baseball team.

e was on the road with the team one season in 1910, when a hotel manager in South Bend, Indiana, refused to provide a room for Rickey's single African American player, Charley Thomas. The way Rickey responded spoke volumes about the man. He did not let the racism slide, and he did not back down. But he refrained from making an angry or even righteous outburst. Instead, he pleaded, he cajoled, and he compromised, finally getting the manager to agree to allow Thomas to share his own room. Like the memory of Follis under pressure, the image of Thomas stayed with Rickey through his life. Rickey recalled many years later that when they shared the room, Thomas would rub and rub his hands. To Rickey, it looked as if he were trying to wash the color off them. He later said that he pointed to the man's hands and swore to him: "Charley, the day will come when they won't have to be white."

After graduating from law school in 1911, Rickey realized he loved baseball more than the courtroom and found a job as field manager of the American League's St. Louis Browns. He was with that team from 1913 to 1915, and then joined the National League's St. Louis Cardinals, serving as club president from 1917 to 1919, field manager from 1919 to 1925, and general manager from 1925 to 1942. In 1943, he left the Cards to become president and general manager of the Brooklyn Dodgers.

● ● ●

Now *he* was in charge—as much as any one man is ever in charge of a major league baseball team. As soon as he assumed the presidency of the team, Rickey made the decision to "cross the color line," as the phrase went. He would sign an African American ballplayer.

His determination was rooted in two sources. First was his close-up experience with the Jim Crow laws of the South, which he found obscene. To him, racial discrimination was, plain and simple, a wrong that cried out to be righted. But there was also a second motive. Rickey was the president of a team in a very competitive sport. He knew there were remarkably promising players in the all-black Negro League. As a businessman, it seemed to him obscenely stupid to turn a blind eye to so much untapped talent. He was not interested in signing just any black baseball player. He was determined to sign up a *great* black player. This would give the Dodgers the moral high ground—as well as an edge on other teams in terms of talent.

But was the time right?

For Rickey, it was a question of *if not now, when?* Late in 1943, the venerable commissioner of baseball, Kenesaw Mountain Landis, convened members of the Black Publishers Association and all sixteen major league team owners, along with the presidents of both leagues, to meet with the African American social and political activist Paul Robeson. He turned over the meeting to Robeson.

"Because baseball is a national game," Robeson declared, "it is up to baseball to see that discrimination does not become an American pattern."

Rickey heard him loud and clear. Rickey expected that Landis would buy into Robeson's message. But he did not. Landis continued to oppose the integration of baseball until he died, in 1944 at seventy-eight.

His successor was former Kentucky governor Albert B. "Happy" Chandler. Rickey decided to confront him. He told the new commissioner that he intended to sign a black player for the Dodgers. It was World War II, and the Battle of the Pacific was at its height. Chandler looked Rickey in the eye and answered "If they can fight and die on Okinawa [and] Guadalcanal . . . they can play ball in America."

That was the kind of thing Branch Rickey wanted to hear. He was also aware that the New York State legislature had just passed the Quinn-Ives Act, which barred racial discrimination in hiring, and he himself was an enthusiastic endorser of New York mayor Fiorello LaGuardia's newly created "End Jim Crow in Baseball" committee.

The iron, it seemed, was hot. But when Rickey, ready to strike, petitioned the owners to allow him to integrate the National League, the vote came back 15 to 1—against. At this, Commissioner Chandler stepped in. He had the authority to override the vote, and he did just that. Nevertheless, Rickey knew his efforts would be met by a great deal of ugly pushback. He decided, therefore, on a course that recalled his approach, years ago, to the South Bend hotelkeeper. He would cajole. He would compromise. He would build a back door.

In the spring of 1945, Rickey founded the United States League, which would be a new "Negro League." The initial response from his own allies was absolute shock. They accused Rickey of turning against the cause of integration by starting a league to encourage continued segregation. Rickey's move, however, was a ruse. The United States League was a paper organization destined by design never to play a single game. It was a fraud, a front intended to allow Rickey to openly scout black ballplayers for a covert purpose. Out of about a hundred players he looked at, he asked just one, Jackie Robinson, to meet with him on August 28, 1945.

"Are you under contract to the Kansas City Monarchs?" Rickey asked the twenty-six-year-old. The Monarchs was one of the original Negro League teams.

"No, sir. We don't have contracts. . . . I just work from payday to payday."

"Do you know why you were brought here?"

"Not exactly. I heard something about a colored team at [Brooklyn's] Ebbets Field." He paused. "That it?"

"No," Rickey answered. "That isn't it. You were brought here, Jackie, to play for the Brooklyn organization. Perhaps on Montreal [the Brooklyn Dodgers' top farm team] to start with—"

"Me? Play for Montreal?"

Robinson found it hard to believe. Rickey explained his plan. He would start Robinson in the minors in Canada, where Jim Crow racism was not nearly so entrenched as in the States. This would polish the rough edges off Robinson's game, as well as prove his merits as a player. That was important. Even more important, though, it would make his transition into U.S. major league play as smooth as it was ever going to get.

"If you can make it, yes," he told Jackie, he would play for Montreal. "Later on—also if you can make it—you'll have a chance with the Brooklyn Dodgers."

Robinson just nodded. When the silence grew uncomfortable, Rickey spoke: "I want to win pennants and we need ballplayers!"

That broke the ice. That reminded them both that baseball was, finally, a game. Yet the meeting was serious enough to last over three hours, as Rickey explained that he had not merely scouted Robinson on the diamond: he had also hired private investigators to research his past. He liked what he found. Robinson went to church regularly. He neither drank nor smoked. He had no criminal record. He had attended UCLA, but withdrew in his third year to help his mother take care of their family.

There was one other thing. Rickey told Robinson that he knew that, in 1942, Robinson had enlisted in the army and was commissioned a second lieutenant in 1943—not all that common for a black man in the segregated U.S. Army of the time. Rickey also knew that both Robinson and black boxer Joe Louis faced court-martial in 1944 for refusing to follow an order to sit in the back of a military bus when both men were posted at a base in the Jim Crow South. The charges were dismissed and, at the end of the war, Robinson was honorably discharged. Rickey admired Robinson for having stood his ground, yet he was concerned about what he might do if he were pushed too far on the field.

"Do you think you can do it? Make good in organized baseball?" he asked.

"If . . . if I got the chance," Robinson replied.

"There's more here than just playing, Jackie. I wish it meant only hits, runs, and errors—things you can see in a box score. . . . Can you do it?"

Robinson knew exactly what he meant by "it." He nodded. But Rickey pressed him, warning that fans would scream insults, slurs, and threats. Worse, so would plenty of players on the opposing team. Runners would slide in spikes-first, Rickey warned, and pitchers would throw at his head.

"Mr. Rickey, they've been throwing at my head for a long time."

Branch Rickey would not let up.

"Suppose I'm a player," he said. "Suppose I collide with you at second base. When I get up, I yell 'You dirty, black son of a'— " Rickey stopped. "What do you do?"

"Mr. Rickey, do you want a ballplayer who's afraid to fight back?"

"I want a ballplayer with guts enough *not* to fight back! You've got to do this job with base hits and stolen bases and fielding ground balls, Jackie. Nothing else!"

Rickey continued to goad Robinson. He drew on his memory to role-play a hotel clerk in the Deep South, a bigoted sportswriter, an insolent waiter.

"Now I'm playing against you in a World Series! I'm a hotheaded player. I want to win that game, so I go into you spikes-first, but you don't give ground. You stand there and you jab the ball into my ribs and the umpire yells, 'Out!' I flare up—all I see is your face—that black face right on top of me. So, I haul off and punch you right in the cheek! What do you do?"

"Mr. Rickey, I've got two cheeks."

Robinson paused.

"That it?"

That was it. Branch Rickey signed Jackie Robinson to a $600-a-month contract with a $3,500 signing bonus to play with the Montreal Royals. He moved him up to the Brooklyn Dodgers at the start of the 1947 season.

● ● ●

Jackie Robinson was an immediate and spectacular success, leading the National League in stolen bases and earning the title of Rookie of the Year. In 1949, he won the batting championship with a .342 average and was voted league MVP. His lifetime batting average was .311, and he led Brooklyn to a total of six league championships and one World Series victory.

Rickey trusted that Robinson could take whatever would be thrown at him. "Whatever" included ugly slurs and heavy glass beer bottles. Hardest to take were the protests from some of his own teammates, who objected not only to sharing the diamond with a black man, but to sharing the locker room and the showers. Opposing pitchers did sometimes throw at his head. Base runners did sometimes come in spikes-first. Southern hotel clerks did sometimes bar the door, and Southern restaurants did sometimes refuse to seat him.

"Plenty of times," Robinson later admitted, "I wanted to haul off when somebody insulted me for the color of my skin, but I had to hold to myself. I knew I was kind of an experiment. The whole thing was bigger than me."

And so it was. An American tipping point was being reached. Racial segregation was no longer immune to questioning. The social-justice conversation had begun.

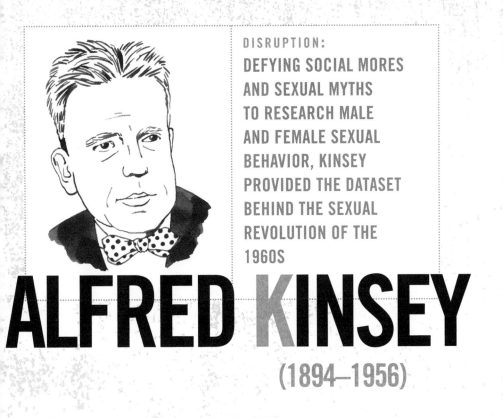

DEFYING SOCIAL MORES
AND SEXUAL MYTHS
TO RESEARCH MALE
AND FEMALE SEXUAL
BEHAVIOR, KINSEY
PROVIDED THE DATASET
BEHIND THE SEXUAL
REVOLUTION OF THE
1960S

ALFRED KINSEY

(1894–1956)

Alfred Charles Kinsey's puritanical father wanted him to become an engineer. The boy tried to be a good son, dutifully enrolling at the Stevens Institute of Technology, where his father was a professor. After two years of misery there, he stood up to the senior Kinsey and took off for Maine's Bowdoin College, where he studied psychology and biology. His father did not attend the 1916 commencement, at which Alfred was awarded his degree with high honors.

N o matter. The young Kinsey began graduate study in applied biology at Harvard. His chief mentor was field biologist William Morton Wheeler, a father figure who was everything Kinsey's biological father was not. Where the senior Kinsey was a fundamentalist Christian, Wheeler was an atheist and ardent disciple of Darwin. Where the elder Kinsey was pious and straitlaced, Wheeler was a close friend of the journalist, social critic, and satirist H. L. Mencken, the epitome of American impiety, irreverence, and skepticism. Guided and encouraged by Wheeler, Kinsey embraced the rigors of science as his one true religion and threw himself into an extraordinary evolutionary study of the gall wasp, based on a huge specimen collection he amassed and taxonomically catalogued. Early in the process, he identified a number of new species of the insect and was awarded a doctor of science degree in 1919. In 1920, he joined the biology faculty of Indiana University.

• • •

As an evolutionary entomologist with a passion for taxonomy, Kinsey hardly seemed destined to shake the world. He shook the world.

Kinsey was born on June 23, 1894, in Hoboken, New Jersey. His mother, Sarah Ann Charles, was not well educated, and while his father, Alfred Seguine Kinsey, was a professor at Hoboken's Stevens Institute of Technology, a well-respected school of mechanical engineering, he was not well paid. The Kinseys did not live well, and the fact that Alfred suffered from poorly treated childhood cases of rheumatic fever and typhoid fever as well as rickets (which left him with permanent spinal curvature severe enough to disqualify him from military service during World War I) suggests the impoverishment of his early years.

The senior Kinsey's social circle did not consist of fellow Stevens faculty members, but fellow congregants of the local Methodist church. Young Alfred became increasingly frustrated by the limitations of his parents' narrow focus on religious routine. His family's move from Hoboken to South Orange, New Jersey, when he was ten enlarged his scope, as he became a member of the local YMCA, which introduced him to camping and nature study.

Fortunately for Alfred, his parents approved of the YMCA—the C, after all, stood for *Christian*—and welcomed their son's joining the Boy Scouts, which was unmistakably founded on Christian principles. Alfred loved scouting because it brought him close to nature, and he excelled in the organization, becoming an Eagle Scout in 1913—one of scouting's very first, in fact. Much as Teddy Roosevelt had embarked on a self-imposed regimen of physical exercise intended to toughen him up after a sickly childhood, Kinsey embarked on long, arduous hikes and camping trips to build himself up—and, doubtless, to distance himself from his family.

In high school, he discovered another side of himself. He was not only a natural student, who thrived on hard study, but he proved to be a talented musician and a pianist of sufficient promise to prompt him to contemplate a concert career. While he ultimately decided on a life in science instead, he remained a lifelong lover of classical music and would entertain fellow faculty members at

Indiana University, an institution celebrated for its superb music department, with impromptu piano recitals.

Quiet and polite as a young man, Kinsey spent much of his time in solitary study. His focus was sharp and sustained. He put in long hours, which gave him great satisfaction. His high school biology teacher, Natalie Roeth, opened to him the wonders of botany and zoology. In later years, Kinsey would credit her with having awakened his passion for the life sciences.

• • •

Kinsey's doctoral work on the gall wasp became the focus of his academic career at Indiana University through the 1930s. He published *The Gall Wasp Genus Cynips: A Study in the Origin of Species* in 1929, the year he was promoted to full professor. His immense collection of gall wasp specimens became a treasured research asset of the Department of Biology. In 1924, he married Clara Bracken McMillen, one of his students. The couple went on to have four children.

His was a successful career and a successful life. Yet he began to feel increasing disappointment at the limitations of being the world's foremost authority . . . on gall wasps. While Indiana University was an excellent institution, he longed for offers from the likes of Harvard and Yale. They did not come. He wanted to make a mark on the world, but he seemed doomed to remain an obscure professor in a midwestern state university.

Then, in 1938, Kinsey nudged his career in a surprising new direction. Students had circulated a petition asking for a "course on marriage." This was coded language for a course on human sexuality. Most faculty members would not consider the request. Kinsey, however, jumped at the opportunity to lead a team-taught course in the subject. He personally prepared and delivered the lectures—illustrated by slides—devoted to the biology and physiology of sexual stimulation, the mechanics of intercourse, and techniques of contraception. Clearly drawing on deep reserves of childhood repression, he also lectured on the damage caused by puritanical laws and social mores. It soon became apparent that he had a theory. If one defined sexuality in a strictly biological context, he argued, it would be apparent that "nearly all the so-called sexual perversions fall within the range of biological normality."

Doubtless Professor Kinsey saw his approach to the subject of human sexuality as no different from his approach to gall wasps. Both were a matter of observing and cataloguing characteristics and behavior. At another level, however, Kinsey was clearly driven by a need to overcome the superego presence that was his joyless, disapproving father, the very embodiment of corrosive Victorian piety. Whether it was the product of objective science or personal passion, Kinsey's "marriage course" was among the most popular offerings in the entire university, with four hundred students packing each lecture by 1940.

Kinsey looked upon the students who attended his lectures as he looked upon his gall wasps. As the wasps presented an identifiable range of variation, so, he decided, would these human organisms. He embarked upon a project of cataloguing, describing, and classifying the varieties of human sexual experience. His first set of "specimens" were his "marriage course" students, who, as a course requirement, were obliged to have private conferences with him in which he took, in exquisite but standardized detail, their sexual histories.

Later, he took his survey farther afield to several midwestern cities. He began presenting his results and wrote grant applications to the National Research Council and the Rockefeller Foundation. Their funding not only gave the project what he considered a highly useful air of academic legitimacy, it also enabled him to hire paid research assistants and fund travel to other parts of the United States. In 1947, he founded the Institute of Sex Research at Indiana University as the center and clearinghouse for this research.

In 1948, Kinsey published *Sexual Behavior in the Human Male* under the imprimatur of Indiana University Press. In contrast to most books published by this or any other university press, the volume made the national best-seller list three weeks after it hit bookstore shelves. The presentation was anything but sensational. Weighing in at more than 800 pages, it was written in the style of Kinsey's gall-wasp studies, using the dry, concise language of a naturalist, with prose anchored by statistics, graphs, and tables. Released in January, it sold 200,000 copies by the middle of March. It embodied data from more than five thousand sexual histories, and it made national news with its revelations concerning masturbation, adultery, and homosexuality, all of which were presented as aspects of normal sexuality.

In 1953, Kinsey followed *Sexual Behavior in the Human Male* with *Sexual Behavior in the Human Female*. This volume was based on even more sexual histories—about six thousand—and was, if anything, an even more profound revelation, especially with regard to masturbation (frequency as well as method), premarital sexual behavior, and the subject of the "female orgasm"—hitherto the single greatest mystery of human sexuality.

Kinsey patterned the second book after the first, laying special emphasis on the gulf that existed between social attitudes and assumptions on the one hand and documented practices and behavior on the other. But while the book on men had provoked both outrage and praise, the study of women motivated a mighty counterattack, the shockwaves of which reached the halls of Congress, which conducted an investigation of Kinsey's financial support. A panicky Rockefeller Foundation swiftly cut off Kinsey's funding.

The tumult, in fact, began to kill Kinsey. His childhood ailments had permanently damaged his heart, and the stress he suffered after publication of the 1953 volume aggravated long-dormant heart failure. He felt neither guilt nor remorse, but great anger and anxiety that his work would be suppressed and that the Institute of Sex Research would be shuttered. (In fact, it not only continued, but was renamed the Kinsey Institute for Sex Research in 1981.) In 1956, Kinsey suffered a serious bout of pneumonia, for which he was briefly hospitalized, but never fully recovered. He died on August 25 of that year, the cause of death reported by the *New York Times* as a "heart ailment and pneumonia." He was sixty-two, cheated out of another decade or two of life. And yet he had changed the world by revealing some of the most intimate secrets of its inhabitants. Although his research upset many social norms, by casting light on hitherto dark taboos, Kinsey's work removed perhaps thousands of sources of unnecessary guilt, bewilderment, and emotional pain. Even Kinsey's pious father would have understood the words of Jesus as the Apostle John reported them: "And ye shall know the truth, and the truth shall make you free."

BETTY
FRIEDAN

(1921–2006)

"Gradually, without seeing it clearly for quite a while, I came to realize that something is very wrong with the way American women are trying to live their lives today," Betty Friedan began the preface to *The Feminine Mystique*, her 1963 book that the feminist health journalist Barbara Seaman called "the most important . . . of the twentieth century." Friedan continued: "I sensed it first as a question mark in my own life, as a wife and mother of three small children, half-guiltily, and therefore half-heartedly, almost in spite of myself, using my abilities and education in work that took me away from home." Then it hit her: "There was a strange discrepancy between the reality of our lives as women and the image to which we were trying to conform, the image that I came to call the feminine mystique." As for the earth-shaking book that flowed from this insight—it came from Friedan's intense desire to answer the question: Did other women face "this schizophrenic split"?

She was born Bettye Naomi Goldstein on February 4, 1921 in Peoria, Illinois, where her father, Harry, owned a jewelry store. When he became ill, her mother, Miriam, took a job with the local newspaper, writing pieces for the society page. While her father's illness was a strain on the family, young Bettye noted that her mother, now working outside of the home, seemed happier than ever.

As a girl, Bettye was attracted to Marxism, which fed into what she identified as a "passion against injustice," a passion that grew in large part out of her resentment of the anti-Semitism she had experienced in Peoria, where Jews were a small minority. Like her mother, Bettye had an inclination toward journalism and joined the staff of her high school newspaper. Her ambition was to have her own column, but the editor turned her down. Undaunted, she gathered six friends and put together from scratch a literary magazine, *Tide*, which enjoyed considerable success within the circle of the school.

Bettye excelled in high school and, in 1938, she was accepted into the exclusive, all-female Smith College. She won a scholarship prize in her freshman year there and, as a sophomore, began writing poetry, which was printed in various campus publications. In 1941, her senior year, Bettye was named editor-in-chief of the college newspaper, a belated fulfillment of her high school journalistic ambition. She churned out left-leaning political editorials. With World War II raging in Europe and Asia but the United States still neutral, she also wrote numerous antiwar opinion pieces, which often stirred controversy. She found that she was quite comfortable with controversy.

After graduating summa cum laude and Phi Beta Kappa in 1942, having majored in psychology, Bettye enrolled for a year at the University of California, Berkeley, on a graduate fellowship in psychology, studying under the developmental psychologist and psychoanalyst Erik Erikson. At Berkeley, her involvement in left-wing politics became more intense. She reached a career crossroads. Should she pursue a PhD in psychology? She had the offer of a full fellowship. Or should she embark on a career in journalism? Her decision (which she claimed had been influenced by her boyfriend) was to abandon academic study, leave Berkeley, and begin writing for leftist and labor-union publications. From 1943 to 1952, she wrote for the Federated Press and then for the United Electrical Workers' *UE News*. By this time, she was married—and had become Betty Friedan—and *UE News* fired her in 1952 when she became pregnant with her second child. Undaunted and still determined to work, she turned freelance, writing for a variety of publications, the most widely circulated of which was *Cosmopolitan*, before it became a women's magazine.

• • •

Her freelance work was beginning to earn her a readership, but it was in 1957 that her writing career took a truly momentous turn. In the months leading up to her fifteenth Smith class reunion, Betty Friedan prepared a questionnaire, which she sent to members of the class. The questions focused on education, post-college employment and experience, and overall satisfaction with the lives they were leading. From her classmates' descriptions of their lives since college and from additional research, Friedan concluded that the women of her cohort—well-educated, bright, relatively affluent—suffered from what she called the "Problem That Has No Name." She wrote a series of articles about it, hypothesizing that middle- and upper-class American women were, for the most part, dissatisfied with their roles as wives and mothers. "The problem lay buried," she wrote, "unspoken, for many years in the minds of American women. It was a strange stirring, a sense of dissatisfaction, a yearning that women suffered in the middle of the 20th century in the United States. Each suburban wife struggled with it alone. As she made the beds, shopped for groceries . . . she was afraid to ask even of herself the silent question—'Is this all?'"

In her 1963 book, Friedan gave the problem a name: the "feminine mystique," a pervasive notion that women could gain satisfaction only through marriage and children. It was a controlling myth, and the book both analyzed it and tore it down, piece by piece, case by case, story by story. The result was the opening of the proverbial floodgates. An obscure, unspoken problem with no name suddenly became an issue that millions of women identified with and embraced. *The Feminine Mystique* was an instant bestseller.

Women had proved themselves in the workplace during World War II, when they showed that they could do any job a man did. Society, it seemed, had changed—until the war ended, and women overwhelmingly returned to their homes, their children, and their homemaking. By the early 1960s, however, women began coming back to the workplace, and publication of *The Feminine Mystique* meshed with their return. It coincided with, even as it fostered, the female reentry into the job market—a market very different from what it had been in the 1940s and 1950s. The earlier work environment had been heavily industrial. The environment emerging in the 1960s was far more service-oriented, propelled by a tsunami of consumerism. As consumerism increased demand and as increased demand stimulated production of a greater variety of consumer goods, families found an economic incentive for an added income. The days of the male as sole breadwinner were numbered. Increasingly, achieving and maintaining middle-class life required two incomes.

Women were up to the task. More of them were enrolling in and graduating from college in the 1960s, and when the first oral contraceptive—"The Pill"—

was approved by the FDA in 1960, it became possible, feasible, and convenient for women to go to work instead of to the maternity ward and the nursery.

The Feminine Mystique disrupted the consciousness not just of American women but of America and the world. As women came to accept that they had alternatives—or additions—to the life of wife and mother, they felt themselves increasingly empowered. Both men and women began to question the values they had been taught as the only "normal" and "acceptable" way to live. Ever the socially committed political activist, Friedan, in 1966, helped to found the National Organization for Women (NOW) and served as its first president.

Riding the tide of insight raised by Friedan's book, NOW began a campaign for full equality for women in every aspect of legal, political, family, and working life. Friedan and NOW worked for liberalized abortion laws and for the passage of the Equal Rights Amendment (ERA). Originally written by pioneering feminists Alice Paul and Crystal Eastman, ERA was first introduced in Congress in 1923 and repeatedly failed to pass until 1971, when it passed both houses of Congress. Submitted the next year for ratification by the states, it was three states short of the necessary 38 ratifications by the deadline of March 22, 1977. The deadline was extended to 1982, but the proposed amendment received no further ratifications.

Today, the fate of ERA remains uncertain. Even within the women's movement that *The Feminine Mystique* had helped to launch and propel, some argued and continue to argue that ERA would actually invalidate many state and federal laws designed to protect women, while others argue that, without ERA, women will never achieve complete equality. Despite the disagreements, the membership of NOW continued to grow, from more than 210,000 members to over half a million today.

The success of *The Feminine Mystique* and the widespread acceptance of NOW among college-educated, liberal women gave rise to another manifestation of the campaign for equality in the 1970s. The popular *Ms.* magazine, edited by Gloria Steinem from 1972 to 1987, became a primary vehicle for the spread of the feminist message.

As NOW became more politically powerful and *Ms.* spread the doctrines of feminism, various strains of the women's movement could be discerned The work carried out by NOW came to be characterized as "liberal feminism." The organization began lobbying not only for women's rights but also for the rights of the LGBTQ community. Most of its attention focused on reform through the electoral process, lobbying, and legislation.

In the late 1960s, a new movement separated from the NOW movement. It consisted of women who doubted that reform could ever be achieved by conventional political means. Most of these women had a history of involvement with the civil rights movement or with the New Left. To their consternation, they found that they were given very little power in these movements. So they broke away. Meeting first in small support-and-discussion groups, the more radically inclined feminists began to define all their relationships with men—in the workplace and in the home—as innately political, and they coined the phrase "sexual politics" to describe these relationships. Labeled by the press "women's liberationists," the radical activists rejected NOW because of what they regarded as its failure to address women's subordination to men in the family and the workplace. In-depth studies by such writers as Shulamith Firestone, Kate Millett, Ti-Grace Atkinson, and others analyzed the debilitating effects of male supremacy on women.

The divide between the women's liberationists and the members of NOW began to close during the 1970s when both groups found themselves working against a common threat—outright antifeminists of the reactionary right, who claimed that feminism of any kind would lead to a society in which men behaved irresponsibly toward women and children.

Despite the differences that have plagued as well as enriched the women's movement since publication of *The Feminine Mystique*, women have made substantial gains in American society. In state legislatures, the number of women elected to office doubled between 1975 and 1988. By 1987, forty states had implemented policies to ensure that women received comparable pay for comparable work. In addition, laws protecting female victims of rape have been strengthened in many states. Still, relatively few women hold national political office or sit in the nation's boardrooms. Rape and domestic violence remain serious problems in American society. And highly publicized cases of sexual harassment and sexual assault in the workplace—with especially high-profile cases in the entertainment industry, in Congress, and, most notoriously, the White House—suggest that the problems of women in societies that are still dominated by men run deep. Doubtless, they will require additional disruptions to resolve—if resolved they will be.

8

POPULAR CULTURE

DISRUPTION:
TRANSFORMED JAZZ,
AMERICA'S MOST
ORIGINAL MUSICAL
ART FORM, FROM AN
EXERCISE IN COLLECTIVE
IMPROVISATION TO A
PLATFORM FOR INTENSE
INDIVIDUAL EXPRESSION

LOUIS

(1901–1971)

ARMSTRONG

A gumbo. That's what natives of NOLA—New Orleans—like to call their city and its culture. It certainly describes the music of that town during the nineteenth and early twentieth centuries, a thick, hot, delicious mélange of sounds. Racially, the mélange was something else again. Not only were blacks and whites segregated by law in the early days, but so were blacks (African-Americans) and Creoles (people of Euro-African ancestry)—not by law, but by tradition. Musically, Creole musicians typically had formal training—in contrast to the people they disparaged as "black Negroes," who couldn't read "those little black dots."

B ut in 1894, the city enacted Municipal Code No. 111, which classed Creoles as "Negroes" and forced them out of segregated white neighborhoods. This had the effect of forcibly mixing African blacks with Euro African Creoles. The result for music was an intense exchange between the tutored Creoles and the untutored "black Negroes" that produced a Euro American hybrid, in which African blacks learned to read music and thereby expanded their musical universe beyond folk traditions, and Creoles were liberated from strict adherence to printed scores. Improvisation came to mark the music of the tenderloin area along Canal Street called Storyville, the "sporting house" district most historians of American music identify as the birthplace of jazz, the nation's most influential indigenous popular music.

Sin was the stock in trade of Storyville—gambling, liquor, drugs, and prostitution. The area was designated a red-light district through legislation drawn up in 1897 by Alderman Sidney Story, who sought to confine "vice" to a single neighborhood. The "mansions," as the district's bordellos were called, needed music, and that music was called jazz, a blend of Creole and African traditions. As the great folklorist Alan Lomax put it, Storyville produced the "master formula of jazz—mulatto (Creole) knowingness ripened by black sorrow."

● ● ●

New Orleans has produced and nurtured a host of musicians. Two of the most famous were Joe "King" Oliver and Louis "Satchmo" Armstrong. Both came of age in NOLA, but they also came from different worlds. But for the music, they would doubtless have had sharply different destinies.

Joseph Nathan Oliver was born in 1881 in rural Aben, Louisiana, and moved to New Orleans when he was very young. He received formal training on the trombone before switching to cornet, and he made a living playing in New Orleans brass bands and dance bands. He was a professional, like most New Orleans band musicians, but, also like most of them, he supplemented his slender income by moonlighting in Storyville. The Storyville gigs were not only essential to paying the bills, they were sources of inspiration, infusing the "legitimate" band music with a certain spice. From 1908 to 1917, Oliver played cornet, and in 1910 he teamed up with trombonist Kid Ory as co-leader of a band that earned a reputation as the best and the hottest in the city. It crossed racial and social lines. Oliver and Ory played black dives one night and white debutante balls the next.

In April 1917, President Woodrow Wilson took the United States into what had been called the "European War" and was now the "Great War" or the "World War." New Orleans became a major U.S. Navy base, and the Secretary of the Navy, a North Carolina progressive named Josephus Daniels, was opposed to the "corruption" of youthful sailors by prostitutes and alcohol. As these were two of the principal commodities served up in Storyville, Daniels, with the backing of Secretary of War Newton Baker, effectively forced the closure of Storyville's "mansions" and drinking establishments. This sent Oliver—and many other New

Orleans musicians—on an exodus to the North. Most, Oliver included, headed for Chicago beginning in 1918.

Louis Armstrong was born in 1901 in a ramshackle house on Jane Alley, between Perdido and Poydras Streets, hard by the Storyville neighborhood. His mother, Mary Albert Armstrong, was sixteen, and his father, William, abandoned mother and son almost immediately, plunging them into deep poverty. Mary's mother took in Louis, raising him to the age of five, at which time he returned to his mother. He began attending public school, where he was introduced to music, but he dropped out in fifth grade. Among the odd jobs he did was running errands for a local Jewish family, the Karnofskys, who ran a junk business and also used their junk wagon to deliver coal. One of Louis's tasks was to deliver coal to the Storyville "mansions." There he discovered the music of the brothels and first heard Joe Oliver.

Over the months and years, Louis's relationship with the Karnofskys ripened. They treated him like a son, and Armstrong wore a Star of David pendant for the rest of his life. It was Morris Karnofsky who advanced Louis $2 on his wages so that he could buy a cornet from a local pawn shop when he was eleven. It is uncertain whether cornetist Bunk Johnson or Joe Oliver taught Armstrong to play the instrument by ear, but he took to it naturally and began performing for tips in a Storyville honky-tonk. He also sang—for spare change—in a street-corner quartet with neighborhood boys.

On New Year's Eve 1912, the street-corner gig got him into trouble. That night, Armstrong got hold of his stepfather's .38 revolver, which he fired into the air to celebrate the New Year. He was immediately arrested and sent to the Colored Waif's Home. The military-style discipline there was harsh, but the school also had a band, and Armstrong received his first "formal" musical training. The band gave public concerts, and Armstrong performed along with trombonist Kid Ory, a fellow inmate.

Released in 1914, Armstrong played in traditional New Orleans parade bands and, in 1918, began performing on Mississippi River excursion boats in the band of Fate Marable, who taught him to sight-read music. But his first big break came in 1918 when Joe Oliver left New Orleans for Chicago, and Kid Ory invited Armstrong to take Oliver's place on trumpet in his band.

● ● ●

By 1918, New Orleans's days as the incubator of jazz were numbered. The closing of Storyville contributed to the demise, but the causes were even bigger than that. Tens of thousands and soon hundreds of thousands of African Americans were leaving the Jim Crow South for the relative freedom and opportunity of the North. In 1922, Louis Armstrong joined that exodus. Like numerous other New Orleans musicians, he went to Chicago, where *Joe* Oliver had already renamed himself *King* Oliver and was a highly successful bandleader.

King Oliver was not a great musician, certainly not a breakthrough musician—except, perhaps, in his genius for invariably attracting great talent to his band. But if you listen to the recordings he made in Chicago during the 1920s with his most important group, the Dixie Syncopaters, you will find the music exuberant and skillful in execution, yet also four-square and a far cry from the highly improvisational jazz that was about to emerge from other musicians. Listen to Oliver's cornet solo on "Dippermouth Blues," his most famous composition, a piece that generations of jazz trumpeters have learned by heart. Clipped, precise, even brilliant, it nevertheless fades in the wake of the far more expressive cornet work of Oliver's most famous alumnus, Louis Armstrong.

Nevertheless, Oliver and his band gave Armstrong a platform and a living. Even more, in King Oliver himself, the young man found the strong, strict, but caring father he had so sorely missed in childhood. Did the older musician influence Armstrong's musicianship? Probably not profoundly. Oliver looked backward, whereas Armstrong was poised to take jazz into the future. But Oliver nurtured the talent he recognized and instilled in Louis Armstrong the discipline he needed to vault beyond *mere* genius and become a *professional* genius capable of disrupting the course of American music.

While playing in King Oliver's orchestra, Armstrong eclipsed his bandmates. The period 1923 to 1924 produced "Potato Head Blues," "Struttin' with Some Barbecue," and "Hotter Than That." In those songs, Armstrong pushed the envelope of popular musical expression, laying down just what jazz, in the hands of a master, could deliver. Lyricism alternated with tommy-gun staccato jabs as Armstrong played in the very highest register of his instrument—a stratospheric region into which early cornetists dared not venture. Above all, it was Armstrong's approach to rhythm—loose enough to come in slightly behind the beat in a manner that invented what came to be called *swing*. The pulse of the music as it

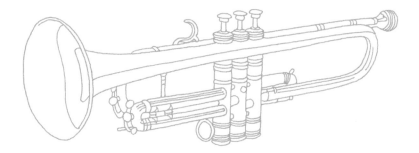

might be notated in a score was never lost, but it was altered, alternately elbowed aside and caressed by Armstrong, a musician with an inexhaustible reserve of invention.

The jazz that migrated north from New Orleans evolved in its new environment in ways that matured the music. The exuberant, spontaneous, but typically down-and-dirty standards of the Crescent City parade bands no longer cut it in the speakeasies of the urban North. Nor did the unpolished approach appeal to the major record producers. Bands and individual performers either became professional or they found themselves cast adrift and left behind. Even more important, performers like Armstrong dramatically raised the bar on improvisation. The catch-as-catch-can collective improvisation of the New Orleans tradition gave way to improvisation born of individual genius. It was more varied, more daring, and just plain harder to do.

It started with Louis Armstrong standing out in the King Oliver band. Throughout the mid-1920s, jazz came to focus increasingly on individual players. The greatest thrill in hearing the music began to come with the solos. What would Louis—or Satchmo or Satch, as his fans liked to call him (short for "satchel-mouth")—what would Satch do next?

The North offered a major market for jazz, and it was within this market that Armstrong became even more than the first great jazz soloist. He became the creator of a new American music, a music whose very individuality made it representative of a people's struggles and triumphs. Oliver gave him his start, and Oliver's band also introduced Armstrong to Lil Hardin, the band's pianist. She became Armstrong's second wife, and she was a source of abundant confidence. When Freddie Keppard, a rival trumpet player, came to hear Armstrong, Lil recalled, he "said to Louis, 'Boy, let me have your trumpet.' So, Louis looked at me and I bowed my head, so Louis gave him the trumpet. So, Freddie, he blew—oh, he blew and he blew and he blew and then the people gave him a nice hand. Then he handed the trumpet back to Louis. And I said, 'Now, get him, get him!' Oooh, never in my life have I heard such trumpet playing! If you want to hear Louis play, just hear him play when he's *angry*. Boy, he blew and people started standing up on top of tables and chairs screaming, and Freddie eased out real slowly." It was Lil who talked her husband into leaving his mentor and father figure to join the far more innovative Fletcher Henderson band in New York. Thanks in no small part to this move, the center of gravity for jazz moved from Chicago to the Big Apple, just as it had earlier moved from the Big Easy to the Windy City.

A year with Henderson in 1924–1925 immersed Armstrong in more modern sounds that were better suited to improvisation. He rocketed to fame, not just with audiences but with his fellow musicians. His evolution as an artist accelerated, and because *it* moved fast, the jazz itself advanced by leaps. To hear the recordings Armstrong made with the Henderson band is to hear an artist veering decisively away from the martial rhythms of New Orleans-style melody into pure jazz invention. What had been a playful dance that shoved against regular meter now became an artist playing with time itself, coming in fractionally before or after the beat. *Swing* was and is ultimately undefinable, yet Armstrong defined it for the next three generations of jazz musicians.

• • •

Before long, even the innovative Fletcher Henderson band became too confining for Armstrong, who moved back to Chicago late in 1925 and, from that year through 1928, recorded more than sixty sides with two groups he fronted, the Hot Five and the Hot Seven. These moved jazz along yet another trajectory.

The original Hot Five consisted of Armstrong on cornet, Kid Ory on trombone, Johnny Dodds on clarinet, Johnny St. Cyr on banjo, and Lil Hardin Armstrong on piano. In 1927, Pete Briggs on tuba and Baby Dodds on drums joined to make the group the Hot Seven. To this day, musicologists lavish well-deserved attention on their recordings in an attempt to pin down just what they mean in the history of jazz. Might as well try to sum up "just what" Beethoven means to classical music. Suffice it to say that the likes of "Struttin' with Some Barbecue," "Hotter Than That," and "West End Blues" revealed to audiences and fellow musicians alike the full range of possibilities for the jazz soloist. With the Hot Five and Hot Seven, Louis Armstrong transformed jazz from an ensemble-oriented, folk-derived music into a popular art form defined by soloists who were extreme in their virtuosity.

Musically speaking, the Hot Five and Hot Seven body of work is the sum and substance of the disruption that brought jazz to its first great maturity, both establishing and changing that musical form forever. The long career that followed brought transformations of a different kind, as Armstrong pushed jazz farther into the popular realm, mainstreaming the music, developing as much as a vocalist as he had as an instrumentalist, and figuring as powerfully as a stage presence, a personality, as he did as a musician.

That Armstrong never pushed racial issues to the forefront of his public persona created some controversy, especially late in his life, during the civil rights era. The truth is that his racial and cultural roots were *in* the music—always. The lyrics of "Black and Blue," a 1929 Fats Waller song Armstrong made his own, plaintively ask, "What did I do to be so black and blue?" The cultural and aesthetic disruption that Armstrong began both embodied and transcended the apartness, the otherness of race to become integral with the fabric of America and its music. The poor black boy from a New Orleans neighborhood so bad that it was called "The Battlefield" was appointed by President John F. Kennedy in 1962 "United States Ambassador of Goodwill" and sent with his biggest band, the All Stars, on a 51-nation world tour. It's possible that no president ever made a better decision.

DISRUPTION:
SHRINKING
THE PLANET BY
COVERING IT WITH
TELEVISION NEWS
IN REAL TIME, 24/7

TED TURNER

(1938–)

William DeVaughn Lucas was the first black general manager in Major League Baseball, and Atlanta Braves owner Ted Turner gave him that job in September 1976. Three years later, on May 1, 1979, Ted got a phone call: Bill Lucas had suffered a massive cerebral hemorrhage and cardiac arrest.

At first, Turner just could not believe it. His friend, a former athlete, just forty-three years old—it didn't make sense. Then, suddenly, it made a lot of sense.

For years, in the back of his mind, Ted Turner, he had been revolving a radical idea. It was to create a new news network for cable TV. What was new about it? It would be national news not for a half-hour an evening, but 24 hours, and it would cover the world, and it would do so, as nearly as possible, in real time, as events were happening and the stories unfolding. There were, however, plenty of reasons the idea stayed in the back of his mind. For one thing, the cable industry during the 1970s was pretty much a technological infant. For another, every time he opened his mouth to someone about the idea, he was shot down. Not only couldn't it be done, they said, it *shouldn't* be done. When he finally floated the idea at a meeting of cable-service operators, fishing for their subscription commitments, he got nary a nibble.

And now Bill Lucas was about to die—in the prime of his life. Ted Turner reached for the phone and dialed Reese Schonfeld, a television news journalist and executive with whom he had spoken about the cable news network idea. In his 1990 history *CNN: The Inside Story*, Hank Whittemore relates the call:

> "Hey, Reese! Do you know what happened today to Bill Lucas?"
> "No. What happened?"
> "He's got a hemorrhage! He's gonna die! And guess what? *None* of us is gonna live forever! So, listen, Reese, let's *do* this thing! With or *without* support!"

An intimation of his own mortality was enough to get Ted Turner over the hump—that and an attitude he once described this way: "I just love it when people say I can't do something. There's nothing that makes me feel better, because all my life people have said I wasn't going to make it."

● ● ●

He was born Robert Edward Turner III in 1938 in Cincinnati, Ohio, the son of a man whose business was billboards. When the outdoor ad business faltered in Ohio, the family moved to Savannah, Georgia, where the market seemed to be better. Nine-year-old Ted was a handful, and his father was a stern disciplinarian who soon packed him off to a series of military schools. From these, Ted enrolled in Brown University. Here, he was less passionate about classroom study than sailboat racing. Suspended during his sophomore year for drunkenness, he impulsively joined the Coast Guard, serving for six months before returning to Brown. He enrolled in liberal arts courses—which displeased his father—until he was expelled for "entertaining" female guests in his dorm room. This sent him back to the Coast Guard, after which he went to work for his father. In 1960, the senior Turner appointed Ted general manager of the company's Macon, Georgia, branch. But on March 5, 1963, with his business near collapse, Ted's father killed himself.

As would the death, years later, of Bill Lucas, Ed Turner's suicide hit Ted hard—and yet it also focused him, giving his hitherto wayward life direction.

He set about rebuilding the advertising company, as if determined to redeem his father's legacy. And then he used the billboard company as a mere platform on which to build a much larger media empire, as if he were determined to satisfy his father at long last by outshining him. Years later, when Ted Turner appeared on the cover of *Success* magazine, he held up the issue and called out "Dad? Do you see this? I made the cover of *Success* magazine! Is that *enough*?"

In 1970, Turner purchased Atlanta's financially ailing WTCG, UHF Channel 17. Six months later, he bought another UHF station, Channel 36, in Charlotte, North Carolina. By 1972, he had made Channel 17 profitable, and the following year he acquired the exclusive rights to broadcast Atlanta Braves baseball games, beating out the city's far larger national network affiliate, WSB.

With these moves, Turner revealed his underdog's talent for making weaknesses look like strengths. In the early 1970s, UHF stations were also-rans, never acquiring the viewership that the longer-established "original" VHF stations enjoyed. Potential advertisers were invariably quick to point this out to him. Turner had a comeback that was surprisingly effective. Fewer viewers, he said, meant more intelligent viewers, because anyone who could actually tune in a UHF station *had* to be intelligent. But those same advertisers had their own comeback. Much of Turner's programming, they complained, consisted of rerun "classic" TV shows, which meant that they were in black and white. "So what?" Turner would counter. Black-and-white programming would enhance the "shock value" of *color* commercials, forcing people to pay more attention to them.

• • •

UHF took Ted Turner a first step beyond the status quo of the era's television technology. What prompted him to take the next step, from broadcast television to cable, came in 1975, when cable pioneer Home Box Office (HBO) announced that it would soon begin transmitting its signal to a new communications satellite, which would bounce the signal back to receiving dishes owned by American cable distributors, who would, in turn, distribute the programming to cable subscribers all over the United States. Turner understood what this meant. "Cable" channel HBO would become a national television presence. Immediately, Turner decided to make his WTCG, Channel 17, the first local broadcast station to go national. He, too, would send its signal to a satellite, which would bounce it to America's cable distributors.

He launched the enterprise in 1976 under a bold new name, SuperStation. Whereas HBO showed *new* movies, he would offer the nation *old* movies from the large and growing library of films he was in the process of amassing. In addition to the "classic" movies and old TV shows, Turner, having just purchased the Atlanta Braves, now owned outright the broadcast rights to the club's games. He added these to the SuperStation's programming mix, and he beamed them to the nation.

But something was missing. He had sports, movies, and (old) series programming. What else did a television station need? *News.*

The traditional broadcast networks had plenty of news shows, but the *national network* news broadcasts occupied no more than one-half hour (22 minutes plus commercials) each evening. News was—well—*news.* It was vital. People were interested in it. Turner proposed to use a satellite/cable station to give the nation what no one else was giving it: 24 hours of news, seven days a week. After all, a number of radio stations were already broadcasting in all-news formats. Why not transfer the format to TV?

Why not?

Because it was unprecedented in television. Virtually everyone he asked about it said it would inevitably fail. Every manager of a major broadcast network knew only too well that news was a loser. News shows were not cheap to produce, and they made little money. There was actually very little demand for news, let alone 24 hours of it. In a way, this is all Ted Turner needed to know: the 24-hour news concept violated common sense and defied received wisdom. For these very reasons, Ted Turner was hooked. Yes, he admitted, market researchers provided executives with the basis for their decisions by asking people what they wanted. The nation's broadcast executives responded with programming based on their responses. Turner argued that this approach created nothing but unoriginal programming. The Wright brothers didn't go about asking people if they wanted to fly: they just went out and built an airplane. Turner believed that if he built a 24-hour news machine, people would use it.

He began collecting his news organization. It started with a cadre of non-network, but nevertheless television-savvy, news people. With them, he hashed out a formula for a 24-hour news station. One thing was certain: setting up the venture would mean sinking into it every penny his media and sports empire produced. Never mind. It was worth it. He was offering a unique value, and unique values make money. He also understood that, even though the vast majority of TV experts consisted of naysayers, the rapid development of cable television that distributed its programming to local providers via satellite would soon prompt somebody somewhere to start the very news network he was contemplating now. Turner believed he had little time to waste. Being first to market with a new idea conferred a great competitive advantage.

As Turner moved closer to the decision, those who worked with him noticed that he began asking ordinary people "Don't you think an all-news TV channel would be terrific?" It was as if he were daring them to answer no. It was as if he were trying to find something wrong with the idea before he took the final, irreversible step. He asked colleagues, and he even asked himself, "Am I crazy? . . . Why am I doing this?" Yet the more he asked, the more he became confirmed in his decision, even if he mostly heard discouraging responses.

The moment of truth came when, after presenting his concept to the cable operators, very few were ready to fork over the relatively modest subscription fee he asked for. This was not encouraging. But then he thought about Bill Lucas. To Turner, 24-hour cable news simply seemed a matter of now or never. On May 21, 1979, he announced to the convention of the National Cable Television Association that CNN, the Cable News Network, would be launched on June 1, 1980, and that it would be a national news network (with "overseas sources" around the world as well), broadcasting news and only news, 24 hours a day, 7 days a week. He put his objective in a context he knew the association members would understand: he explained to them that he was about to bring to fulfilment, at long last, the promise of television that legendary media guru Marshall McLuhan had articulated back in the 1960s. It would, he said, transform the world into what McLuhan had called a "global village."

No doubt, Turner's passion at the convention was contagious. But that was probably not the reason the operators rushed to subscribe—including all those who had balked even a short time earlier. Turner was no longer asking them for support. He had crossed the Rubicon. He was announcing a decision already made. No longer was 24-hour news an idea: Turner presented it as a world-disrupting reality, and, suddenly, no one wanted to be left out of the global village. Ted Turner had convinced them that he was about to position television to shrink the planet.

CREATING A NEW ROOTS MUSIC THAT DEFINED A GENERATION OF URBAN YOUTH AND REWROTE MUSIC INDUSTRY RULES

DJ KOOL HERC

(1955–)

This is what happened. Clive Campbell was born in 1955 in Kingston, Jamaica. All around him were the sounds of neighborhood parties called "dance halls"—the echoes of records played through public address systems, and the DJ "toasting," chanting over the beat of the music. It was the soundtrack of Clive's life until he moved with his family at age twelve to a large apartment building at 1520 Sedgwick Avenue, the Bronx, New York, in November 1967.

H e enrolled in the Alfred E. Smith Career and Technical Education High School, where his impressive physical presence and basketball prowess got the kids to calling him "Hercules"—Herc, for short. The late 1960s and early 1970s in New York saw an explosion of graffiti, which the cops and the city fathers condemned as vandalism but the teens who were doing it called "tagging," an artistic form of branding, of self-expression, of declaring your presence to the city and to the world while also just saying hello. Herc joined a tagging crew named the Ex-Vandals, and it was here that he perfected *his* tag. Herc became Kool Herc.

With his sister Cindy, Kool Herc started hosting back-to-school parties in the common rec room of 1520 Sedgwick Avenue. The sound system was the standard one for dance-party DJ's back in Kingston: two turntables wired to two amplifiers playing through a PA system featuring two big columnar speaker arrays. The records were James Brown, Jimmy Castor, and Booker T. & the M.G.'s. But they were played the way DJ Kool Herc played them.

This is what happened.

From the record—James Brown's "Give It Up or Turnit Loose" was an early favorite—Kool Herc picked out the "break," the most percussive segment of the cut. This was the part partygoers loved. It was the part they danced to—provided they were "breaking" or "break dancing," performing the hyper-athletic, super-show-off-style moves that were about to become familiar on New York City street corners.

After picking out and isolating the break on the record, Herc would prolong the break by rapidly changing between two turntables. As record *A* approached the end of the break, he cued record *B* to the beginning of the break, creating what he called a "five-minute loop of fury" by going back and forth between the records. Herc worked his twin turntables the way a symphony conductor works the orchestra; but, unlike the symphony conductor, he also conducted the crowd. Using multiple breaks and even multiple records to build what he termed "The Merry-Go-Round," he ran one break after another and switched back and forth between them. This climactic span of music and dance was introduced into DJ Kool Herc's performances in 1972 and involved three records on three turntables. At this point, he added the style of chants he had heard back in Kingston, calling over the music the rhyming phrases of street slang that would become the pattern for hip-hop.

• • •

It caught on, big, and DJ Kool Herc assumed the status of "founding father of hip-hop," the most culturally expressive, fresh, and original genre of American popular music since jazz. Even more, it emerged as a new roots music, going by the alternative term to hip-hop, a term less favored today: rap. It is a word that predates hip-hop music by many years. For some African Americans, *rap* described a highly stylized manner of speech, using braggadocio and double entendre that had its origin in the nineteenth century. As a style of speech, rap evolved from jive talk, a feature of African American urban speech heard during the 1930s and 1940s. Jive is highly metaphorical, witty, improvisational, and fast-paced. It gained currency through its use by popular black jazz musicians. The militant civil rights leader H. "Rap" Brown energized his fiery political speeches with a more barbed form of jive, which became modern rap.

Following Herc's Bronx inspiration, in the late 1970s and early 1980s, a number of "rap" groups, usually featuring a pair of toasters, or "MCs," and a DJ working a pair of turntables, started dominating the charts. Without instruments, the groups had to rely on the MCs' verbal combat and the DJ's turntable prowess to get the crowds going. The new music caught on, not just in America but around the world. Soon, rap groups were going platinum and the funk and R&B bands that had defined black music in the 1970s began to lose cultural relevance.

Like any other popular music genre, hip-hop went through a number of permutations over the following decades as it deepened in complexity and cross-pollinated with other musical trends. But many of those changes were played out in far more dramatic shifts than was seen in other schools of modern American music.

In the late 1980s, so-called gangsta rap (a popular term often disowned by the performers themselves) burst onto the scene as a powerful—and, to some, offensive—musical vehicle for conveying angry political messages and hard-bitten stories of life in gang-ridden neighborhoods, sometimes escalating into calls to violence. In the 1990s, the rappers of the East Coast brought out hardcore hip-hop, while the West Coast artists were softer. A feud developed between exponents of the East Coast and West Coast styles, which sometimes turned violent among fans, performers, and, quite possibly, even record labels. Many believe that the "East Coast/West Coast" feud as played out between Death Row Records (based in New York) and Bad Boy Records (based in Los Angeles) resulted in the fatal drive-by shooting of Death Row star Tupac Shakur in Las Vegas on September 7, 1996, and the fatal drive-by shooting of Bad Boy Records artist The Notorious B.I.G. (Christopher George Latore Wallace) in Los Angeles on March 9, 1997.

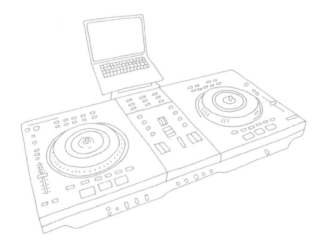

To be sure, by the 1980s, hip-hop, or rap, was widely recognized as an import-ant and often complex means of social expression subversive of the dominant white culture. For DJ Kool Herc, however, "it was just something that we were doing for fun," as he explained in his introduction to Jeff Chang's history of hip-hop, *Can't Stop, Won't Stop* (2005). Herc believes that "hip-hop . . . bridged the culture gap," bringing "white kids together with Black kids, brown kids with yellow kids. They all have something in common that they love. It gets past the stereotypes and people hating each other because of those stereotypes." Never-theless, Herc saw hip-hop as an outgrowth of James Brown ("Say It Loud—I'm Black and I'm Proud") and civil rights and Black power. "It has become a pow-erful force. Hip-hop binds all of these people, all of these nationalities, all over the world together."

Herc never grew wealthy from the musical genre he innovated. He never moved into commercially recorded hip-hop. Never even tried. But a lot of other people did. The music that struck an emotional, cultural, and political chord exploded into a major industry. As the business magazine *Forbes* reported in 2017, hip-hop had become the "dominant genre in the U.S. for the first time." What started as the musical equivalent of graffiti, self-expression on the level of the individual and the neighborhood street, was, by 2017, responsible for roughly a quarter of all music consumption in America.

**ABSORBED THE
MAINSTREAM ELEMENTS
OF POP-CULTURE
SUCCESS AND BECAME
THE MOST PROVOCATIVE
AND ENDURING OF
POP-CULTURE ICONS**

MADONNA
(1958–)

Her name is the one her parents gave her, Madonna Louise Ciccone—with two thirds of it lopped off. Just enough to transform her into the combination of an object worthy of spiritual adoration and an affront to the Holy Mother herself. Michelangelo spoke of seeing the sculpture he wanted in the block of marble before him, his task being to carve away the unnecessary. Madonna did much the same. She became a dancer, songwriter, singer, actress, filmmaker, and businesswoman. Those are professional credits. Most of all, she crossed the bright red lines of American mainstream pop music, leaving enough to make a mainstream fortune, but presenting herself as a *sui generis* provocation, pure image become pure cultural phenomenon, a celebrity who carries along her own altar. She became the objective correlative of fame in an age that worshipped precisely that. Quantitatively measured, she is the richest woman in the music business, with sales north of 300 million records and a net worth even farther north of half a billion dollars. As a live attraction, she still holds the distinction of being the highest-grossing solo touring artist—ever.

Madonna Louise Ciccone was born on August 16, 1958, in Bay City, Michigan, the daughter of a second-generation Italian American father—an engineer and designer in the Detroit auto industry—and a mother whose parents were French Canadian. She was one of six children in a devout Catholic family. The death of her mother, of breast cancer at the age of thirty when Madonna was just five years old, left her with the impulse (she later explained) to search "for something . . . to be somebody."

Educated in Catholic elementary schools, Madonna went on to a public middle school and high school, achieving standout grades in both—yet also acting out by performing impromptu acrobatics in the hallways and pulling up her skirt in class to show boys her underwear. Yet her high-school record was straight A's. She went on to the University of Michigan School of Music, Theatre & Dance on a scholarship. Her initial ambition was to enter the ballet, and in 1977 she moved to New York City and studied with famed choreographer Alvin Ailey. She earned extra money by modeling and, in 1979, was hired by a disco group, the Patrick Hernandez Revue, with which she performed in New York and Paris.

In the City of Light she met Dan Gilroy, with whom she formed the Breakfast Club pop/dance group. Madonna started out with the band on drums before morphing into its lead singer. She formed a new band, Emmy, in 1980, and then moved on to dance/disco. A demo led to a contract with Sire Records in 1982 and her first single, "Everybody," which, with "Physical Attraction" and "Holiday" the next year, established Madonna as a club presence. Her first album, *Madonna*, landed in 1983, with "Holiday" getting her into the Top 40 and, in 1984, "Borderline" making the Top Ten.

At the dawn of her fame, Madonna signed on to star as a brash, gum-popping downtown New York hipster in Susan Seidelman's much-admired film, *Desperately Seeking Susan*. *Like a Virgin*, Madonna's second album, came out at the end of 1984. But it was in 1985 that Madonna became a global celebrity on the basis of her catchy songs, sexy music videos, brash film presence, colorfully unique fashion sense, and provocatively in-your-face personality. In March, "Material Girl" hit number two, and she embarked on her first tour. She had a number-one hit with "Crazy for You" and, with the release of *Desperately Seeking Susan* in July, became a movie star. Two assaults on her evolving image followed: the video release of *A Certain Sacrifice*, a cheapo erotic drama from 1979, and a suite of 1977 nude photos published by *Playboy* and *Penthouse*. The rising star took these in her stride and, in August, married actor Sean Penn.

Even as Madonna fed a pop-culture hunger for celebrity for celebrity's sake, she worked assiduously at developing her songwriting and performance, releasing the *True Blue* album in 1986 to critical acclaim as well as great commercial success. In November, however, *Shanghai Surprise*, a comedy in which she co-starred with husband Sean Penn, bombed, as did her third feature film, *Who's That Girl?* (1987), which nevertheless occasioned the hit single of the same name.

Always looking for new challenges, she retreated into Broadway in 1988, acting in distinguished playwright David Mamet's *Speed-the-Plow*. Her marriage to Penn ended in divorce at the beginning of 1989. That same year, she released *Like a Prayer*, which critics and hardcore fans consider her most ambitious album, expanding from the era's pop to styles embracing dance and rock. The album produced three Top Ten hits, which ensured that her 1990 year-long Blonde Ambition tour would create a sensation. The same year, her fourth feature film, the highly stylish and stylized *Dick Tracy*, directed by co-starring Warren Beatty, scored a welcome success and was followed at the end of 1990 by the release of a greatest-hits album, *The Immaculate Collection*.

But this was not the usual retrospective. Two new songs were included, including the number-one single "Justify My Love," which was debuted with a video sufficiently sexy to draw both praise and condemnation. "Rescue Me," the other new song, was the highest-debuting single by a female artist in U.S. chart history. The greatest-hit album, combined with the chart-topping new songs and the sexy video, made a frame for what came next year, the documentary film *Truth or Dare*, which chronicled the Blonde Ambition tour.

The year 1992 put the pop spotlight on sex with the *Erotica* album, which was balanced by Madonna's featured appearance in the hit comic film *A League of Their Own*, whose soundtrack included her number-one single "This Used to Be My Playground." But the year ended with the release of a costly, steel-bound "art book" titled *Sex*, a collection of erotic photographs of her and others. While *Sex* was universally panned by critics, *Erotica* sold in excess of two million copies.

● ● ●

For some, *Sex* marked the beginning of Madonna's decline. The album *Bedtime Stories* (1994) seemed tame after *Erotica*—and yet "Take a Bow" was her biggest single yet, and the album went multi-platinum—though other singles failed to crack the Top 40. It was at this point that Madonna demonstrated her remarkable ability to reinvent herself. With *Something to Remember* (1995), she presented a sophisticated and lyrical side, which persuaded composer Andrew Lloyd Webber to approve her to play Eva Perón in the film adaptation of his stage musical *Evita*, released later in 1996. Although she did not win the Best Actress Oscar she coveted, Madonna did win the Golden Globe for Best Actress (Musical or Comedy).

She reinvented her persona yet more radically in the well-reviewed comeback album *Ray of Light* (1998), which brought her into the realm of electronica and techno. In 2000, the album *Music* explored even more contemporary styles. She married filmmaker Guy Ritchie at the end of the year and, two years later, she starred in Ritchie's *Swept Away*, a remake of the 1974 Lena Wertmüller classic. The remake was not a success, and her 2003 album, *American Life*, failed to spawn any hit singles in the U.S., though its number one *Billboard* debut showed that the public was still eager to see what she would do next.

The early 2000s saw a couple of new albums that met with middling success, as well as a number of ever-more-elaborately staged concert tours, and the latest in Madonna's never-ending reinventions, this time as the author of children's books and director of feature films.

Now Madonna, at fifty-three, began work on her twelfth album, *MDNA*, in 2011, which was released in 2012 just after her live performance at Super Bowl XLVI and was followed by the year-long MDNA Tour, which covered much of the world and spawned a TV special and live album, *MDNA World Tour* (2013). Her thirteenth album, *Rebel Heart*, was released in March 2015, reaching number two in America and Britain, and launching a tour during 2015–2016.

From the beginning, Madonna disrupted everything about the "girl" singer. That breakthrough was only her first. Her career is quite simply one of the most important in the history of popular music. The mark she made is as a breaker of boundaries who never ran out of boundaries to break. A genius? Perhaps. But, far more important, a living influence on the generation rising around her.

INDEX

ABOUT THE AUTHOR

Alan Axelrod is the author of more than 100 books, including the CEO and Real History series. He was the coauthor of *the New York Times* bestseller *What Every American Should Know About American History* as well as the *Businessweek* bestsellers *Patton on Leadership* and *Elizabeth I, CEO.* He has appeared on numerous TV and radio programs and in magazine and newspaper articles.